"Major Bowes, Ted Mack, Arthur Godfrey – all were synonymous with old-time talent shows. Nowadays, open-mike nights and cable TV public access and shows like 'Star Search' are the main venues for new talent to get off the ground. Cliffie Stone, longtime country musician and promoter, has joined with his wife, Joan Carol, to put together easily the most comprehensive book on this subject imaginable. What's a talent show like when it's held in a nightclub? A comedy club? A local access show? What kind of act do I put together? Where do I find my material? Do I have any talent to do this in the first place? All these questions and many more are answered here, accompanied by anecdotes about Cliffie's colleagues in entertainment (including Tennessee Ernie Ford, Minnie Pearl, Roy Rogers and Gene Autry) and how they did it. The folksy, chatty style is mixed with real nuts-and-bolts theatrical advice; if you go ahead and join Cliffie on his front porch, you'll be rewarded with solid pointers."

BOOKLIST
AMERICAN LIBRARY ASSOCIATION
(DECEMBER 1999)

"Cliffie Stone serves up practical advice and encouragement for aspiring musicians, country style, in this amiable, posthumously published meditation on talent shows. Known throughout the country music business as a tireless promoter of emerging artists, Stone was Historian of the Academy of Country Music for many years; the ACM has awarded its annual Pioneer Award ("The Cliffie") to people who have made unique contributions to country music.

"Drawing on his experience as a musician, songwriter, publisher, booking agent and producer of radio and television programs that launched careers for a number of well-known performers, Stone and his coauthor/wife provide guidance along with anecdotes and homespun humor. From overcoming stage fright and hiring a manager to avoiding a major pitfall for performers – alcohol and substance abuse – the Stones cover all of the bases from beginner to seasoned pro...Stone's easygoing, conversational tone will help take the edge off newcomers' anxiety and self-doubt...Despite the focus on talent shows, it's Stone's exuberance as a cheerleader for fledgling artists that will likely remain in readers' minds."

PUBLISHERS WEEKLY

(January 24, 2000)

"Cliffie Stone (*Everything You Always Wanted To Know About Songwriting But Didn't Know Who To Ask*) has enjoyed a versatile career as DJ, bassist, comedian, songwriter, and booking agent; served as one of the founders of the Academy of Country Music and an original member of the Country Music Association; has a star on the Hollywood Walk of Fame; and was inducted into the Country Music Disc Jockey's Hall of Fame in 1979. Needless to say, he has 'been there and done that.'

"His latest book, coauthored with his wife – a songwriter with over 100 published songs – provides the nitty-gritty details about how to use local talent shows to push your dreams into reality. Coverage is thorough; they explain rules and guidelines, how to prepare for performances and deal with stage fright, where to find talent shows, and the ins and outs of artist financing, managers, and audiences.

"This book is simply a goldmine of information, as well as a tome of encouragement toward self-esteem. Recommended for music and/or vocational guidance collections in academic and public libraries."

LIBRARY JOURNAL

(January 2000)

From Cliffie's Friends

"Discovering and encouraging new artists is important. It ensures that the music will never stop. Cliffie spent his life nurturing talent. He found it. He presented it. He promoted it. He made an extraordinary contribution to our musical lives."
-DICK CLARK, Legendary Emmy & Multi-Award Winning TV Producer/Host
Emmys: Producer & Best Show, "American Bandstand"; Lifetime Achievement, 1994
Hall of Fame - Academy of Television Arts & Sciences, 1993

"Cliffie was one of the best artists and friends I ever knew. Our pioneering trails have crossed many times on radio, television and music publishing. Aspiring artists will benefit from his straight-shooting advice in his book."
-GENE AUTRY, The "Original" Singing Cowboy & Western Artist Icon
Hall of Fame - Country Music Association (CMA), 1969
Pioneer Award - Academy of Country Music (ACM), 1972

"Cliffie's diverse knowledge of the music business, along with his many talents and kind heart, made him one of country music's best assets."
-ERV WOOLSEY, Manager of George Strait
-GEORGE STRAIT, MCA Recording Artist
Entertainer of the Year - Country Music Association, 1989 & 1990
Entertainer of the Year - Academy of Country Music, 1989

"Cliffie was one of those special people who gave newcomers a chance. He was an inspiration to so many, and he certainly was to me!"
-BARBARA MANDRELL, Multi Award-Winning CMA & ACM Artist; Actress
Entertainer of the Year - Country Music Association, 1980 & 1981
Entertainer of the Year - Academy of Country Music, 1980

"When I was young, I'd sit in with local bands whenever I got the chance. I also sang on the Dixie Jamboree in Louisiana, and it fueled my fire to be an artist."
-TIM McGRAW, Curb Records Artist/Songwriter/Producer
CMA Male Vocalist of the Year, 1999; ACM Top Male Vocalist, 1999

"Cliffie Stone was a master at helping performers hold onto their dreams. He encouraged them to keep getting on stage to hone their skills and perfect their profession. We are lucky he was able to bless us with this new book, which is destined to become a talent show Bible."
-RAC CLARK, Senior VP/Product & Programming, dick clark productions, inc.
Co-Executive Producer of TNN's "Prime Time Country"

"Cliffie Stone was the most wonderful man who ever walked on the face of the earth! We shared the same passion - to promote country music to the utmost!"
-FRAN BOYD, Executive Director, Academy of Country Music

"Cliffie knew more about talent and people than anyone I ever met. He believed that everyone deserved a chance, and he had the ability to get the best out of everyone. Following the path that he lays out in this book can make your journey to success a shorter, sweeter trip."
-GENE WEED, Premier TV Director/Executive Producer
Board of Directors' Chairman, Academy of Country Music

"I won my first talent show at Rockhill High School in Ohio by singing 'Shot Gun Boogie.' Little did I know that someday I'd be a good friend with one of the writers, Cliffie Stone. Talent shows are important because they give you confidence and reaffirm what you suspect about yourself - that you have talent!"
-BOBBY BARE, RCA Recording Artist/Songwriter/Publisher/TNN Host

"When I was growing up in Waco, Texas, I used to participate in the programs at schools, churches, outdoor activities and other music functions. The real boom was the 'Kiddie Matinee' at the local movie theater, which was preceded by a 30-minute amateur show. I used to enter them because it gave me the opportunity to perform in a professional atmosphere on stage and broadcasting on the radio. Most of the time, I'd win first prize. Youngsters need these types of opportunities, and Cliffie provided them for many fledgling artists. He assisted in my first recording session for Capitol in 1947, and we became lifelong friends."
-HANK THOMPSON, Entertainer; Hall of Fame - Country Music Association, 1989

"In 1950, I entered a talent show and placed 2nd to none other than Faron Young. I've judged many talent contests on the 'Charlie Daniels' Talent Roundup' shows on TNN. I don't know why, but the winners, in most cases, never made the big leap to major labels, and many who came in 2nd or 3rd went on to become big stars. That's show biz! Cliffie was one of my all-time heroes and role models. I'm so glad his knowledge will be kept alive in his books and that he included a chapter about management."
-MERLE KILGORE, Manager of Hank Williams, Jr./Artist/Songwriter
Hall of Fame - Nashville Songwriters Association Int'l, 1998

"No one is more qualified to write about any aspect of the music business than this beloved Country Music Hall of Fame member. He has done it all! New artists will enjoy his sense of humor along with the tried-and-true advice. They will find much to help them as they travel their own long winding road to success."
-JO WALKER-MEADOR, Hall of Fame - Country Music Association, 1995

"I was playing very few gigs in Bakersfield when I decided to enter a talent show on a dare at the Rainbow Gardens one night. Although I came in second, the backup band's fiddle player, Jelly Sanders, asked me if I was interested in getting any jobs, and this led to many gigs for me around town. I am proud to have known Cliffie. He was my good luck charm. Whenever he was in the studio while I was recording at Capitol, my song would become a hit. His advice in this book could become your good luck charm."
-**MERLE HAGGARD**, Legendary Award-Winning CMA & ACM Artist/Songwriter
Hall of Fame - Country Music Association, 1994
Pioneer Award - Academy of Country Music, 1996

"If you could write down the name of every artist, songwriter, musician, producer, promoter, manager, agent, etc...that Cliffie Stone spoke an encouraging word to (and I was no exception), it would probably extend from here to the hereafter...where I'm sure if encouragement is needed, he's still at it!"
-**BUCK OWENS**, Pioneer Award - Academy of Country Music, 1988
Hall of Fame - Country Music Association, 1996

"I sang 'The Glory of Love' and 'Twilight on the Trail' in a talent show at Spirit Wood Lake, North Dakota and won $5.00. You'll enjoy reading Cliffie's informative book because he knows whereof he speaks."
-**PEGGY LEE**, Legendary Pop Entertainer/Capitol Recording Star/Songwriter
Star on the Hollywood Walk of Fame, 1960; Pied Piper Award - ASCAP, 1990

"Roy and I were blessed to know Cliffie. We appreciated the integrity and honor that he brought to the profession. But most of all, we prized his sense of humor and what a joy he was to work with."
-**DALE EVANS**, Mrs. Roy Rogers - 1st Lady of the West
TV Host/Actress/Singer/Songwriter

"Cliffie lived a life of respect. He respected the music, the artists, and the entire process (both good and bad) of the business. This is a man who stood out by opening his heart to everyone and conducted himself, always, with grace."
-**LORIANNE CROOK**, Premier Television/Cable Host (TNN's "Crook & Chase")

"Cliffie's book on the importance of talent shows is the closest an aspiring artist can get to professional advice from one of the most beloved men in the music business. His career-building suggestions bring the reader up close and personal to a man who was involved in the careers of hundreds of successful artists."
-**FRANCES W. PRESTON**, BMI President and CEO
Hall of Fame - Country Music Association, 1992

"Cliffie was positive about everything! There wasn't anything he wouldn't try or figure out how to do! To follow a dream is a gift and he reached beyond his dreams to create a unique and lasting legacy. This book is that 'gift,' which may inspire you to get on stage, refine your craft and stand tall among the successful."
-PAUL CORBIN, VP/Music Industry Relations/CBS Cable - TNN/CMT

"As Tennessee Ernie Ford's manager for the last thirty-five years of his life, after taking over from Cliffie Stone, I attribute almost all I know about 'the business' to Cliffie. His manner, his patience and his encouragement are all part of what I learned from him. There will never be another executive like him."
-JIM LOAKES, President, Bayshore Music; Former Manager of Tennessee Ernie Ford

"I was in the tenth grade when three buddies and I decided to form a band and enter the high school talent show. How excited I was when we won! But another one of my talent show experiences should encourage anyone who loses in a talent competition! I had entered the University of Georgia's talent contest, which had been broken up into different divisions, and I competed against one other student in the 'Talent & Original Song' division. I lost, and I was embarrassed and hurt.

But this story has a footnote. The boy who beat me also decided to move to Nashville, as I did, to pursue a songwriting career. I figured I got the last laugh when, two or three years later, I went to purchase a pair of shoes at a downtown shoe store and the guy who had defeated me in the two-man contest was the shoe salesman. I never saw or heard of him again."
-BILL ANDERSON, Entertainer/Musician/Songwriter/Actor/Author/TNN Host
Hall of Fame - Nashville Songwriters Association Int'l, 1975

"Cliffie and I worked together for some twenty years in a rather stressful business; and he gave us the 'humanity' we all needed to survive the transition from creative independence to corporate 'accountability.'"
-SAM TRUST, President, Trust Management, Inc.; Former President/ATV Music Group

"I finally had the opportunity to meet Cliffie Stone at an ACM awards show after years of admiring him and his career. I can identify with his passion and joy for presenting new talent. I've been producing the 'Johnnie High Country Music Revue' and broadcasting it nationwide on radio for years, which has launched so many careers, such as John Anderson and LeAnn Rimes. LeAnn was six years old when she auditioned for my music revue show and she became a cast member. I remember one night when she came off the stage and a lady asked her what she wanted to be when she grew up. LeAnn looked up at her and said with conviction, 'I'm going to be a star.' Like Cliffie, I encourage not only new artists to perform on stage, but also potential producers to present new talent to the world."
-JOHNNIE HIGH, Producer, "Johnnie High Country Music Revue" (Arlington, TX)
Disc Jockey/Musician/Booking Agent

"Cliffie Stone's name is synonymous with integrity and musical vision. He was a contemporary of my father, Si Siman, in the pioneer days of country music - they wrote the book figuratively and now literally. Those of us traveling down the music road today owe them so much. So pay attention! Cliffie's words of advice come from his vast knowledge and heartfelt passion for creative people."
-SCOTT SIMAN, ACM Board Chairman/President of rpm management
Manager of Tim McGraw

"Cliffie's influence is immeasurable! In some way, he was associated with or responsible for many of the most important milestones ever recorded in pop and country music, radio and television. But for the hundreds of artists and musicians that came under his wing, the strongest memory is his guidance, enthusiasm and support. If Cliffie believed in you, you not only had his backing, but his loyalty and friendship - usually sealed with nothing more than a handshake and his word. This I know from personal experience, because if it hadn't been for his handshake, friendship, encouragement and the spotlight that he gave to my Dad, the world would never have heard the name Tennessee Ernie Ford. Thank you, Cliffie."
-JEFFREY "BUCK" FORD, Producer/Writer/Executive/Actor
Producer, "Tennessee Ernie Ford's 50th Anniversary Show" for TNN

"I met Cliffie in the late 60's in Hollywood, and he was already a legend. He was a beacon for country talent, and our most effective voice to the L.A. entertainment industry. Doors for country music opened wider and sooner because of him."
-BRUCE HINTON, Chairman, MCA Records Nashville

"Cliffie brought many new artists to Capitol Records/Hollywood. He played bass on many of my recording sessions as well as his own. He, along with Lee Gillette and myself, had a publishing company called Central Songs and it wouldn't have been successful without him. He was a fantastic man and a dear friend."
-KEN NELSON, Producer/Head of Country Division - Capitol/Hollywood, 1951-78

"When Cliffie gave me the opportunity to work under his tutelage, he impacted my life. His belief in me not only influenced my work, but also my work ethics. I credit him for playing a big role in my success as a songwriter, publisher and producer."
-GEORGE RICHEY, Manager/Husband of Tammy Wynette
Record Producer/Award-Winning Songwriter

"Cliffie and I became dear friends when he was the executive producer of Tennessee Ernie Ford's NBC television show and I was the MCA rep. Later, we formed our own corporation for other television production ventures. He gave more people opportunities to present their talent than anyone I ever met!"
-DALE SHEETS, President of International Ventures, Inc.
Agent/Manager - Mel Torme, Roger Williams

"Cliffie was the Ed Sullivan of the West Coast and the future stars that he has discovered through his radio and television shows read like a 'Who's Who.' They either appeared as a special guest or were introduced as a new artist. He was the most important influence on country music the West Coast will ever have."
-JOE ALLISON, Jim Reeves Memorial Award - Academy of Country Music, 1969
Hall of Fame - Nashville Songwriters Association Int'l, 1978

"I knew Cliffie when he was just a pebble, long before he became a gemstone in c/w music. Although I can't carry a tune in a bucket, my brand of entertainment is trick roping and riding. Every new artist needs a stage and an audience. Mine was small town rodeos where, as a youngster, I stood on a platform and gave a rope spinning exhibition while learning to smile and be at ease in front of people."
-MONTIE MONTANA, World Famous Trick Roper and Cowboy

"Cliffie was a neighbor rancher of mine, and there would have been a big hole in my life if I hadn't known him. He hired me to play on many albums as well as club gigs, which always included new talent that he had discovered. I'll treasure the duet we did on the 'Drifting Clouds' album that he produced for the Riders."
-BUCK PAGE, Founder/Member - Riders of the Purple Sage

"Cliffie was a good friend for many years. He always presented local talent on his free annual c/w concerts that he'd have for the community. His contributions to country and western music genres will be cherished. I was proud to participate in inducting him in Santa Clarita's Walk of Western Stars, which honors other great Westerners like Gene Autry, John Wayne, Dale Evans and Roy Rogers."
-JO ANNE DARCY, Mayor of Santa Clarita

"As a boy, I grew up listening to and admiring Cliffie Stone. Later, I had the opportunity of becoming his friend, and he became my supporter when I was elected Los Angeles County Supervisor. It was an honor to join with his family and friends and give a Eulogy at his Memorial Service."
-MICHAEL D. ANTONOVICH, Supervisor Fifth District
Los Angeles County Board of Supervisors

"It's always a thrill to see the faces of new talent when we tell them they have been selected to appear on national television. It's a golden opportunity, and they know - win or lose - that the experience and exposure is the most important thing."
-SAM RIDDLE, Producer
"Star Search" and "From Hawaii...Destination Stardom"

"I had the great pleasure of knowing Cliffie for many years in the Santa Clarita Valley. As much as I enjoyed his music, I admire him most for his dedication to his family and to his community. Through selfless dedication, he worked hard to make the Santa Clarita Valley area a better place. I'll always think of Cliffie as a larger-than-life figure, riding off into the sunset with his guitar slung over his shoulder and a warm grin on his face. He was truly one in a million."
-HOWARD P. "BUCK" McKEON, U. S. Representative
25th District of California, Santa Clarita

YOU GOTTA BE BAD
BEFORE
YOU CAN BE GOOD!

Talent Shows & Beyond
Career-building Advice
for the
"Stars of Tomorrow!"
Artist Financing
Produce "Fun" Money-Making Shows!

CLIFFIE STONE
with JOAN CAROL STONE

A SHOWDOWN BOOK
N. Hollywood, CA USA

Library of Congress Catalog Card Number: 99-96801

ISBN 1-880152-01-0

Published by

Cliffie Stone's SHOWDOWN, INC.
P.O. Box 9657 • N. Hollywood, CA 91609-1657
www.cliffiestone.com

Manufactured in the United States of America

First Printing January 2000

Distributed by

BEEKMAN PUBLISHERS, INC.
P.O. Box 888 • Woodstock, NY 12498
1-888-BEEKMAN • www.beekman.net

Unless otherwise indicated, photographs are taken by Joan Carol Stone and/or are from the "Cliffie and Joan Carol Stone Collection." Grateful acknowledgment is made to those photographers so credited. Cliffie Stone caricatures by Charlotte Huffine.

Grateful acknowledgment is also made to the people listed in "From Cliffie's Friends" for their permission to reprint excerpts from their letters, conversations and/or books (*"Whisperin' Bill"* by Bill Anderson/Published by Longstreet Press, 1989; *"Not Without My Horse"* by Montie Montana/Published by Double M Company, 1993; this also includes poems by Shawnie Wise-Hawkins and Marie Wise-Hawkins).

Bibliography appears on page 239, which constitutes an extension of this copyright page.

Book Design and Layout - KATY GOULD/Katy, Ink.
Book Bindery/Printing - ZACH MARTINEZ/Swell Graphics, Inc.
Cover and Photo Insert Concept - JOAN CAROL STONE
Front Cover Photo by PHIL POOL
Editor - JOAN CAROL STONE
Copy Editors - JOAN CAROL STONE and KATY GOULD

OTHER BOOKS BY CLIFFIE STONE

with Joan Carol Stone

"Everything You Always Wanted To Know About Songwriting But Didn't Know Who To Ask"

$16.95   ISBN 1-880152-00-2 (1992)

▲ "To record a song like 'Sixteen Tons' is a dream come true for every artist. I urge you to read this book and learn firsthand from a man who truly knows about country music." -TENNESSEE ERNIE FORD

▲ "Who better to write a book about songwriting than Cliffie Stone! He's been involved in all aspects of the music business with not only great success, but also great integrity." -KENNY ROGERS

▲ "Cliffie's book will be of much assistance to any new writer because of its valuable content. He's a professor and a publisher and this book is long overdue." -MERLE HAGGARD

▲ "Attention all music schools. This is a very important piece of literature and it should be mandatory reading for anyone who wishes a career in songwriting or music publishing." -BOBBY BARE

▲ "...gives beginners practical advice on everything on the country field from composition to royalties...Stone's charming, just-folks style helps music business intricacies seem less intimidating to the novice..."
-PUBLISHERS WEEKLY

▲ "This wonderfully informative and entertaining book is exploding with tips for beginning and aspiring songwriters, music students, those wanting to put their poetry to music and inquisitive music fans...This masterpiece is destined to be a basic tool for musicians."
-LIBRARY JOURNAL

A SHOWDOWN BOOK
P.O. Box 9657
N. Hollywood, CA 91609-1657

Dedicated To Entertainers!

"God gave you a gift, and what you do with it is your gift to God."

"There is nothing more fun or more gratifying
than seeing, hearing and feeling
an audience's love and appreciation
after doing a successful show where I've given
my best to entertain and make them laugh!
And as I stand next to the stage and look up at the sky,
I think to myself, 'Thank you, Lord. I feel so good
about myself and have such high self-esteem!
It's a wonderful world!'"

Cliffie Stone

Table of Contents

A Personal 21-Gun Salute to "The Cliffie!"

1917 - 1998

Cliffie was magical and simply the best! We lived a lifetime "as one" during the inseparable years that God granted us. I'll forever treasure those loving memories, as well as a Valentine's letter that he wrote me:

"To Joan and Carol, my other self: I will always go where you go, think what you think, dream when you dream, feel what you feel...Because I love you, my heart continues to beat to the rhythm of your heart. Without you, I do none of these glorious things because you are my other self. God bless you for your love, understanding and respect.
Your other self, Cliffie"

To Cliffie, my other self:

"If I Had Never Loved You"
Words & Music by Joan Carol Stone

From what I can see in the world around me.
Not many will love unconditionally.
Thank God there is you with a love forever true.
Oh, what I'd have missed if I had never loved you.

If I had never loved you...if you had never loved me
We wouldn't have known love's glory and all that love can be!
The day I take my last breath, I'll thank the Lord above
for giving me the gift of you...for I have loved.

Words don't come easy, so please hold my hand.
As I try to tell you how lucky I am.
Our love deserves a 21-gun salute!
I wouldn't have lived if I had never loved you.

Chorus

© 1998

"I'll Be Just Around the Corner"

A Poem by Cliffie Stone

I now know there comes a time in every person's life
when they have to move on...
But I'll be just around the corner.

I now know what a long run my life's show has been.
And even though my show is a hit, it will eventually close.
The marquee will be dark, the seats empty...
But I'll be just around the corner!

I don't intend to go far – the great producer has me
booked beyond the stars...there's always another stage
and a place where someone will remember me
and the hit that I once was...
So I'll be just around the corner!

©1997

A Special Acknowledgment

Cliffie had a heart as big as the universe and an endless capacity to love life and people. I'll never forget the passion in his voice when he once said, *"Oh, how I love life! I just love it!"*

He also commented to me that he felt so lucky to have been married to two loving ladies at different seasons of his life. Likewise, I feel that his late first wife, Dorothy, and I were both lucky to have known his love.

Cliffie was always in awe of the miracle of life itself. He and Dorothy were lovingly devoted to raising their four children, Linda, Stephen, Curtis and Jonathan. They were so proud of their children's accomplishments, which I feel reflected their own character traits and family values.

Well done, Cliffie and Dorothy!

Cliffie loved to share his philosophy with everyone: *"God gave you a gift, and what you do with it is your gift to God."* He made the most out of all the gifts God gave him and his accomplishments speak for themselves.

However, sharing the gift of love was always first on Cliffie's agenda. Although the Lord loves all his children equally, he must be so proud of Cliffie, who has truly fulfilled one of his Biblical commandments: *"You shall love your neighbor as yourself."* I can just imagine God saying:

Well done, Cliffie, my son! Well done!

Acknowledgments

All of his life, Cliffie loved to discover and encourage new talent to be all that they can be. This talent show book, which was so near and dear to his heart, was to have been our top priority in 1998. However, God had other plans and on January 16, 1998, Cliffie made his transition.

About a year later, I started transcribing and editing his talent show tapes. It was my honor to complete this book for my brilliant husband so that the very essence of his passionate thoughts and ideas will live on and be passed on to anyone interested in pursuing a music career.

Although it breaks my heart that he's not physically here to see it in print, I believe and feel that he spiritually knows.

◆◆◆◆◆◆◆

I, along with Cliffie's children - Linda, Stephen, Curtis and Jonathan - give our heartfelt thanks to the Academy of Country Music's Board of Directors for designating the ACM Pioneer Award as 'The Cliffie' on their May 5, 1999 CBS awards show. They are: John Blassingame, Ray Benson, Carol Bowsher, Fran Boyd, John Briggs, Dixie Carter, Bill Catino, Kenny Chesney, David Corlew, Mike Curb, Steven Dahl, Tim DuBois, Rod Essig, Jerry Fuller, Joe Gehl, Cathy Gurley, Mark Hartley, Bob Heatherly, Clint Higham, John Hobbs, Gayle Holcomb, Debbie Holley, Brian Hughes, Wade Jessen, T.K. Kimbrell, Bob Kingsley, Fran LaMaina, Jack Lameier, Joey Lee, Brent Maher, Joe Mansfield, Bill Mayne, Melissa McConnell, Marge Meoli, Paul Moore, Gary Morris, Ken Mueller, Buddy Owens, Ray Pilszak, Fred Reiser, Bob Romeo, Paul Shefrin, Shelia Shipley-Biddy, Scott Siman, Paige Sober, Clarence Spalding, Jonathan Stone, James Stroud, Bonnie Sugarman, Pat Surnegie, Butch Waugh, Gene Weed, Selma Williams and Tim Wipperman.

A special thank you goes to Fran Boyd, Marge Meoli, Linda Zandstra, David Young and the rest of the wonderful ACM office staff who are always there to help in every way they can.

I deeply appreciate and thank all of Cliffie's friends and associates who took the time to write their loving and respectful thoughts, which have been incorporated into this book. (See "From Cliffie's Friends.")

A million thank you's go to my new friends, Katy Gould, Katy, Ink. and Zach Martinez, Swell Graphics, Inc., for going above and beyond the call of duty in the design, layout, bindery and printing of this book.

◆◆◆◆◆◆◆

The deeply felt sentiments that Cliffie had about life and his immediate family are as true today as they were yesterday and forever will be:

Here I am Lord! Thank you for this beautiful day and all my blessings:

My talented second wife and best friend in the world, Joan Carol. Your love has brought new meaning and dimension into my life. Without you, this book would not have become a reality. Thanks for everything;

My beloved mother, Nina Belle Snyder, whom I adored with all my heart. Her selfless love and understanding inspired me to be all that I am;

My charismatic father, Clifford H. Snyder (AKA Herman, "the Hermit") who introduced me to music and encouraged me to become a professional musician. What fun we had performing together;

My beautiful late first wife, Dorothy, who gave me roots by standing, lovingly and faithfully, by my side while I chased my elusive dreams;

My bright daughter, Linda, whose inspired poetry I dearly enjoy and who truly gives of herself by teaching hearing impaired children;

My three "buddy" sons - Stephen, Curtis and Jonathan - who followed in my musical footsteps to find "their place in the sun," and now I'm learning from them;

My grandchildren - Katy, Susan, Mandy, Amy, Melinda, Jonathan Jr., Rachael, Seth and Abby - to whom the "song of life" has been passed on.

On Cliffie's behalf, I thank all the people who have been a part of our lives. You know who you are. (See page 241, "Tapestry of Friends.")

◆◆◆◆◆◆◆

I, too, want to thank God for the gift of life and for all my blessings:

My prince-of-a-husband and best friend, Cliffie - thank you! Our songs, "A Little Sooner" and "If I Had Never Loved You," say it all;

My angel-parents, Daisy and Leo Kiczenski, who showed me what love was all about through action. Thank you for the great lessons in courage;

My brother/friend, Ronald Kiczenski - I value our loving sibling relationship with all my heart. You are quite a man;

My sister-in-law, Cory - You've added so much to our family;

My nephew, Ronald Kiczenski, Jr. - Know that I love you;

My niece, Marie Roark - You've made your mother so proud;

My niece, Natasha Powers: Welcome! You bring joy to many people;

My extended family of sisters: Ann Powers, Mary Salamone and Jody Milligan - All of you are so special! Thank you for always being there;

Treasured friendships include: Marilyn Ball, Evelyn Ballard, Bob and Rochelle Brooks, Margie Evans, Annette Fuller, Teresa Jacobs, Neddy and Porky Johnson, John King, Laurie King, Jo McFadden, Marilee Montana, Rosemary Oehmler, Jim Powers, Maryrose Smochek, Bill Snipes, Cathy Stone, Tommi Stone and the Stone family. (See "Tapestry of Friends.")

To Steve, Linda, Curtis and Jonathan: Well done, Cliffie and Dorothy!

To all my cousins, aunts and uncles: Thanks for the great childhood memories. (See "Tapestry of Friends.")

To our four pawed family members - Tempo, Melody, Viva, Cappy, and Tasha. Unconditional love doesn't get any better than this;

I'd like to thank all the musicians, artists and songwriters that Cliffie and I were associated with down through the years, who are too numerous to mention here. (See "Tapestry of Friends.")

I acknowledge the great sport of tennis, which has been and continues to be a joyful passion. I thank all my tennis friends for sharing moments of their lives on and off the court with me. (See "Tapestry of Friends.")

I thank all the professional people who participated in their individual ways with my various projects. They include: Carol Anderson, Bonnie Balloch, Jeannie Bare, Paula Benjamin, J. R. Boyd, Chris Caravacci, Fred Ciporen, Jane David, Barbara Evans, Holly Foster-Wells, Jesse and Barbara Hogan, Brad Hooper, Steve Katz, Deirdre Kline, Mark Landis, Rebecca Miller, Victor Muschetto, Sandy Niles, Kathy Nolan, Dottie Oelhafen, Chip Peay, Hope Powell, Cheryl Rogers-Barnett, Patricia Schultz, Jim Shaw, Amy Striebel, Sunny Wise and Connie Woolsey.

Cliffie believed that a sense of humor was essential to enjoying and surviving life. From my heart, I thank Jay Leno for his "Tonight Show" monologues, which brought the first smile and laughter into my life when I needed it the most.

About The Author

Cliffie Stone brought country music to Sunset & Vine! He has been the most important influence on country music that the West Coast has ever had, which is now an integral part of country music's history.

This beloved jack-of-all-trades wore all the musical hats: bassist; disc jockey; radio, television and record producer; master of ceremonies; comedian; singer; songwriter; publisher; artist's manager; agent; author; Board of Directors' trustee for the Musicians Union Local 47; and executive positions at notable publishing and recording companies.

In Hollywood, he was one of the Academy of Country Music's founding fathers and has served on its Board of Directors as president, vice president and historian. In Nashville, he was one of the original members of the Country Music Association and has served as its vice president.

The honors that his peers have bestowed upon him include:

Academy of Country Music's Pioneer Award, 1972,
aka "THE CLIFFIE"

Hall of Fame - Country Music Association, 1989

Star on Sunset & Vine - Hollywood Walk of Fame, 1989

Country Music Disc Jockey's Hall of Fame, 1979

Walk of Western Stars, 1990

Shriners' Man of the Times, 1982

Hall of Fame - No. American Country Music Asso. Int'l, 1999

Los Angeles Music Week Honoree, 1998

Cliffie Stone was born Clifford Gilpen Snyder on March 1, 1917, to Nina Belle and Clifford H. Snyder in Stockton, California. He was raised in Burbank and his main interests in high school were football and music, namely the bass.

In 1939, he married Dorothy Darling and they had four children, Linda, Stephen, Curtis and Jonathan.

Cliffie's career began at age sixteen when he became Stuart Hamblen's permanent bass player on his "Lucky Stars" radio show. At one time or another, he was on twenty-eight radio stations in California.

One of his radio programs was the "Hometown Jamboree" show, which became one of the most popular, long-running variety shows on radio and television (1946 to 1960). It literally was a launching pad for a multitude of singers, musicians and songwriters that reads like a Who's Who in the music world. Over the years, many were regulars; others were featured guests, which include: Tennessee Ernie Ford, Merle Travis, Molly Bee, Billy Strange, Joanie O'Brien, Dallas Frazier, Tommy Sands, Ferlin Husky, Lefty Frizzell, Eddy Arnold, Johnny Cash, Jim Reeves, Barbara Mandrell, Johnny Horton, Johnny Bond, Tex Williams, Eddie Dean, Tex Ritter, Wesley and Marilyn Tuttle, Freddie Hart, Liberace, and even Elvis made an appearance at the beginning of his career.

Cliffie was a master at juggling three or four musical hats. In the mid-1940's one of his most fulfilling achievements occurred when Capitol Records signed him as a recording artist as well as head of their country/western department. He became a major influence in building Capitol's country roster with history-making artists.

In the ensuing years, he became a legendary force in all areas of the entertainment industry and developed a lasting reputation for being one of its most respected and beloved music men.

His passionate love for music and life was unceasing and after his first wife passed away, he married writer Joan Carol and continued to be involved in all areas of music. This array of activities includes: appearances on "Hometown Jamboree-Today" concerts; CBS and NBC music award shows; top-rated TNN cable shows; countless radio stations worldwide, including the Larry King Show; consultant and director of Gene Autry's publishing empire; and Historian on the ACM's Board of Directors. In the midst of all this, he produced seven albums, co-wrote forty songs and authored two books with Joan Carol: *Everything You Always Wanted to Know About Songwriting But Didn't Know Who to Ask* and *You Gotta Be Bad Before You Can Be Good*. Both books are lasting legacies that are geared toward perennial aspiring artists, which embodies his life-long passion of helping new talent to be all that they can be.

RADIO CREDITS include: "Lucky Stars," "Covered Wagon Jubilee," "King Cowboy Revue," "The Cowboy Church of the Air," Cliffie Stone's "Hometown Jamboree" (number one on KXLA), "The Cliffie Stone Radio Show" (KLAC), "Radio-Rodeo," "The Cowboy Hit Parade," "Dinner Bell Roundup," "Country Junction," "The First Western Quiz Show," "Harmony Homestead," "Hollywood Barn Dance" (CBS for eighteen years) and "Pot Luck Party" (CBS).

TELEVISION CREDITS: He produced over 14,000 television and radio shows during his career. They include: "Hometown Jamboree"; "Tennessee Ernie Ford Show" (five years - NBC-TV and CBS radio); "Molly Bee Show"; "Gene Autry's Melody Ranch"; "Songs for a Lusty Land" (T. Ernie Ford); "Christmas Songs" with Mel Torme; "Cross Country"; and two "Great American Gospel" shows (T. Ernie Ford).

He has made hundreds of appearances on television shows, which include: "Hometown Jamboree," "Tennessee Ernie Ford Show," the "Lawrence Welk Show," "Merv Griffin," and "Hee Haw."

More recent appearances include: "Academy of Country Music Awards Show" (NBC-TV); "Country Music Association's Awards Show" (CBS-TV); KTLA's Morning Show; The Nashville Network's (TNN) "Nashville Now" with Ralph Emery; TNN's "Crook & Chase"; TNN's "Prime Time Country"; and the "Tennessee Ernie Ford's 50th Anniversary Show."

RECORD COMPANY affiliations include: Capitol Records, RCA Records, Warner Bros. Records, Beltone Records, Granite Records, Lariat Records, ARA Records, Newhall Records and Showdown Records.

ALBUM PRODUCTION includes: Notable artists such as: Tennessee Ernie Ford, Merle Travis, Molly Bee, Sons of the Pioneers, Roy Rogers and Dale Evans, Stan Freberg, Tex Ritter, Tommy Sands, Stuart Hamblen, Tex Williams, Pat Buttram, and Kay Starr.

PUBLISHING COMPANY affiliations include: American Music (writer); Central Songs (owner); Beechwood Publishing; Executive Director & Consultant of Gene Autry's Western Music Publishing Co., Inc. and Ridgeway Music; ATV Music Group (Beatles catalog); Bayshore Music; Old Mill Music; Showdown Publishing Group.

ARIST CREDITS/Singles include *Billboard's* Top-Charted Songs:

"When My Blue Moon Turns to Gold Again" - *Cliffie Stone;*

"Silver Stars, Purple Sage, Eyes of Blue" - *Cliffie Stone & his Orchestra;*

"Peepin' Through The Keyhole" - *Cliffie Stone & his Barn Dance Band;*

"Little Pink Mack" - *Kay Adams with the Cliffie Stone Group*

ARTIST CREDITS/Capitol Records' Albums include:

"Cool Cowboy" - *Cliffie Stone*	Capitol T1230
"The Party's On Me" - *Cliffie Stone*	Capitol T1080
"The Cliffie Stone Singers Present the Great Hank Williams Songs"	Capitol T2159
" Cliffie Stone Presents the Original Country Sing-A-Long"	Capitol SKAO 15
"Cliffie Stone's Waltzes"	Capitol BD-4001
"Cliffie Stone & His Square Dance Band"	Capitol H4009
"El Ultimo Rodeo" - *Cliffie Stone*	Capitol TM-20770
"Dancing With A Memory" - *Cliffie Stone*	Showdown SD-1111

SONGWRITER CREDITS: Three of Cliffie's collaborations reached *Billboard's* Top 5 country charts: (See page 238.)

"Divorce Me C.O.D." - #1, Merle Travis (1946)

"Divorce Me C.O.D." - #5, King Sisters, 1946)

"Divorce Me C.O.D." - #4, Johnny Bond (1947)

"No Vacancy" - #3, Merle Travis (1946)

"New Steel Guitar Rag" - #5, Bill Boyd & the Cowboy Ramblers (1946)

PUBLISHER affiliated award-winning songs include: (See page 235.)

"Try a Little Kindness"	Glen Campbell/*Sapaugh & Austin*
"Mama, He's Crazy"	The Judds/*Kenny O'Dell*
"Put Your Hand in the Hand"	Anne Murray/*Gene MacLellan*
"Snowbird"	Anne Murray/*Gene MacLellan*
"Together Again"	Buck Owens/*Buck Owens*
"I'm Just An Old Chunk of Coal"	John Anderson/*Billy Joe Shaver*
"Silver Threads and Golden Needles"	Linda Ronstadt/*Rhodes & Reynolds*
"Wrong Time to Leave Me, Lucille"	Kenny Rogers/*R.Bowling/H.Bynum*
"Shot Gun Boogie"	T. Ernie Ford/*Cliffie Stone/TEFord*
"He'll Have to Go"	Jim Reeves/*Joe & Audrey Allison*

About the Co-Author

JOAN CAROL STONE, songwriter/singer/publisher/author has over one hundred and fifty published songs to her credit, many of which have been recorded and label-released by various artists.

She was born in Dearborn, Michigan, the second child of Daisy and Leo Kiczenski. A few years later, her father left the Ford Motor Company and moved his family to Punxsutawney, Pennsylvania. During this happy farm environment childhood, she became exposed to country music and sang with her guitar-playing uncles and cousins at family gatherings.

When she was twelve years old, her parents decided to make their home in Southern California. While in junior high school, she had an emergency appendectomy and contracted hepatitis. During her recuperation period, she developed a passion for books and music.

Carol attended San Fernando High School with her brother, Ronald. She excelled in sports and competed in the Women's Track and Field events in Southern California. Olympian, Stella Walsh (holder of 65 world and national track and field records for women) had high hopes for her in the 100 and 200-yard dashes and was grooming her to compete for the Nationals and future Olympic games three years down the road. However, she wasn't dedicated enough to go through the rigorous training schedule that was required. Instead, she concentrated on high school and became a cheerleader as well as Vice President of her senior class. Her brother, Ronald, became an all-city football player and later he graduated from the University of Southern California on a football scholarship.

After graduation, she became a managerial assistant at one of the Bank of America branches. Two years later, she decided to go into the Aerospace Industry where she worked with top flight engineers on various space programs. She also married her high school sweetheart, Carl Riefler, who played major league baseball for the Houston Astros after he graduated from college. In time, they amicably went their separate ways.

She decided to give the Entertainment Industry a whirl and she worked at various companies for years as an executive assistant, which includes the A&R and promotional departments of Capitol Records in Hollywood. It was here she briefly met Cliffie Stone, who had come to see Tennessee Ernie Ford when he was recording a gospel album.

During this time frame, she took singing, piano and guitar lessons and started writing her first songs. She also developed a passion for tennis as well as rekindling her love for books, which took her on a self-imposed spiritual journey to increase her self-enlightenment.

Years went by and Cliffie and Joan Carol's paths crossed again at a c/w club called the Silverado where he was emceeing a talent show. Ironically, this was to be his last night as an emcee, because he had been hired by Gene Autry to be the Director of his publishing companies. He told her to call him for an appointment, which she did a month or so later. Cliffie met with her and her co-writer, Marc Levine (bassist for Barry Manilow) and published six of their songs.

After Cliffie's wife, Dorothy, passed away, they started dating and were married in 1989. It turned out to be a marriage made in heaven because she preferred being the "wind beneath Cliffie's wings," and enjoyed turning him loose and watching him revel with boyish delight whenever he was in the spotlight on center stage.

For nine priceless and precious years, this versatile and beloved country music legend groomed her in all areas of the country music industry via his numerous projects (songwriting, publishing, artist management, record production, concert production and performing, publicity, advertising and promotional work). She has also co-authored two books with Cliffie, *Everything You Always Wanted to Know About Songwriting But Didn't Know Who to Ask* and *You Gotta Be Bad Before You Can Be Good*.

After her beloved Cliffie ascended, she took over the reins as President of their music publishing company and administers their song catalog as well as continuing to be involved in the creative areas of the business.

She is an avid tennis player and lives in Southern California with her two musical Shih Tzu dogs, Melody and Tempo.

Introduction

What and where is the most important stage in the world for new talent? Is it the Hollywood Bowl or the Dorothy Chandler Pavilion in Los Angeles? Is it the Radio City Music Hall in New York? Is it the London Palladium in England? Is it the Grand Ole Opry in Nashville? Is it the Las Vegas show stages or the multitude of television/cable stages such as TNN, CNN, NBC, CBS or ABC? Although they are world famous, it's none of the above!

I believe that the most important stage in the world for aspiring artists is their local talent show stage - be it in a nightclub or some other organizational venue! Without these stages, where can the "stars of tomorrow" go to serve their apprenticeship? Where can they go to get the initial experience and confidence in themselves so that someday they may be able to perform on some of the aforementioned prestigious stages? In short, where can they go to make mistakes and then correct them?

Because of my multi-faceted sixty-year music career, which included being involved in talent shows in one way or another at various times in my life, I feel that I can speak with authority on this subject. Since it appears to me that talent shows are on the *endangered species* list, I've had this urge to write a book about its importance.

Before proceeding, I decided to do some mini-research in a couple of bookstores and libraries to see if I could find anything up-to-date about talent contests and basic outlines for producing them. As far as I could tell, there wasn't anything that could help give amateurs some guidance.

Then I asked myself, "If I write this book, who is really going to care?" In my business, this is what we call a giant question because whenever we're producing an album, writing a song or a book, there has to be a market for it. Although I had my doubts, I kept seeing signs that convinced me there really is a need for this book.

One of those signs was the success of our first book, *Everything You Always Wanted to Know About Songwriting But Didn't Know Who to Ask*, which was published in January 1992. My darling wife, Joan Carol, and I spent a year promoting it, and I gratefully say that in its successful aftermath, we received hundreds of complimentary letters from readers.

In this book, I wrote a chapter called, "A 21-gun Salute to Talent Night Shows," which touched upon the importance of talent contests and their role in the development of future artists. In many of those letters, there were a variety of questions about the subject that I didn't cover.

To further validate the potential need for this book, in 1996 I was on TNN's "Prime Time Country" show and I talked about the talent show book that I was in the process of writing. As the saying goes, we got letters! So I knew there were people out there in the world who cared, which means there is a market for it. Why? Because there will always be new talent budding on the musical landscape who will be asking the same age-old questions. *"How do I get started with my career?"* *"Where do I go to get experience performing before an audience?"* *"How do I go about producing a show?"* *"Someone wants to sponsor my album, so how do I go about doing that?"* *"Do I need a lawyer or a manager?"* Once I realized that the talent show chapter could be a sequel to my songwriting book, a title popped into my head - *You Gotta Be Bad Before You Can Be Good!*

This book has had an incubation period of over five years for that's how long I've been thinking about it and recording my thoughts on tape. I've done this so that I could answer, to the best of my ability, every conceivable question that anyone could possibly ask.

As I said before, I feel that talent shows are on the endangered species list. So I've included a chapter that gives a thumbnail sketch about talent show production, which I hope will encourage potential producers.

Since "artist financing" is another subject that I'm constantly asked about by aspiring entertainers, I've devoted a chapter to it as well.

My friend, it's my desire that my book will help guide you to the realization of your dreams. But you don't need to become "world famous" to be a bona fide entertainer, because fame, at best, is nothing but the flicker of a firefly on a hot summer's night. Everyone has their own definition of success, and it's my belief that the most important thing for anyone is to *be all that they can be*, regardless what level they finally attain. Simply live each day to the max and enjoy each step along the way while maintaining your sense of humor because *You Gotta Be Bad Before You Can Be Good!* Welcome to my world!

Chapter 1

Caveman Boogie Band: Historically Speaking

"No one is more qualified to write about any aspect of the music business than this beloved CMA Hall of Fame member. New artists will enjoy Cliffie's sense of humor, along with the tried-and-true advice."
-JO WALKER-MEADOR, Country Music Association Hall of Fame, 1995

"Although our caveman didn't know any 'Achy Breaky Heart' songs in those days, he might have done something like 'Achy Breaky Heads' with his club."
-CLIFFIE STONE

I've been the Academy of Country Music's official Historian for the past several years, and I write a column for their monthly *Country Focus* newsletter called *Historically Speaking*. I'm proud of this title because I believe in caring for and watering the roots of traditional Mother Country Music. Young aspiring artists and fans should be aware of its foundational roots, which were built out of pure love by its pioneers. This is what has made country music what it is today! I'm thrilled to say that I've had wonderful feedback from the Academy members, which proves that people respect and sentimentally identify with their roots. Should you ever go to Nashville someday, I strongly urge you to pay a visit to the Country Music Foundation's Hall of Fame Museum, because they've done and continue to do a great job in preserving the integrity of its forefathers and foremothers!

They say that history repeats itself. Therefore, whatever feats have been done by anyone in the past can also be accomplished by someone today or in the future. Since I believe that the most important stage in the world is the talent show stage for new talent, let's take a few moments to reflect on its historical importance in the world of entertainment.

I fantasize that talent shows probably got started back in the days of the caveman. Reminds me of that motion picture, *2000 BC* (I never forget movies that have a beautiful lady in them). So let's use our

1

imaginations and travel back in time to the Stone Age.

Let's assume that the emotional makeup and basic genes that are in all of us human beings today were also in our Neanderthal ancestors. So I would imagine that any time two or more cave dwellers are huddled together, one of them would have an uncontrollable urge to sing or grunt or strut their stuff in some sort of a fashion under the moonlight. Maybe Caveman Sam found himself a four by eight-foot flat rock that could serve as his stage. If nothing else, he got on it to show off his cool Tarzan-like body and personality for the cave-woman he'd been chasing lately, but hadn't been able to convince her to swing along with him yet.

I certainly can't imagine Caveman Sam being a suave Cary Grant-type. He would probably be doing some wild and funny things like Robin Williams or Mel Brooks and Carl Reiner (whose classic "2000 Year Old Man" character is just hilarious). Although our caveman didn't know any "Achy Breaky Heart" songs in those days, he might have done something like "Achy Breaky Heads" with his club.

If Caveman Sam had any rhythm pounding through his veins at all, then maybe he put together a little group called the Caveman Boogie Band. Possibly they hit their hairy chests with their hands while grunting in harmony, or pounded their clubs in rhythm against the floor or walls to keep in time with the distant drummer they heard somewhere inside their heads. Whatever they did can only mean one thing: they felt the need to express themselves, which means the beat was a happening thing way back when; and here we are today, thousands of years later, and the beat still goes on!

But let's get serious here. Since the beginning of life and recorded time, there have been artistic people from all cultures worldwide who need to express and/or show off their talent in some forum. (Maybe that's how the name "talent show" came to be.)

I'm sure you've heard the word "vaudeville" mentioned at one time or another in your life and you may or may not know what it was all about. Well, vaudeville was the very heart of early America's history of entertainment in which the stage show would consist of a variety of unrelated acts, such as comedians, singers, musicians, dancers, animal acts, magicians, acrobats, etc. There were countless theater circuits, which were probably tiered from the prestigious to the mediocre to the less mediocre. This golden era's heyday was from about 1890 to 1915, and it continued into the 1930s. This is where the expression, "he was born in a trunk" originated, because many vaudevillians took their families on the road with them as they traveled the various theater circuits. They literally lived out of trunks, and since their children were exposed to show biz, many followed in their parents' footsteps.

The reason I mention vaudeville is because it seems to me that it was probably the granddaddy and/or the start of the talent show concept. After all, it had the same basic formula and format wherein it was entertainment in a public venue where a variety of aspiring acts could try out their talent, develop it and improve themselves and then move on to more prestigious theatres.

Anyway, when one evaluates the importance of talent shows in the history of the entertainment world (and I can only speak from my own life and times), they keep cropping up in all mediums and avenues of expression. They have certainly been an integral part of the script in countless movies.

There was the historical long-running series of comedy shorts called *Our Gang,* which the ingenious Hal Roach produced for theaters. Apparently he sold the rights to MGM in 1939, and when television came on the scene in the 1950s, about a hundred of the Roach shows were eventually released for television and the comedy series name was changed to *The Little Rascals.* You've probably seen these series on television at one time or another. (If you haven't, check out the cable stations that cater to the classics.)

This show consisted of a group of little kids who were always getting into amusing and mischievous situations. The main characters were Spanky, Buckwheat, Alfalfa and Darla. If I remember correctly, Darla imagined herself to be a dancer and Alfalfa fancied himself a crooner. Although Alfalfa is an awful singer, he and his buddies think he's just great, which is a running joke throughout the series; and, from time to time, they would stage talent shows in barns or wherever. I loved this series because it goes to the heart of this book: the most important stage in the world is your local talent show stage - be it in a barn, your own backyard or wherever the setting may be!

I've always loved all the movies that Mickey Rooney and Judy Garland starred in together when they were teenagers, which have become classics. One of my favorites was *Babes on Broadway*. At one time or another you may have seen it on one of the television or cable movie channels (or possibly video). Mickey and Judy portray a couple of young, unknown, star-struck kids who want to make it as actors on Broadway. So they decide to put on a benefit show in an urban building for an orphanage or children's home and they invite a big time Broadway producer in hopes that he'll discover them. Their set has a very countrified look to it, with a white picket fence and the cast members are all dressed up in overalls and cute funny clothes. The movie centers on them overcoming all odds as they happily follow their hearts.

Speaking of following one's heart, there was a 1994 motion picture starring Ann-Margaret called *Following Her Heart*. The title speaks for itself, and one of the most important scenes is near the end of the movie when Ann-Margaret wins a talent show at Buddy Killen's Stockyard nightclub in Nashville with one of country music's current stars, Travis Tritt, awarding her first prize.

As I said before, I can only speak from my own life and times. Goodness, I feel ancient when I say this, but let's a take look at talent shows at the beginning of radio, when it was the entertainment centerpiece in the family home, before there was television.

I don't know the exact date when radio was invented, but I do recall that my folks didn't get one for a long time because money wasn't easy to come by in those days. But it was around 1930 when my dad (whose show biz name was Herman, "the Hermit") bought one. My mother, dad and I would sit and listen to the radio, just like families watch television today (unless they're online and surfing the Internet).

I got hooked on the radio and listened whenever I could. Since my dad played so many musical instruments, I inherited my love for music from him, and I started playing the bass at an early age. I guess this is when my own fantasies about being a musician started to blossom, which is why I really enjoyed listening to the talent show programs.

Back in those days, there was a big time talent show on network radio called "Major Bowes and His Original Amateur Hour." After Major Bowes presented the new artists on his weekly show, the listening audience would call in their votes by telephone and this is how the winner was chosen. I don't think there was any way of knowing or tracking how many calls any one person made. I suppose if you had a lot of family and friends in radio land, you could be the winner even if you weren't the best performer.

However, best performers certainly did get discovered on this show. Frank Sinatra (in my opinion, the greatest popular singer/entertainer of our generation and possibly any future generations) has always credited "Major Bowes and His Original Amateur Hour" for giving him his first big career break. He was a hit when he appeared on the show in 1935 as part of a vocal quartet called the Hoboken Four, which lead to a cross-country tour with other variety acts.

After Major Bowes retired, a gentleman by the name of Ted Mack came on and replaced him. Many big stars of yesterday got started on "Major Bowes and His Original Amateur Hour" and "Ted Mack's Amateur Hour" show.

A most important radio talent show (and, eventually, television) was "Arthur Godfrey's Talent Scouts." I thought his show was really a neat way to present new talent because its premise was so uniquely formatted. A celebrity would come on his show and Arthur would interview him (or her) for a few minutes. Then he'd say, "Now, who have you brought us today?" The celebrity would respond with something like, "Well, it's a young man I heard sing in church, and I think he's got what it takes to be a star." Then the artist would come out and do his act.

Arthur was always my favorite because I felt we were alike in so many respects. Both of us had the same respectful attitude and passion for discovering new talent. I even entertained the thought that if I ever had my own television talent show some day, I would be the country version of him.

Many stars from that era were launched from "Arthur Godfrey's Talent Scouts" show, including the McGuire Sisters. This trio became regular cast members on Arthur's popular television variety show, before striking out on their own. They had several big hit records, as well as becoming a headline act for years at the most prestigious nightclubs in Las Vegas and throughout the country.

After "Arthur Godfrey's Talent Scouts" went off the air, there seemed to be a lapse in television talent shows.

Although I don't know the exact time frame, I was so pleased to see new creditable talent shows start to emerge on television and cable, which, thankfully, are available to the future stars of tomorrow.

For years (until the mid-1990s), one of the classiest talent shows was "Star Search," which Sam Riddle produced for Al Masini's company TeleRep. (Currently, Sam is the supervising producer of "From Hawaii...Destination Stardom," with Al Masini and Byron Allen as its executive producers.) The emcee on "Star Search" was Ed McMahon (Johnny Carson's sidekick on NBC's "Tonight Show" until Johnny retired). If I'm not mistaken, it had several category divisions, such as singers, dancers, comedians, etc. It ran in twenty-six week episodes, and the challenger would compete with the previous week's winner. The highly successful country act, Sawyer Brown, was once a winner on this legendary talent show.

Of course, I'm very partial to TNN (The Nashville Network), who have programmed a number of talent shows over the years, and I'd like to mention a few of them.

TNN had one about five or six years ago called, "You Could Be A Star." Their format consisted of a panel of three judges (usually prominent music industry people) who would give points to the contestants. If I remember correctly, they presented three artists in each half-hour segment and each one got so many points. Some of their winners have also had a chance at country music's brass ring.

Then there's my good buddy, Charlie Daniels, who has a talent show on TNN called the "Charlie Daniels' Talent Roundup." (I can't say enough good things about Charlie, who continues to stay true to the traditional roots of Mother Country, regardless of what the current trend is in country music.)

I've known many of the producers of the talent shows that I've just mentioned. One of them, whom I wish I could have gotten to know better, is the multitalented entertainer/songwriter, Bill Anderson, one of the co-producers of the aforementioned "You Could Be A Star." He also has written many hit songs, which landed him in the Nashville's Songwriters Association International Hall of Fame in 1975. His country hits include "The Tips of My Fingers," "City Lights" and "Still" (and he still is writing hits for the current stars of today). At the beginning of his career, Bill had entered several talent shows, which he mentions in his autobiography, *Whisperin' Bill*. He has a deep respect for talent because he is a great artist himself.

So I salute all these big time, history-making network talent shows and their producers, for they have done such a wonderful job presenting talent with dignity and respect.

I'm sure that some of you are wondering, "How do I get on one of these television talent shows?" I don't want to put the cart before the horse, but I will make a slight detour from the historical premise of this chapter to briefly talk about how you go about it (which may spur you on to continue reading this book).

If you wish to be on any of these shows, one of the first things you'll have to do is contact them for the standard procedures. They will probably want you to submit a cassette tape. If you pass their listening ears, they'll notify you and will probably set up an audition date and/or have you submit a video, which may be a prerequisite.

If it's the latter and you're a beginning professional, you may not be ready yet to put out a lot of dough to do a video at this stage of the game. But once you feel you have enough experience under your belt, then it may be worthwhile, because this is the only way a producer and/or a member of his staff can see how you will look on television and/or how well you interact with the camera. (I suggest that you pretend the camera is your friend, so look at it with love.)

This is just a brief outline of the various stages it may take to get on any of these television talent shows, and I'm throwing it in here so you'll have some knowledge about it, regardless what entertainment level you're currently at.

As I said at the beginning of this chapter, history repeats itself. What another artist has done in the past - be it pop, R&B or country - you, too, can do. This is why I felt it was important to give you a brief dissertation on the history of talent shows via vaudeville, radio, television and motion picture mediums during my lifetime. These talent shows (some are no longer on the air and have become a part of music history) can become a goal that you can work towards.

But, first things first. Don't forget that the artists who have appeared and who are currently appearing on some of these aforementioned television talent shows have had to get experience somewhere in order to become professional enough to qualify.

So where do you go to get this essential experience? Get on any stage that's available to you, particularly your local talent show, because *You Gotta Be Bad Before You Can Be Good.*

Chapter 2

"Hometown Jamboree"
My Talent Show Experiences

"Cliffie was the Ed Sullivan of the West Coast, and the future stars he discovered through his radio and television shows read like a 'Who's Who.'"
-JOE ALLISON, Hall of Fame, Nashville Songwriters Assn. Int'l, 1978

"In all talent shows and auditions, you'll find the good, the bad and the gifted. Oh, how I love to watch this parade of talent! And however long their fantasy may last, it makes me feel so good to see people letting their God-given talent shine."
-CLIFFIE STONE

Whenever the media is interviewing me, I inevitably bring up the subject of talent shows and I'm usually asked why I'm so passionate about them. Why, indeed, especially to warrant me writing a book about them! I think I've answered that question in the Introduction, because I know where you, the aspiring artist, are coming from.

Likewise, I would like you to know where I'm coming from, so I thought I'd share some of my experiences with talent shows and what originally got me interested in them in the first place.

The more I think about it, the more it seems as though I've been exposed to talent shows in one way or the other all my life. When I became semi-retired, I decided to devote more time to them. It's my way of giving back to a business that's been so good to me.

As I recall, my first encounter with a talent show occurred when I was a deejay on my own radio show on KIEV, a local 250-watt station in Glendale, California. My boss, Loyal King, decided to start a new Saturday afternoon talent search show; and since I was a deejay, which apparently qualified me, he asked me to be one of the judges. It was called "Stairway to Fame," which I thought was a great name. I really enjoyed the experience, but I found out that being a judge can be a thankless job at times. Since there can only be one winner (if there are extra prizes, there can be second and third places), it's only natural that there are going to be disappointed contestants. When I saw how upset some of them got, I developed my own attitude early on towards these two fickle imposters called *winning* and *losing*, which is for aspiring artists to think in terms of gaining invaluable experience regardless of whether they win or lose.

While taping my thoughts for this book, it occurred to me that my life-long penchant for discovering talent truly took root a few years later during my thirteen-year musical variety television show, "Hometown Jamboree." Although this wasn't a talent show, I presented new talent. In hindsight, my show was actually a launching pad for many artists, songwriters and musicians. They include superstars like Barbara Mandrell, Tennessee Ernie Ford (who had a worldwide hit with "Sixteen Tons"); Merle Travis (writer of "Sixteen Tons"); Molly Bee; Tommy Sands; Bobby Bare; comedian Stan Freberg, and the list goes on.

I would like you to have a feel for the exciting decades of the 1940s and 1950s, because I believe that at the time television was the most incredible invention since the wheel. When it was unleashed to the unsuspecting innocent masses of the world, it changed everyone's life forever. (Not to mention the fact that it was the granddaddy or catalyst to the incredible computer/Internet world explosion that we're experiencing today.) In the Southern California area alone there were originally seven channels: 2, 4, 5, 7, 9, 11 and 13.

Many of you are too young to have watched my "Hometown Jamboree" show, which aired on Channel 13 (and later Channel 5) on Saturday nights. If you have parents or grandparents who were residents of Southern California in the 1940s and 1950s, you may want to ask them if they remember, because it was truly a fun and wholesome show for the entire family.

However, the fly in the ointment was World War II, which was a horrific event, as all wars are. So during the early 1940s, California was inundated with hundreds of defense plants and its share of Army, Marine and Naval bases. These plants and Armed Service bases were primarily staffed and filled with people from every state in the union. Of course, it's only natural that these displaced folks were homesick and missed their own hometowns. I realized this so I decided to call both my radio and television show "Hometown Jamboree." I tried to give the audience what they wanted, which was a place for them to come so that they could forget their troubles. So I made it a homespun, fun-loving environment that would remind them of their close-knit communities back home.

It was this influx of people from all over the United States that made me very aware that talent isn't limited to any particular part of the world, but is within everyone everywhere. Since the television station was getting telephone calls from aspiring artists who wanted to know how they could get on my show, I decided to have a talent audition night. After all, if you don't audition people, how on earth are you going to know what they can do? So I would announce on my Saturday night show that if anyone wanted to audition, they should come down to the Channel 13 studio on Monday nights. Like clockwork, there would be thirty or forty people showing up ready to sing or play an instrument. There were three of us from the show who were involved: my keyboard player, Billy Liebert; my producer, Milt Hoffman and myself. Oh, how I loved to sit there (as I do today) and watch the parade of talent!

As I think about it, I guess you could say that my "Hometown Jamboree" audition night was my very own personal talent show. Not only would some of them "win" the audition, but also I had the "grand prize" of being able to present them professionally on local television to the immediate world. It was at these auditions that I discovered some wonderful artists and many of them became regulars on my show, while others were occasional guests.

I also had waltz contests that became a regular part of my shows, which was a huge hit with both the live and viewing audiences at home! Before the show, we'd play some waltzes and choose about four or five couples. At the allotted time slot during my television show, I'd interview each couple by asking their name and where they were from, etc. Then my band would play a waltz and I would let the audience decide who they thought were the best dancers. Regardless who won, they all received prizes.

One time I decided to have a talent contest for housewives on my show and it turned out just great! In order for the housewives to enter, they had to audition, at which time we would pick out three to appear on my show. I was amazed at all the talented housewives out there and it was wonderful to see their husbands, families and friends supporting them. Once again, I let the audience determine the winner. It was great fun and, regardless of who won, they all got prizes from my show's sponsor.

In essence, my "Hometown Jamboree's" audition night and its subsequent waltz and housewife talent contests were my first exposures to really working with raw untrained talent.

Somewhere in that time frame, I was also a judge on a talent show called "Stairway to Stardom," which was on one of the local channels. They would present about five talented artists and we'd have to choose who we thought deserved first place.

Whenever I think of "Stairway to Stardom," I recall a cute story that my dear friend, Jeannie Bare, once told Joan Carol and me when we were having dinner with her and her star hubby, Bobby Bare. When Jeannie was a fledgling singer/songwriter, she appeared on this talent show and she had stage fright so bad that when she started to sing, nothing came out. She mouthed the words until she got to the chorus and, finally, her voice came to the rescue. But the folks at home must have thought they were having audio difficulties with their television sets for a while! With time, Jeannie got over stage fright and appeared on my "Hometown Jamboree" show, as well as "Town Hall Party," and she was terrific! Her story is a wonderful example of the importance of talent shows, which give young artists the necessary experience to become true professionals.

Of course, there was a large time period in my life when I didn't have time to think about talent shows, because I was Tennessee Ernie Ford's manager. He was on his way to becoming a major star, and I was involved in a million things while on that trip to the moon with him. I was also managing several other artists, as well as running my publishing company, Central Songs, which garnered more than its share of BMI and ASCAP award-winning songs.

I decided to retire in my fifties, but that got boring. So when my good friend, Sam Trust (President of ATV Music Group) asked me if I wanted to head up the country division at ATV, I jumped at the chance.

Somewhere in that time span, I started producing and performing in a weekly Friday and Saturday night show called "Country Showdown" during the summer for about three or four years at a wonderful venue called Alpine Village in Torrance, California. Although this wasn't a talent contest, I was always presenting new talent along with established acts that I had on these shows.

Then my good buddy, Steve Tharp, who was a producer/engineer at KLAC, asked me if I'd help him put together a talent search contest for the radio station. At the time, he was producing biweekly remotes for KLAC from popular and well-known venues such as Disneyland, Knotts Berry Farm, Magic Mountain and the Palomino club. Since I love working with aspiring talent, I gladly got involved and it turned out to be an annual event for three consecutive years.

A year later, I became the Entertainment Director for an outdoor facility called Rivendale in the Santa Clarita area. Although I was hiring major acts like Merle Haggard on the weekends, I also decided to produce a "Battle of the Bands" contest, which was very successful. (I'll go into more detail about the two above contests in Chapter 10, "How and Where Do I Find Talent Shows?")

Around 1984, I produced and emceed talent shows at the legendary Palomino club in North Hollywood, California, which lasted over four years. I also emceed some prestigious talent contests that had big time sponsors as well as smaller ones at other clubs, the last one being the Silverado, which I decided to relinquish. (I had just been hired by Gene Autry to be the director/consultant of his vast publishing companies and I wanted to devote my full time to it.)

Dear reader, you now know something about my experience with talent shows, which has been a life-long avocation with me.

I have always enjoyed helping and encouraging new artists to follow their dreams because I know how tough it can be to get a break in the business. You can call me a Pollyanna, a pied piper or whatever, but however long anyone's fantasy may last - be it ten minutes, a month, a few years or a full-fledged career - it makes me feel so good to see people letting their God-given talent shine!

Chapter 3

Believe and Be! It's Your Call!

"God gave you a gift, and what you do with it is your gift to God."
-CLIFFIE STONE

"When Cliffie gave me the opportunity to work under his tutelage, he impacted my life. His belief in me not only influenced my work, but also my work ethics. I credit him for playing a big role in my success as a songwriter, publisher and producer."
-GEORGE RICHEY, Manager/Husband of Tammy Wynette
Record Producer/Award-Winning Songwriter

My friend, regardless of your age, it is possible for you to become a doctor, lawyer, dentist, athlete, pilot, carpenter, teacher, actor, musician or whatever your heart's desire!

Many talent show contestants who are pursuing their musical fantasies are already successful in some of the aforementioned occupations, and I've always been astounded at the unique variety of careers. One guy was a very successful building contractor in Burbank, but what he really wanted to be was a country singer. Another man was a big executive from one of the Hollywood trade magazines. One lady was a secretary. As they say in show business, "Don't quit your day job." One must make a living to pay the bills while pursuing a career in the entertainment industry.

Regardless of your age or what you do for a living, I'm assuming that since my talent show book has found its way into your life, you must be attracted to the music business in some way, shape or form. If any of my suggestions can help you "to be" whatever it is that you want "to be," then I've accomplished what I've set out to do.

I'm not going to make any bones about it! This is going to be a no frills, hard-hitting book about your possible future in the entertainment industry. I really believe that deep down behind the kneecaps in all of us there exists a nagging desire to express ourselves. One that says, "Maybe I can make it in the exciting world of show business!" You must have felt that way or you wouldn't be reading this book.

Since I'm semi-retired from country music, I'm very interested in spending the rest of my life writing books to impart some of the knowledge that I've acquired during my exciting sixty-plus years in this wonderful business.

To give this my best shot, I've had to do some deep thinking about all kinds of things relative to this book and to you, the aspiring artist (producer, manager, investor or whatever role you've chosen). During my extensive career, I've seen and have also been personally involved with thousands of people in all aspects of the music business - musicians, singers, songwriters, producers, managers, executives, etc. Some of the ones that I thought would make it, didn't. Others that I thought wouldn't make it, did. I finally came to the conclusion that it's anybody's ball game!

How and why does someone overcome all the odds and become a star? Is it talent? Personality? Promotion? Luck? No one really knows the answer. It's my opinion that it's a combination of the foregoing, coupled with essential components such as self-esteem, self-respect, confidence, and an *unwavering belief* in yourself as the underlying magical glue that keeps it altogether.

It's one thing to say that you believe in yourself; it's another to feel it at gut level and live it through action. You see, it's all too easy to have your belief system watered down over a period of time for whatever reason, including a series of so-called negative experiences and/or remarks.

This may sound totally irrelevant to this chapter's subject matter, but let's stop to consider for a moment the miracle of life. (If this doesn't encourage you to believe that anything is possible then I don't know what will!) We're all born with a physical body, a mind and a soul - all of which houses our precious God-given emotions.

All things being equal, we basically have a body that physically functions the same way so that we can live in this earthly form of existence. We eat, and our body will digest the food automatically without any help from us whatsoever. We have eyes and ears and the same moving parts such as arms and legs to help us go about our business on this planet. We all have a heart that beats so that our blood can flow throughout our body and, needless to say, without the ability of the lungs to breathe, it would be a no go.

Each of us is born with an incredible computer-type brain (some use it more than others). Now I'm not going to sit here and go into detail about the miraculous wonders of the conscious and subconscious areas of our mind. I don't know how it works nor do I care. It just is! If you want to pursue this subject, there are scores of books available to you in libraries and bookstores. The important thing to remember is that it's all in how you use your mental abilities. For every action, there's a reaction; for every cause, there's an effect. We're all subject to these immutable universal laws of nature. It's as simple as that.

Now for the greatest and most glorious miracle of all - the emotional, soulful aspect that is within each one of us. Master poets, such as Kahlil Gibran, are more adept at describing the "singing of the soul," as I like to call it, than I am. If you haven't read his classic masterpiece, *The Prophet*, then I highly recommend that you do.

We are sensitive human beings who are endowed with a variety of emotions that encompass love, hate, laughter, tears, anger, fear, etc. In a nutshell, somewhere within your body, mind and soul is your God-given gifts, and it's up to you to discover them so that you can let your talent shine before the world. I firmly believe that regardless what your area of interest is - be it a musician, singer or songwriter - we all have the same shot at the "big time."

I can hear some of you giving me excuses as to why you can't do this or why you can't do that! You might be saying, "I can't do this because I'm not good looking enough;" or "I can't do that because I come from a poor family;" or "I can't do this because I have this situation or this problem." What is the problem? I have always believed that you don't have a problem until you "think" you have a problem. But if you do have a problem, it's up to you to accept the responsibility of dealing with it. The only thing other folks can do is give you advice from their own point of view. In the final analysis, it's entirely up to you to make the decisions because you're the one who has to live your life. Just don't sabotage yourself with excuses or set up roadblocks on your journey to being all that you can be.

One of the most important things you can do is to eliminate the words "I can't" from your vocabulary and replace them with "I can." It's quite obvious that you'll never be able to succeed at anything if you constantly say, "I can't." By thinking and saying "I can," you have set the positive law of belief into motion, which can produce magical results. Even if you're fearful of trying something, you must gather up the courage to do what you love to do. The key word here is "love." When you love something enough, it will give you the courage to go into action. Once you experience baby successes, you're on your way to building a belief system that will make you stand tall whenever life's trials seem to overwhelm you.

Let's take the word *believe* just one step further. I'm going to talk about someone who believes in you and your abilities other than yourself. Let's face it: we all carry our own little bag of rocks and insecurities, and to have someone on your side during the difficult times is a blessing. It helps to have your own personal support system who will be there cheerleading you on whenever you waiver in the belief department or when things aren't going right.

When you were a child, do you remember the first time you ever did anything that required courage? For instance, if you played piano for the first time at a recital in front of an audience or if you played baseball and it was your turn at bat. Your hands and knees were shaking so you quickly searched the audience for your mom and dad and there they were - giving you the thumbs up sign. They *believed* in you! Do you remember how this gave you additional confidence and belief in yourself? So the importance of someone believing in your talent is vital because it will give you that added boost of confidence whenever your belief system falters.

One of the highlights of my life occurred in 1989 when I received the Country Music Association's Hall of Fame Award on the Grand Ole Opry Stage in Nashville. I enjoyed all the people congratulating and talking to me afterwards at the numerous parties that Joan Carol and I attended. I still smile whenever I think of this one lady who came up to me and said, "Cliffie, if you hadn't believed in me, I never would have come to Nashville to pursue my career." For the life of me, I couldn't remember ever meeting her nor did I ever see or hear from her again. However, I'm glad that whatever I said somewhere in time helped her to believe in herself.

Of course, there are those people who believe in themselves from the get-go and aggressively move toward their goals. My longtime friend and associate, Stuart Hamblen (who wrote one of my favorite religious songs, "It Is No Secret"), was one of them. But for most of us, it's an acquired attitude that needs renewing from time to time.

17

And tuning into Dr. Robert H. Schuller's (Pastor of the Crystal Cathedral in Garden Grove, CA) weekly "Hour of Power" television ministry is one of the ways you can renew yourself! For years, he's shared the secret of God's power and how to move toward one's goals and dreams, through his enthusiastic sermons as well as his inspirational books! Two of his uniquely titled books that come to mind are *Move Ahead with Possibility Thinking* and *Tough Times Never Last but Tough People Do*, which were on my nightstand while I read them.

Sammy Davis, Jr. was one of the most multi-talented entertainers ever to grace a stage. He, along with his good buddies, Dean Martin and Frank Sinatra, made unforgettable history in all areas of show biz for decades. But Sammy had his share of tough times, which he wrote about in his inspiring autobiography entitled, *Yes, I Can*. I've never forgotten that title, because those three simple but powerful words say it all!

As I said before, take the words "I can't" out of your vocabulary and replace it with "yes, I can." Make it a daily habit. When your belief batteries really need to be recharged, look into the mirror and say them over and over. You'll be amazed at the results.

It's my desire to encourage you to do something with your potential talent so that you, hopefully, will get a chance at the "big time." But my words of encouragement will be to no avail unless you take action. If there is no action, there is no reaction.

I believe that it's anybody's ball game. We all start out in life, more or less, with pretty much the same physical, mental and emotional equipment. It's what you do with what you've got that counts! If someone has become a star, you can bet that he *believed* in himself, which made him stand out above the crowd. This thing called *belief* is absolutely magical, and it's yours for the taking.

God gave you a gift, and what you do with it is your gift to God. So boldly believe in your talent as you step onto the stage of life and let your talent shine. Believe and be! It's your call!

Chapter 4

You Don't Have to Be Born in a Trunk!
Getting Started

"I met Cliffie in the late '60s in Hollywood, and he was already a legend. He was a beacon for country talent, and our most effective voice to the L.A. entertainment industry. Doors for country music opened wider and sooner because of him."
-BRUCE HINTON, Chairman, MCA Records Nashville

"There are a thousand answers to the question, 'How do I get started in show business?' And whatever helps you to get your foot in the door is your very own personalized answer."
 -CLIFFIE STONE

"He was born in a trunk" is an expression that originated in the vaudeville era, which was the very heart of early America's history of entertainment. As I said in Chapter 1, "Caveman Boogie Band," these vaudeville performers and their families traveled the various theater circuits. They lived out of trunks and many of their children followed in their footsteps.

Dear reader, *you don't have to be born in a trunk to get started in show business*. Yes, it would be nice if you had relatives in the business to help you, but where there's a will, there's a way.

Here's one of my favorite sayings that I've used for years: "If you want to be successful in show business, simply listen to the audience, and then give them what they want to hear."

So, I've let you, the audience of aspiring talent, tell me what you want to know about making it in show business. One of those questions I'm constantly asked via letters or in person is "How do I get started in show business?"

Now that is a great question! I don't want to scare you, but that question potentially has a thousand answers, and whatever helps you to get your foot in the door is your very own personalized answer.

What I mean by the foregoing statement is this: although I don't personally know you, I don't hesitate for a second in saying that you are very special! Just as I am special and everyone else, too. Each of us has our own individual likes and dislikes, which is why we have chocolate, vanilla and an endless variety of ice cream flavors. All of us have different backgrounds, religions, nationalities, etc. I have never been able to understand why people would get inferiority complexes because they felt or looked different than others. You are unique, so objectively find those wonderful attributes that are yours alone. Once you acknowledge them, they will stand you in good stead in any situation that confronts you.

So how does this relate to your personalized answer to the question, "How do I get started in show business?" As I said before, your answer may be different from other folks. My first opportunity, which was my answer, was unique unto me.

Having said that, you may be curious as to how I got started. I guess you could say I was sort of "born in a trunk." My father was an individualist who made a living in a variety of ways, including being an actor and a musician. He had small parts in many movies and there wasn't an instrument he couldn't play! He even built some of his own instruments, and I developed a love for music by being around him. I tried out several instruments, but it was the deep tones of the bass that stirred something within my soul. So I practiced religiously until I turned out to be a pretty good gut bass player.

One of my dad's gigs was playing banjo on Stuart Hamblen's "Lucky Stars" radio show. One day the bass player quit and my dad told Stuart that he had a sixteen-year-old son who could play bass. So Stuart gave me a chance, and after a few weeks he asked me to be a member of his show. As it turns out, I had a natural flair for comedy and it wasn't long before Stuart and I started trading quips throughout the radio show. In one of our off-the-cuff humorous retorts, he called me Cliffie Stonehead and the name found a home with me. Somewhere along the line I shortened it to Stone and now you know how Cliffie Stone came to be.

Although it was my dad who opened the door for me, I'm the one who had to walk through it. This was my entrée into show business, wherein I became associated with other people in the music field, which, ultimately, led to many other opportunities.

But let's get back to you! If you're an aspiring singer, musician, comedian or whatever who has had little or no experience in front of an audience, where do you go to get started? Now, I'm not talking about sitting around the piano and having fun singing with your family and friends, which is a memorable thing to do. I'm talking about an audience that is made up of strangers who aren't bias and will react to you as they perceive you to be (although most artists usually bring a few friends for support when they perform).

I can only think of two places. One is church choirs, where many country stars (and artists from other music genres, such as the R&B singer, Aretha Franklin) have gained invaluable experience; the other is your local talent show stage, which I talked about in my Introduction. It's my opinion that the latter is the most important stage in the world for the stars of tomorrow!

Why? It's here that you and all aspiring artists can take your first step up the show biz ladder. Here is where you can learn to deal with stage fright. Here is where you can get a feel for and a glimpse of what it's like to be an artist. Here is where you can make mistakes and then correct them. Never be embarrassed about starting there, because many stars have done so at the beginning of their careers.

Yes, you'll be making mistakes because *you gotta be bad before you can be good.* But always remember that you're the captain of your ship and when you find you're going in the wrong direction, adjust your sails to get back on course to your destination. Never let anyone knock the wind out of your sails by something they may have said, either unwittingly or intentionally.

Let's pretend that you forgot a lyric line or you sang out of tune. Or maybe some drunk made a remark and you got flustered. I'm sure you've heard the expression, "just like water off a duck's back." With more stage experience, you'll be able to handle any adverse situation "just like water off a duck's back." In other words, you'll rise above it and won't let it affect you. As they say in tennis, you'll be getting *match tough*, but in this case, each time you perform, you'll be getting *stage tough*. Once you start experiencing one little success after another, you'll soon build a large bank account of priceless belief in yourself.

Personally, I think it's easier for people to get started in the music industry than any other phase of the entertainment world, such as

21

acting, which I tried myself at one time. To me, it was more rewarding creatively to become a singer or musician, wherein you can sing or play at the drop of a hat. In contrast, an actor has to depend on casting directors, a script, and then has to worry about his facial expressions and saying his lines right, etc.

Since you're reading this book, you must have an interest in being a singer or a musician. If that doesn't work out for you, there are many other areas of the industry that are open to you. Regardless what end of the music spectrum you end up participating in, it would behoove you to know something about music.

Maybe some of you are saying to yourselves, "But I'm not very musical" or "I can't sing a note or play an instrument." Have you really tried? You don't know what you're capable of doing until you've given it a fair chance. Music is built on mathematics, and if you can add two and two and get four, you should be able to learn how to play an instrument.

You may be surprised to know that most of the classic country songs are made up of three or four simple chords. After all, there are only eight notes in a scale. In my first book, *Everything You Always Wanted to Know About Songwriting But Didn't Know Who to Ask*, one of my chapters is "You Don't Need a Ph.D. in Music to Write a Melody." It will give you encouragement if you read it.

The guitar is one of the most popular instruments because it's so versatile (and easy to carry). Let's say that you've always wanted to learn, but never had the time or opportunity. However, it seems to me that if you really want to do something, you'll make the time. You can do this by simply putting aside fifteen minutes a day to practice, and you can build from there.

If you can't afford to take lessons, you could become self-taught. One of the greatest self-taught guitar players and songwriters of all times is Merle Travis (writer of "Sixteen Tons"), who became a regular member of my "Hometown Jamboree" television show. Merle has always been a big influence on so many guitar players down through the years, such as Capitol Records' Steve Wariner - a multi-talented artist who can do it all, including songwriting and producing.

There are thousands of inexpensive and easy to understand "how to" music books (some include CDs so that you can hear how the various practice lessons should sound) and videos. They, as well as my above-mentioned songwriting book, are available at music stores, libraries and bookstores. Don't forget to surf the Internet, because it can inform you about any subject matter.

Also, look in your TV guide, because I've seen guitar being taught on public broadcasting and cable stations. From time to time, The Nashville Network (TNN) has well known country guitarists who are plugging their own "how to play guitar" commercials.

You've probably seen experts and pundits on television talking about every subject imaginable. You, too, could become an expert on music by keeping up with what's happening on the music scene, so that you can, as they say in show biz, schmooze up a storm.

To give you an idea of what's available to you other than being a singer, songwriter or musician, I've made a list of related areas in the music industry. They include: record producer, manager, music publisher, song plugger, publicist, booking agent, entertainment lawyer, music accountant, disc jockey, record companies (executive assistant, marketing, sales, advertising, receptionist), photographer, television and/or video producer/director, magazine editor, artist, investor, and the list goes on. So there are numerous opportunities that can help you get started in the business.

Down through the years, I've known so many people who have chosen the executive side of the music industry simply because they're dyed-in-the-wool country fans. I'll name a few of them, because there's nothing like examples to build a fire under you.

I met Jo Walker-Meador when the Country Music Association first opened its doors in Nashville, and we became close friends as the years went by. She started there as a secretary and, through unceasing devotion and hard work, became its executive director; she continued in that capacity for many years before retiring three or four years ago. She deservedly was inducted into the Country Music Association's Hall of Fame in 1995.

Another lady I deeply admire and respect is Frances Preston, who started out as a receptionist at WSM-AM-TV in Nashville. From there, she became involved with BMI (Broadcast Music Incorporated, a performing rights society). Today, she's the CEO and president of BMI. And because of her enormous contribution to the music industry, she was inducted into the Country Music Association's Hall of Fame in 1992.

In Hollywood, I was one of the founding fathers of the Academy of Country Music. Further on down the road, I met Fran and Bill Boyd when they first joined the ACM as members. From the get go, they dedicated their lives to the Academy and the promotion of country music. Through dedication and hard work, both of them worked their way up to executive positions. Sadly, Bill passed away long before his time, but his wife, Fran, courageously carries on and she's now the Academy's executive director.

Many people (even those with college degrees) started out in lower positions, such as in the mailroom or janitorial departments in order to get their foot in the door. One of my favorite artist/songwriters, Alan Jackson, worked in the mailroom of The Nashville Network for a while. The multi-talented artist/songwriter/actor Kris Kristofferson was a janitor at CBS when he first went to Nashville to break into the business.

Whether you aspire to be an artist or end up choosing another area of the music business, I certainly hope that my aforementioned examples will inspire you to take full advantage of any opportunity that comes your way. With a lot of hard work, as well as a little luck, you can lead a very fulfilling and successful life in the entertainment field.

You don't have to be born in a trunk to get started in show business. Hopefully, somewhere in the pages of this book, you will find your personal answer to the question, "How do I get started in show business?" And when you do, welcome to my world!

Chapter 5

The Key to Success: Pre-Show Preparation!

"Cliffie's career-building suggestions will bring the reader up close and personal to a man who was involved in the careers of hundreds of successful artists."
-FRANCES PRESTON, BMI President and CEO; CMA Hall of Fame, 1992

"You're always auditioning whenever you step on a stage. If you're prepared, any number of magical things can happen to you."
-CLIFFIE STONE

When I started writing this talent show book, I knew that my title, *You Gotta Be Bad Before You Can Be Good*, struck at the very heart of show business itself. I wanted it to have "key" road-tested suggestions that could help unlock the seemingly hard-to-open entertainment door, which could guide the truly interested people to try out their creative wings - be it as an entertainer or possibly in the executive area of the business. Should it be as an entertainer, one of the keys to unlocking that door is "pre-show preparation."

In one of my chapters in my first book, *Everything You Always Wanted to Know About Songwriting But Didn't Know Who to Ask*, I refer to being in the right frame of mind as being in the process. This is also what you're doing when you're trying to make the hundred-and-one decisions with regard to your adventure into the fantasy world of entertainment. Assuming that you've decided to go for it, you're now in the process of figuring out how and what you're going to do. If you're truly a newcomer, maybe I should define a couple of common music terms, as I perceive them to be.

Amateur show: The word "amateur" implies that someone pursues an interest more or less as a hobby instead of a profession. In short, they're not as experienced as a professional who is able to do it for a living. Talent contests offer amateurs (I prefer to call them "aspiring artists" or "beginning professionals") that experience so that someday they may be able to perform for a living.

In amateur shows, there could be anywhere from ten to thirty acts participating and they are usually on stage about four minutes. I'm glad that some of the contest names have replaced "amateur" with other sundry titles like "Opportunity Time" or "Showcase."

Showcase: However, there is a slight difference between "showcase" and "amateur" shows. When you hear someone say, "We're going to showcase some talent," this usually means that the artists are more experienced and that there will be one or two people performing who will sing five or six songs, which could take about twenty-five minutes per person. In other words, they showcase their entire talent. However, the word has been kicked around a lot, and I guess it really doesn't make that much difference anymore.

Regardless of whether they call a talent contest an amateur show or use the word "showcase," you may want to know what is required of you when you enter one. Since I was primarily involved as an emcee and producer of talent shows in a c/w nightclub setting, that's the venue to which I'll be referring. (I'll go into more detail on the requirements in Chapter 7, "Sides to the Bridge.")

In a nutshell, you simply sign up when you go to the club on the evening of the scheduled talent night show. There is no band rehearsal, so if you are planning to sing, it would be helpful to have sheet music to give to the bandleader, especially if it's a relatively new song. When the emcee calls your name, you get up on that stage and perform to the best of your ability.

However, before you step out on stage, there are numerous "preshow" things for you to consider, and I'll discuss some of them.

CHOOSE YOUR CATEGORY: First of all, you have to choose the category you'll be participating in - singer, vocal duet, musician, comedian, dancer, magician or whatever. Since singing is the most popular, I'll use that as the example and most of the things I say about it can be applied to the other categories.

There are some important questions that you should be asking yourself. First of all, what singer or singers do you admire? This, of course, would indicate what genre of music you're interested in. Do you want to sing rock 'n' roll, a pop ballad, a country standard, R&B, gospel or a Broadway show tune?

Personally, I enjoy numerous singers who are in various music genres. In the pop field, it's Frank Sinatra and Barbra Streisand. In the country field, it's hard for me to choose because so many artists from various time frames of my life come to mind. Naturally, Ernie Ford is one of my favorites because I discovered and managed him. But others include Merle Haggard, George Jones, Tammy Wynette, George Strait, Patty Loveless, Vince Gill and Alan Jackson.

I'm very partial to Merle since he's both a premier country singer and songwriter. He's been called the "Poet of the Common Man" and he truly is! Listening to the songs he recorded when Ken Nelson was head of the country division in Hollywood for Capitol Records brings back memories, because I frequently dropped in on his sessions. And whenever I did, the song that he was recording would become a hit, so he started calling me his good luck charm, which always flattered me to no end.

Quite frankly, I believe that country music is the easiest genre for aspiring artists to enter because it's so diversified nowadays - from traditional country to country rock to country pop to whatever. This gives you a broad spectrum of songs to choose from, which leads to the next question: "What is your favorite country song?" You undoubtedly have several favorite songs for different moods.

If you're a girl singer, I venture to say that "Crazy" will be the one you'll choose to sing. I know for a fact that "Crazy" is a winner because it's won more talent shows than any other song I know of, which is the only reason I'm plugging it. I didn't publish it and Willie Nelson wrote it years ago. (This reminds me of an inside joke among musicians: "How many girl singers does it take to sing "Crazy?" Answer: "All of them!")

If you've chosen "Crazy," do be aware that it's not the easiest song in the world to sing because it has a large melodic range and it requires a little vocal gymnastics. Should you have difficulty hitting all the notes, you may want to choose an easier song.

The reason I'm saying this is because I want you to have every possible chance of succeeding. It's going to do nothing for your confidence when you're in front of an audience and you can't hit a high note or if you do, it's flat. The important thing is for you to feel comfortable with whatever song you've chosen to sing.

If this should be your first time or first few times on stage, I would suggest you pick a standard song that the house band will know, because when they know a tune, you are halfway home. (Believe me, they will know "Crazy.") But if you've chosen an original song or one of the current hits that they're not familiar with, I suggest you get a copy of the sheet music from your local music store. If it's an original, make up a lead sheet with the lyrics, chord and melody. If you don't know how yet, then have a musician do it.

To make things simple, let's assume that you've chosen to sing "Crazy." (If you haven't, let's go with "Crazy" because I'd go crazy trying to cover the thousands of great songs that are available.) Do you know your key? Do you know all the lyrics? Do you know the melody line? If you're not sure, then buy Patsy Cline's version of "Crazy" and listen to it, because it's a classic!

If, by chance, you can sing like her, then you're pretty well down the road. But chances are you can't, because not many vocalists can. Besides, you're just learning, so just observe how she's phrasing the lyrics. Then sing along with her to learn how to phrase. (Phrasing means the way a vocalist delivers or sings a group of words.) Practice by playing that record over and over while you're driving a car, washing dishes or whatever. If at all possible, rehearse with a musician until you know it inside out.

YOUR IMAGE: Let's talk about you personally. Never forget that your show business image is of the utmost importance, because whenever you get up on stage, you're saying, "Look at me."

Have you given any thought about what kind of an image you'll be projecting to the audience? If you haven't, then you should. It can be difficult to evaluate yourself, especially if you're new at the game and feel insecure. However, try to be objective.

Do you think you're the girl-next-door type, or are you the sexy type? (We all like to feel that we have sex appeal.) What is your age group? Does your hairstyle become you? Do you have the proper show clothes? (I'll be discussing wardrobe later in the chapter.)

For example, let's say that you're a beautiful young lady who has always wanted to enter the Miss Teen or the Miss America contest. Therefore, having a wholesome look about you would be just as important as your talent, whether it's singing, dancing or playing an instrument. And if you are past the age of entering the Miss America contest, then maybe you could be in the Mrs. America contest. I feel that anyone who has a few years on them will have more poise and dignity because they've experienced more of life.

28

Whenever I talk about image, I can't help but think of this guy who faithfully came to my Palomino talent shows month after month and he wasn't even close to coming in third place. I smile affectionately whenever I recall the evening that he said to me, "Cliffie, I think I'll change my image." I couldn't believe my ears, but I tried to be tactful yet truthful when I said, "With all due respect, John, you don't have an image. How can you change something you haven't got? So, buddy, go ahead and start off fresh." Bless his heart! I truly admired the guy for thinking and trying.

Your image is something you've got to consider and those people closest to you, your support system, can be helpful. However, in the final analysis, you have to feel comfortable with yourself.

SELF-ESTEEM: Self-esteem is how you truly feel about yourself deep down inside your kneecaps from which there is no escape. What I've said about "believing" in Chapter 3, "Believe and Be," also applies to self-esteem. But I still want to make a few comments about it because it's a big part of your image and it's vital for your success on and off the stage.

I've never forgotten an interview that I saw with a very talented, intelligent and beautiful actress years ago. At the height of her career, she had a successful television series and she shared the fact that even though she had professional success, she had an unhappy relationship with a man, which affected her self-esteem. She candidly talked about that period in her life. Once she made a number of personal changes in her life, she felt better about herself, and her professional work reflected it from that time onward.

Oh, what a battle these two words have been for so many people and I venture to say that all of us, at one time or another, have had to deal with it whether we want to admit it or not. I've had my own bouts with it, especially when I was in my early teens.

So let's cut to the chase: all of us human beings are emotionally fragile! Basically, we all want to be loved and appreciated. No matter how old we are or how thick-skinned we think we've become, unkind or thoughtless remarks as well as negative experiences can have their effect on us if we choose to let them.

My friend, I care about you and I want you to have high self-esteem. If you aren't feeling good about yourself, then consciously start to work at building your self-esteem so that you do.

29

One of the things you can do is to treat yourself kindly and have respect for yourself. You're different and special, so carry yourself with dignity! Be proud of what you look like! Be proud of how you dress! Be proud of how you sing or play the guitar no matter what performance level you're at! Be proud of everything you do that's of a positive, constructive and loving nature.

I'm not talking about an "attitude" that's on the borderline of being egotistical. I'm talking about knowing, accepting and loving yourself for whatever you have found yourself to be. There are those people who seem to enjoy saying negative things about other people. So take a stand within yourself and never let anything that anyone may say or do to you diminish that precious self-esteem part of you.

Whether you're in a talent show or doing a regular gig, be proud of yourself for having the courage to get on stage and doing the best you can at that moment in time. Wherever you stand is holy ground! That's the kind of self-esteem I want you to have. Yes, this is soul stuff I'm talking about. So love yourself unconditionally!

STAGE PRESENCE/BODY LANGUAGE: Stage presence and body language reflect a big part of your self-esteem and self image so let's give it some attention. Your physical demeanor, how you act and your body language while you're performing all add up to stage presence. So from the moment you make your entrance until the time you exit the stage, project confidence!

I read somewhere that the subconscious can't tell the difference between a real and an imagined experience. So in your mind's eye, see yourself moving around on stage with poise. If you are about to go on stage and you don't feel confident, then act "as if" you were. Doing these simple mental exercises will help to keep your energy forces moving in a positive direction and it will be a matter of time until you are what you have imagined yourself to be.

This is why being prepared is important because it will give you confidence. Yes, it can be a difficult thing to do when you're first starting out, because you're unsure of yourself in so many areas. But this is the beauty of talent shows, because here is where you can practice every time you step on the stage until you get it altogether.

How you put over a song to an audience so they can identify with it is made up of not only singing, but also your entire body language. I recommend that you observe the master entertainers either in person or via concert reruns on television.

To celebrate our fourth wedding anniversary, Joan Carol and I were fortunate to see Frank Sinatra perform at the MGM Grand in Las Vegas. He totally mesmerized the entire audience! After he sang his last number and walked off the stage to another standing ovation, my darlin' and I just sat in our chairs for about twenty minutes (as many others did) relishing the performance we had just witnessed. His show was an event and none of us wanted it to end. Talk about leaving an audience wanting more!

Frank has done a lot of television specials at various stages of his career, which are classics, and if you ever see them scheduled in your TV guide, especially the Public Broadcasting channel, tune in.

George Strait is a multi award-winning artist. He won the ACM and CMA Entertainer of the Year in 1989 and 1990, respectively. He's so cool and keeps it simple with the minimum of movement, whether it's an up-tempo or a ballad. Less is more and he just stands there with his guitar and flat out sings while captivating the audience with his facial nuances, which has a powerful impact on them.

I just have to mention Barbara Mandrell, who performed on my "Hometown Jamboree" show a few times at the beginning of her career when she was a youngster. She's also a multi-award winning CMA and ACM artist. In 1980 and 1981, she was the CMA Entertainer of the Year. She sings and plays a variety of instruments and is so full of energy on stage! She proves that big talent comes in small packages, and she's my Entertainer of the Year forever.

I could go on and on with wonderful examples, but there's nothing like observing the top current artists like George, Garth or Reba with your own eyes. Then go to the drawing board and work out your own body language and stage presence. The bottom line is for you to do whatever feels natural and fits your personality.

WARDROBE - DRESS THE PART: When I studied acting, (see Chapters 11 and 23), I learned to "dress the part" of whatever role I was acting out. All my life, I've believed in having a quality stage wardrobe. In my generation, dressing sharp is what television sponsors, recording company employers, club owners and fans expected of entertainers, which still holds true today but is more lax.

31

I'm pleased to see that most country artists and stars "dress the part of an entertainer" on award shows or when they're doing a concert. However, many of today's artists and musicians in all music genres don't dress as classy for the occasion as they should.

Dressing sharp is never out of style and I want you to stand out in a crowd. If you're going to audition for a commercial, a talent show, and a gig or if you're meeting with an executive, please don't show up in tennis shoes, blue jeans, a dirty T-shirt and a baseball cap. Okay? Always dress appropriately for the occasion, especially when you're doing a gig, because first impressions count!

Some of you may say, "But this is how everyone dresses now" or "I'm making a statement" or "I don't want to do that." Well, I know you don't want to do that, but why do you want to be like everyone else? And what kind of a statement do you think is being made when you dress sloppy? You may be a talented artist as well as a nice person, but dressing shabbily robs you of a positive first impression and people will remember, especially if they're considering hiring you. There's a time to dress up and a time to dress down. If you look like a bum, you're probably not going to get the gig.

I'm now speaking from an employer's point of view. Whenever my band and I were performing in nightclubs, television or show concerts, I always had my musicians wear matching country shirts and trousers. From the moment we walked on center stage, we got their attention. There was no mistaking who the entertainers were!

When I had auditions for my "Hometown Jamboree" television show and other shows I was involved with, I always remembered what they wore because I believed it reflected their general attitude about themselves. There were some talented people that I didn't hire. If they're going to give me a hard time about my show's rules and regulations, why should I? There was an array of talented artists that I could choose from and the same holds true today.

Country: Some of the sharpest dressers were the early legendary artists who appeared on the Grand Ole Opry in their fancy tailor-made sequinned suits, such as Hank Williams. Porter Wagoner is from the old school and still carries on that tradition with dignity whenever he appears there or in concert somewhere.

I've always thought that entertainer/guitarist, Marty Stuart (who is also President of the Country Music Foundation's Board of Trustees),

32

dressed with such style from the very first time I saw him when he played in Johnny Cash's band. He deeply respects country history and its traditional values. He's a great example for aspiring artists because he's also a walking encyclopedia of our genre's history, and I know he'll be representing country music to the best of his abilities for the rest of his life.

Out here on the West Coast, there was a family hillbilly act called The Maddox Bros. and Rose, whom I knew quite well. They were famous not only for their unique hillbilly music, but for the flashy outfits they wore. They'd come driving up to the nightclub in two or three Cadallics with the neck of the bass sticking out of one of the windows! They were a delightful sight to behold. Real show biz stuff! Rose Maddox was a no-nonsense performer. She would get up on stage and start tapping her foot to the tempo she wanted for each song and say, "Play it in the key of G, boys."

Western: I've had the pleasure of knowing and working with many Western cowboy (and cowgirl) icons such as Gene Autry, Roy Rogers, Dale Evans and Montie Montana (world famous trick roper). Whenever they appeared in motion pictures, rodeos or at any other public venues and events, they proudly dressed to the hilt in Western attire (as did their horses with their fancy silver saddles).

I've known Montie Montana since I was in my teens, and if anyone was born a cowboy, it was Montie! Joan Carol and I have attended numerous Western functions with him and his lovely wife, Marilee. Whenever he was performing with his lariat on stage or horseback, he always dressed the part with class and style.

Because of his dress code, he gave the world a wonderful image of the American cowboy, especially when he roped President Eisenhower during the 1953 Inaugural Parade in Washington D.C., which was in every newspaper worldwide. This image prevailed for decades because millions of viewers would see him perform his rope tricks on his horse in the Rose Bowl Parade for years.

One of the most memorable Hometown Jamboree Today concerts that Montie and I ever did together was on July 24, 1997 at the Ramona Bowl, which is an outdoor Western-style amphitheater that's nestled at the foot of the mountains overlooking Hemet, California. My other guest stars were Molly Bee and the Riders of the Purple Sage. Talk about a cast of well-dressed Western folks - we were it! An old pro like

Montie knows how to get the audience's attention with his trick roping and witty cowboy sense of humor. However, his three-year old grandson, Jason, who was dressed exactly like him in boots, hat and a fancy red cowboy shirt, stole the show when he came out on stage with his mother, Trudy Johnston, to do a few rope tricks! It was quite a visual sight and showstopper!

Pop field: Dressing for the occasion was prevalent during the big band era (ala Tommy Dorsey, Glenn Miller, Harry James and Lawrence Welk). The musicians always wore tuxedos or other matching show outfits. Legendary entertainers like Frank Sinatra and Peggy Lee always dressed immaculately and they set a standard for others to emulate. Even today, the pop stars and great stage entertainers still get all decked out when they appear in concert or on prestigious hotel casino stages.

BE AN AGELESS LATE BLOOMER: I want to say a few things about age, because many people use it as an excuse for not trying and, therefore, have defeated themselves before they're out of the starting blocks. I don't know how many times I've heard people say, "I'm too old to start" or "I'm too old to be an entertainer." That's not true! There have been many "late bloomers" in all areas of show business who became successful in their later years.

Actor Harrison Ford is one of the biggest box office draws in motion picture history. The sweet smell of success didn't blossom for him until he was about thirty-five years old, when George Lucas cast him in *Star Wars* in 1977. He's in his fifties now and is still going strong and being handsomely paid for it.

A perfect example of defying age is the "Follies" show in Palm Springs, which has been a huge success for years. A very talented producer/host, Riff Markowitz, has a brand new show each year, which keeps his audiences coming back for more! The cast members have to be over fifty years of age. About halfway through the show, Riff will start introducing the cast members and they, in turn, tell the audience a little something about themselves, including how old they are, which always gets a gasp from the audience. It's unbelievable how young they look, which proves that if you exercise, eat properly and have an interest that keeps you mentally alert and enthused about life, you can delay the aging process.

Yours truly is still out there doing his thing! I may move a little slower and sometimes I have difficulty climbing on that stage but with a little help from my friends, I get up there and perform my heart out! It makes me feel good and the natural high I get whenever I hear the audience applause is beyond words. Hey! It's what I am and what I do!

The point I'm trying to get across to you is not to worry about age, because whatever age you are when you decide that you want to be in show business is a good age and you want to make the experience fun. The older one gets, the more one realizes that having fun makes you feel like a kid again and keeps you interested in life.

SUMMARY: These are some of the main pre-show preparation aspects that you should be considering before you step out on stage.

Never forget that you're always auditioning whenever you're on stage, even if you've become a professional. If you're prepared, any number of magical things can happen to you. You could live to be a hundred years old and be asked to appear on Jay Leno's "Tonight Show" on NBC. It's your big break! You've been ready for years and you know all the words to "Crazy." Start tapping your foot and say to the band, "Play it in the key of G, boys."

Chapter 6

A Little Ignorance Goes A Long Way!
Just Do It!

"Cliffie was the most wonderful person who ever walked on the face of the earth! We shared the same passion, which was to promote country music to the utmost!"
-FRAN BOYD, Executive Director/Academy of Country Music

"Sometimes you can worry or analyze things to a point where you talk yourself out of experiencing the experiment. A little ignorance goes a long way! Just do it! Be like the guy who didn't know it couldn't be done and he did it!"
-CLIFFIE STONE

Yes, a little ignorance does go a long way! Why not be like the guy who didn't know it couldn't be done and he did it? If you've prepared yourself the best way you know how, there comes a time when you should stop thinking about it and, with blind faith, enter a talent show, get up on stage and see what happens. Whatever happens has to be good - even if you are bad. After all, *You Gotta Be Bad Before You Can Be Good!*

There's really only one way for you to find out if you're cut out for this type of career and that's to take your first step. One step for you and possibly a step for all mankind in the future! Maybe you could end up being an entertainer who brings happiness into the lives of people - be it on a small or grand scale. However, it's one baby step at a time, and then another. Maybe show business is for you! Then again, maybe not. One thing is for sure: if you give yourself a fair crack at it, you'll get your answer sooner or later.

No one ever forgets the first time they've done anything in their lives that means something to them, and this certainly applies to anyone who appears on stage in front of a live audience for the first time or first few times.

I've never forgotten the time when I, more or less, auditioned for my first gig, and it's of no consequence that it wasn't a talent show. The important thing was there came a moment in time when I had to make the decision on whether or not to experience the experiment. Although I've mentioned it in a previous chapter, its importance bears repeating. That decisive moment came when I was sixteen and Stuart Hamblen gave me, a young inexperienced bassist, a chance to play with his band on his radio show, "Lucky Stars." And I was so thrilled when he asked me to be a permanent band member!

Was I scared and nervous the first time in front of a mike, especially since it was a radio show? You bet! What was my reaction to the experience? I loved it! Being part of a musical team where everyone played as one unit turned me on! Did I decide then and there that show business would be my life? No. But it hooked me enough so that I kept on doing it and my career just happened. I thank my lucky stars and Stuart Hamblen for that unforgettable experience, which was a defining moment in my life.

There will come a time when you, too, will have to make a decision to experience the experiment. It may take you months or years to decide whether or not show business is for you. Maybe you'll say, "Yes, this is for me," and for a couple of months or a year, you pursue it. Then the day may come when you decide that it's not for you, and that's okay. After all, we have to go with the flow of life's ever-changing circumstances. "Now" is all we have.

So the choice is yours on whether or not you're going to experience the experiment "now." The bottom line is this: if you've secretly wanted to be a performer and have a desire to be in the spotlight, then it's time for you to get on with it. So, I'm going to have you take my very own Litmus test and/or Cliffie's "just do it" musical prescription. All you have to do is read the directions, make the decision and then go into action.

STEP NUMBER ONE: Make a personal commitment to take three months out of your precious life to get on any stage that you have access to, such as your local talent show or church choir, or enroll in theatrical workshops or whatever.

I'm very partial to talent shows, especially when they're held in a nightclub, because you'll be getting used to the venue that you'll most likely be performing in should you become a professional. Talent shows are places where you can be free to make mistakes. This is how you will learn, which is the premise of this book.

A thousand questions will be racing through your mind during these three months as you appear in front of the public, especially if you've never had much experience on stage. Do I really want to do this? Will I forget the lyrics? Will the audience like me? My friend, expect to make mistakes and don't get upset about it when you do.

For instance, if you're a singer, you may try to hit a high note and you don't quite make it. Or maybe you sing out of tune. Whatever you do, try not to panic. Keep listening to the music and keep on singing and moving with the beat and you should instinctively get back on key. Don't worry if you forget some of the lyrics. This, too, has happened to all professionals at one time or another.

This reminds me of the time when I was emceeing as well as performing at a fundraiser. For the most part, the people did a lot of dancing. However, a drunk kept coming up and asking me to sing the "Tennessee Waltz." Since, I only knew the first two lyric lines, I kept putting him off, but the drunk was persistent, so I finally gave in. All I did was sing the first two lines over and over. The people were so busy waltzing, they didn't know the difference and the drunk was so happy that he gave me a twenty-dollar tip!

If you're an aspiring musician who's never played in front of an audience or with a band before, you may make a few mistakes on your chords or possibly forget part of the melody on your solo. Or maybe you don't stay in rhythm with the rest of the band. It's okay. It's not the end of the world. You'll do better with more experience.

Maybe you're an aspiring comedian and you didn't get any laughs from a couple of your jokes when you delivered the punch lines. You might have to get funnier jokes or practice your punch line timing. I've certainly had a few jokes that didn't make it so I know what it feels like when no one laughs. I also know what a great feeling it is when they do laugh, which motivated me to keep on doing it. The best of comedians don't always get laughs from their jokes either. It's a real hoot to watch Jay Leno whenever any of his jokes go south on him, because his reaction and comments are usually funnier than the joke would have been. And he's got millions of viewers watching, but that's why he gets the big bucks.

Possibly you've entered a talent show that has a dance category and maybe you forgot a few steps during your dance routine. It's okay! Who's going to know, other than your partner? The audience won't, because it seems to me that it might be fairly easy to fake a few steps. Or maybe your worst nightmare came true and you tripped and fell on your face. Now that could be a little embarrassing, but as long as you didn't hurt yourself, it's okay. Just pick yourself up and laugh about it; the audience will mirror your attitude and laugh along with you - but not at you.

Here's an example of what the atmosphere will probably be like in a talent show when it's held in a nightclub. Let's pretend that it's a packed house with people who, number one, don't know you (unless you happen to bring in a few friends). Number two, they are not related to you. They are not your parents or family and they have no desire whatsoever to be related to you. These are people who have never seen you before and, in some instances, they may be irritated that you're up on that stage singing or dancing in the first place, because you're bothering them. They can't talk, drink, eat or smoke (heaven protect us smokers). Maybe some guy has his eye on a gal and he's trying to make a move on her or vice versa and there's some clown up on the stage jumping around saying, "Look at me." Somehow, you've got to get their attention. Since time began, the professional entertainers have had to deal with situations like this and it goes with the territory.

As I light up my pipe, I'd like to digress a bit and give a little thought to what I used to think about when I was in your shoes as an aspiring artist. You've probably heard or read those old classic statements when the talent wasn't entertaining enough and what they would do to get people off the stage - statements such as "bringing the curtain down" or "a big hook that comes out of the wings" and crudely pulls the artist off the stage. Across the ocean in merry old England, they would say things like "get on with it" and then they'd start stumping and applauding right in the middle of an artist's act. When that happens, it's over - the artist is out of there!

I don't personally remember the Old West era, but I do remember the stories my dad told me that he had heard about those rugged pioneering days. They had music halls that were part of a saloon. (I'm sure you've seen this scene a hundred times in various Western movies and television series.) Anyway, the men would sit in the audience and if they didn't like the act, they might throw vegetables, eggs, tomatoes or pickles at the performer.

Goodness, time does fly, because it doesn't seem that long ago when

I personally knew of a couple of places here in Southern California where they put chicken wire up between the audience and the entertainer in case somebody threw something. Sometimes they might throw a penny, which is an insult to an entertainer. But that's just the way it goes. However, take heart, dear reader. Most of the above doesn't happen anymore. Oh, you may have to deal with a heckler or a drunk from time to time, but ignoring them is the best way to handle the situation, unless you've got a quick wit like Jerry Lewis, Rosie O'Donnell, Robin Williams or Jay Leno.

The last time I was a presenter on the Academy of Country Music Awards show, I had finished naming the nominees and was about to announce the winner when a man in the balcony yelled something. I quickly came back with a humorous reply, which made the audience laugh and applaud. Of course, I've had years of experience in dealing with audiences, as well as having the innate ability to think on my feet. So there's nothing anyone can say that could ever throw me off stride or upset me for I can usually make a joke out of it.

I certainly hope I haven't scared you to death with the above horror stories and what entertainers might have to go through. However, my friend, it will take a certain amount of courage to get up on stage, but don't think about it! Just do it!

STEP NUMBER TWO: At the end of three months, take your own Litmus test and evaluate yourself. How do you feel about what you've done so far? Are you still enamored with the stage, lights, audiences and the people you have to work with? Be totally honest with yourself because this is important to your future and, more importantly, to your personal fulfillment. You don't want to wake up one fine day with regrets and say, "I wish I had done this or that" and feel as though life has passed you by.

If you've had fun these past three months, regardless how bad you think you were and you still want to keep trying, then you've got the right stuff because you've got the heart and determination. Now you're ready for the next step.

STEP NUMBER THREE: Repeat step number one.

SUMMARY: If you've lasted the six-month course that I've prescribed, good for you. Realize, however, that it's not going to happen overnight, so be patient and gentle with yourself. You're a novice and you're taking baby steps. If you believe that you could be the next Elvis, Garth Brooks, Reba McEntire, Jay Leno, Alan Jackson or Shania Twain, then continue to aggressively go after it.

Talent shows are worldwide and the main thing is to enjoy the experience of being on the stage, which is the most important one in the world. It's a safe haven where you can get your feet wet. You're probably going to trip and fall a few times, but that's okay. Just pick yourself up, regroup and have at it again.

Sometimes you can worry about something and analyze things to a point where you run the danger of not doing it at all, thereby talking yourself out of "experiencing the experiment."

Be like the guy who didn't know it couldn't be done and he did it! With a little luck, talent and hard work, you could become a genuine, certified entertainer. Just do it!

Chapter 7

Sides to the Bridge:
Talent Show Guidelines and Suggestions

"Cliffie knew more about people than anyone I ever met! He believed that every one deserved a chance and he knew how to get the best out of them. Following the path that he lays out can make your journey to success a shorter, sweeter trip."
-GENE WEED, Premier TV Director/Executive Producer

"I've always had fun emceeing talent contests in nightclubs and I respect what the artists are trying to accomplish. But there are rules or guidelines that I've used to tighten up my show to keep it running smoothly."
-CLIFFIE STONE

I prefer to use the word "guidelines" whenever "rules" or "regulations" are mentioned. Otherwise, it's a turn off because it sounds so formal and dictatorial. It certainly doesn't sound like much fun, and if you can't have fun doing something, don't do it.

I've always thought of "rules" as "sides to the bridge," which was the image I used when laying down the ranch rules to my kids as they were growing up. So imagine, if you will, a wooden bridge that goes from one side of a mountain to the other over a deep canyon and it's the only way you can get to the other side. I don't know about you, but I'd be shaking in my boots if that bridge didn't have sides that I could hang onto.

None of us likes to be told what to do. I guess it's all in how you tell someone how you want things done. There's an old saying that "a spoonful of honey will attract more flies than a cup of vinegar" (and if it's not an old saying, it is now). Whether we like it or not, in all areas of our lives we have to have some sort of rules, protocol or guidelines to follow - whether it's in our homes, offices, sports arena or wherever. Otherwise, there would be chaos.

With regard to talent shows, I've always had so much fun being an emcee and working with aspiring artists. I have a deep respect for what they're trying to accomplish for I know how much this means to them. Most of them are nervous and some are just downright scared, so I try to make them feel as comfortable as possible on stage because I want this to be a positive learning experience.

However, there were rules and protocol that I used to tighten up my show to keep it running smoothly while giving it that added kick to keep the audience interested. Although all talent show venues have their own set of rules and regulations, mine are simply common sense guidelines and suggestions, which I feel are important. So consider this as "required reading" - just like you had to do in school in order to pass a course. Hopefully, mine will be more fun and interesting.

PERFORMER GUIDELINES AND SUGGESTIONS

Although the legendary Palomino club (where I had a four-year weekly talent show gig as emcee) was a good-sized place that was large enough to seat about two or three hundred people, the way it was set up had an intimacy about it. It had a big stage, fairly large dance floor, excellent lighting and sound systems. The pool table area was off to the side and far enough away from the stage so that it never interfered with entertainment. It also had a medium-sized backroom that could be used for a variety of things, such as a small band rehearsal, meetings or a dressing room. This nightclub setting is what I'll use for the talent show rules and general protocol.

If you, your family and/or friends are planning on going to a talent show (and I hope you are), it's good to be aware of the protocol that takes place, which make things easier for both the contestants and the people in charge. They also give it that added zest to keep the crowd entertained, which helps to broaden audience and contestant appeal.

Check out the talent show club or venue: To ease you into the talent show scene, I'd like to start with a suggestion, which has nothing to do with contest rules. Don't sign up the first time you go to a talent show, especially if it's at a nightclub. I can't stress this too strongly, especially if you're a newcomer to talent contests.

It's always been my habit to go three or four days ahead of time (if possible) to check out the venue where I'm going to do a gig so that I could get a feel for it. I like to feel comfortable when I do a gig and walking in cold turkey to perform was always unsettling to me. I suggest that you use the same principle before you participate as a contestant in a talent show.

Let's say that you've never been to a club you've heard has talent shows, and it's located about sixty miles from your home. If you're planning on entering one in the near future, I suggest that you drive down to the venue a week in advance before you plan on entering, and case the joint. Look it over and really check it out. Sit down and be aware of what's happening. What time do they start? Where is the stage and the dance floor? Get used to seeing where the audience is sitting. Listen and get used to the sound system, the lights and the entire environment in general.

Thoroughly familiarize yourself with that particular location, its stage and the band. By checking it out, you'll have a certain amount of confidence when you finally do decide to participate.

While you're at it, find out who's in charge. Who is the manager and/or assistant manager? Who is the soundman? What kind of a personality does the emcee have? One of your biggest sources of information will be waitresses and bartenders, so strike up a conversation with them. Then when you enter the contest, you'll feel as though you have a friend who will be in your corner.

If you've had some experience with talent shows in the past, and circumstances prevent you from checking out a venue that you've never been to before, you'll be able to wing it.

Critique contestants and professional entertainers: Once again, this is a suggestion and certainly not a contest rule.

Although the definition of "critique" basically means a "critical estimate," the word, itself, sounds classy and has a way of taking the sting out of what it really means. So after casing the venue as well as having all your senses accustomed to its entire environment, start "critiquing" or observing the singer who's currently performing on stage (whether it's a contestant or a professional).

To the best of your ability, objectively observe their attitude and stage presence. What are they wearing? What songs are they singing? Note their good points as well as their bad points. What are they doing that makes them that good or that bad? You'll know by the audience's reaction after they are through performing.

44

If you didn't have the opportunity to case the place and other performers (be it a weekly or a one-time contest, regardless of venue), you can still do so on the evening you actually perform. I know you'll be nervous and probably self-absorbed with what you're going to sing or play, but it might help to take your mind off yourself for a while as well as relax you. So while you're waiting, critique other contestants who are going on before and after you. After all, you and the other aspiring artists are here to learn.

Entering a nightclub talent show: The first two suggestions were warm ups to get you pre-show ready for the big day.

Generally, when you're entering a talent show at a local nightclub, you merely show up at their club a few hours before it starts. At the door, you'll be given an entry card to fill out, which is a must. (If it's another type of talent show venue that's a one-time event, you will have to fill out a form ahead of time and mail it in.)

Now this card will have blank spaces that indicate where to write your name, e-mail, phone number, mailing address as well as the category you'll be entering. Most contestants enter the vocalist division so there will be a place to list the song and its key. This info will be going to the emcee and/or whoever is in charge of the show.

Since this type of talent show is on the fly, the emcee, manager and/or producer won't know how many people will be entering. However, if it's a weekly show, they'll have a fairly good idea. It's been my experience with weekly contests that there will usually be about twenty or thirty contestants and many of them will be coming on a regular basis.

One of the reasons why I recommend you get there an hour or two early, especially if you've never seen the place before, is because it can get quite hectic as show time approaches. The contest schedule has to be made up. If the show starts at 8 p.m., then the talent will probably start signing in before 7 p.m. By being there early, you'll probably get a better spot on the show, which is an edge up on the competition as well as making a good impression on the emcee and the folks running the show.

Many times, you may be taking your own support system, such as family and friends. So after you get a table where all of you can sit together, go sign up for the contest. After you've signed in, you can rejoin your friends. However, when it's your time to shine, be ready to leave them because from that point on, you're flying solo.

There are no band rehearsals in a talent show of this type, so before the first set and subsequent sets, the contestants will meet with the band in the club's backroom or in a corner somewhere as far away from the audience as possible. During the last twenty minutes before show time, decisions have to be made as to who goes first, etc. This is done so that the show can move along without unnecessary interruptions as well as being entertaining.

Know your key and have sheet music for the band: If you're a singer, you should have your sheet music (lyrics, chords and melody) on paper in some manner so that it's ready to give to the band. This is particularly important if it's an original tune or one of the new top forty hits. (Some country musicians can't read music and if they do, let's hope they can read just enough so that it doesn't hurt their playing). If it's a standard country song, the band will probably know it. In either case, be sure you know your key.

If you don't follow these guidelines, the band may have to stop for five minutes between acts to discuss the song they're going to play next and/or try to figure out the key to your song, which takes away from a professional and smooth-running show. By knowing your key and having your sheet music ready, you're on your way to developing a professional attitude, which will get the immediate respect of the band. It will also give you added confidence to know that the band is not going to play the wrong chord.

By the same token, if they do, so what! They're so professional that they won't make a big deal out of it and will quickly recover and move on, which could be a lesson for you to observe and apply when you make a mistake in the future.

Talk to the soundman prior to the show: If you're going to accompany yourself with a guitar or sing along with a track tape Karaoke-style and you don't need the band, then you should talk to the soundman prior to the show. If that's not possible, then get with him during the break after the first set if you're scheduled to appear on the second set. Don't wait until the last minute because things go at a fast pace and can get hectic once the show starts. The soundman has to concentrate on a number of things and, as I keep stressing throughout this chapter, the flow of the

46

show shouldn't be interrupted with the band's idle chitchat such as, "What are we going to play now?" This is a good way to lose the interest of the audience, which is hard to get back.

Stage fright: This is another suggestion, because one of the most important things you can learn in talent shows is to overcome stage fright, or at least get a handle on it. Realize that all performers - singers, speakers and athletes - get nervous, no matter how long they've been doing their thing. If this nervous energy is properly channeled, it helps the artist to give an electrifying performance before an audience. Regardless of performance level, any artist who is worth their salt will get butterflies in the pit of their stomach just before a show. But as soon as they step on the stage and get past that first song, they usually calm down.

I've found it helpful to substitute the word *excitement* for *nervous and/or stage fright*. Tell yourself that you are excited about what you're going to do! Being excited simply means that you care about your performance and the audience. So center yourself by slowly inhaling and exhaling. Then go out on that stage in a relaxed alert manner so that you're aware of what's happening around you.

After you've performed, you'll probably be feeling a "natural high," especially if you've connected with the audience. This is what hooks you into becoming an entertainer, which will keep you coming back for more. It's one of the greatest feelings in the world.

Master of Ceremonies: Talent shows will have an emcee and, often times, it's the bandleader or a local disc jockey. Sometimes, they bring in a professional emcee as in my case. Whoever it is, observe him (or her) because it's important that you become aware of his stage-side manner and style.

When the emcee introduces you, quickly come up to the mike. Naturally, he'll ask your name and a few other questions such as, "What do you do for a living?" "Why do you want to be in show business?" and "What are you going to sing?" Personality is everything, so bear in mind that these simple but important questions are being asked so that the audience can become aware of your personality.

If you've ever watched any beauty pageants, such as Miss America, then you'll be aware of the importance of personality. They always have a talent section wherein the emcee interviews the ladies. He will ask questions of each contestant and since they're on big time television, they really need to be able to talk, smile, laugh and, most important of all, be themselves. They're letting the world see their personality. So take your cue from them, because this is what you have to do at your local talent show. Someday, you may be on a big time talent show or in a Miss America contest yourself!

I cannot stress the importance of being yourself, so follow the emcee's lead. Get to know and work with him. If you go back to the same talent show week after week, you will have developed a little friendship with him. This will make you feel more relaxed as you're being interviewed, which will carry over when you perform.

Often times, an emcee will joke around with and about the talent in an entertaining way, which happens to be my style. And, as an aspiring artist, it's important for you to learn to relax and not take yourself so seriously. You will be making mistakes and it's not the end of your potential career when you do. Laugh and learn from your mistakes. If you can do this, you'll also be developing a great attitude. So don't be surprised if the emcee makes a few cute or comical remarks about you before or after you perform, which would be in the spirit of fun, and not meant to be demeaning in any way. After all, the audience needs to be entertained, and there's nothing like laughter to loosen up and create a bond between you and everyone else in the room.

Now, what I'm about to say is for all master of ceremonies everywhere: always treat the aspiring talent with dignity and respect. Honor them for what they're trying to accomplish. You're a pro at this and it's within your power to encourage and inspire them, and that in itself is your priceless gift to them, which they'll deeply appreciate and remember forever.

I humbly say this from my experiences with people down through the years. I've had many accomplished artists and songwriters thank me for the encouragement that I gave them at a certain point in their lives when they needed it the most. This is why you, the emcee, should be aware of the vital role you play in these talent contests.

You, the artist, should understand how important it is for the emcee to keep the show moving. So when he introduces you, get up on that stage as quickly as you can without appearing rushed. You certainly don't want to be in such a hurry that you trip over your own feet. Of course, that could be a way to get your audience's attention, but I'm sure that it would be rather embarrassing for you.

Getting the audience's attention: Although you're an aspiring artist whose main goal at this point in time is to develop your talent and gain invaluable experience on stage with a live band, you're also there to learn how to entertain an audience. So you may as well start learning how to get their attention and how to keep it from the get go. Sometimes this is easier said than done. However, if you can do that, then you're on your way to being a true professional.

Whenever I think about getting the attention of an audience, it always reminds me of a cute story that I once heard about a farmer who had a mule that wouldn't do anything but eat and sleep. So he called a horse trainer who also trained mules from time to time and asked him to come over and see if he could train his mule to be useful. The trainer shows up and the farmer takes him out to the barn and says, "There's Clyde, my mule." Now Clyde is standing in his stall, nonchalantly eating. The farmer goes on to say, "I can't get Clyde to do anything. He won't pull a plow. He won't let me ride him. He's just a waste of time. Can you do anything about it?" The horse trainer scratches his head and says, "Yep! I can do something about it." So he goes to his truck, gets a two by four and takes it into the corral and proceeds to hit Clyde on the head about five times. The farmer is shocked and says, "What are you doing? You'll hurt him! You can't train him that way!" The trainer says, "Yes, I can, but first I have to get his attention!"

Now I don't recommend that you hit the folks in your audience with a two by four. However, the first thing you have to do is to get their immediate attention! But how?

I refer you to Chapter 5, "The Key to Success: Pre-Show Preparation," in which I discuss your image, self-esteem, stage presence, body language and your show clothes. All these factors contribute to getting and keeping the audience's attention.

In due time and with each new experience, you'll be learning the tricks of the trade. Consider yourself an intern or an apprentice because there are some things that can't be taught in books; the actual experience itself will be the greatest teacher. And so it goes with getting and keeping the attention of an audience.

Your entrance and exit: I cannot emphasize enough about the importance of how you begin and end your act because this is what will stay in the minds of the audience. Yes, the stuff in the middle is important too, but it's your entrance and your exit that the audience will remember.

So when it's your turn, get up there as quickly as possible while projecting poise and confidence. If you have lead sheets, quickly give them to the bandleader, who will take care of handing them out to the other band members. Meanwhile, the emcee will probably start talking to you and you've got to have all your wits about you.

However, once he says, "And now here is Mary Worth," that's when the band will play the intro to your song and you should be at the microphone and ready to sing. For goodness sake, at that point, don't turn around and start talking to the bandleader or walk off somewhere and decide to do something else before you sing. The audience is sitting there and you have their attention. If you fool around for thirty or forty seconds after he says your name, you're going to lose their attention and probably never get it back. So act like a professional. The moment you're introduced, it's your time to shine, so go to work!

When you're finished, don't rush off like you have to catch an airplane. The audience will be clapping, especially your entourage who has been sitting proudly at your table. So acknowledge the audience and savor the wonderful moment. Then walk off with poise and dignity.

Alcohol and/or other substance abuse: Be aware of your time slot on the show. Don't be sitting around so engrossed in chitchat with your friends that you're caught off guard when you're introduced and you say, "Oh, it's my turn! Wait a minute!" Then you go grab a quick drink in order to get the nerve to go up there.

While I'm on the subject, let's discuss alcohol for a moment. Being relatively new to the performing arena, you may get so nervous when you're about to get on stage that you may be tempted to take a drink or two to calm your nerves down, because you think it will give you courage to stand before an audience. First of all, you never want to become reliant on it. Although alcohol (as well as any other stimulant) will give you false courage, it will dull your senses. Secondly, you want to be able to remember the experience so that you can relish it as well as correct any mistakes you've made, which will improve your next performance. Thirdly, as I've stated before, all entertainers who are worth their salt will always be nervous (or excited) before they perform. So get used to being in front of the audience with all your senses intact and under your own self-reliant control without the aid of a foreign substance such as alcohol. You should be in total control of yourself. You owe it to your audience and to yourself.

By the same token, I understand what a temptation alcohol can be. I've seen some contests in nightclubs where someone is programmed at number twenty-six, and once the show gets underway, he probably won't get on stage until about 11 p.m. He's got a long time to wait, so maybe he starts having a few beers and by the time it's his turn, he's not who or what he really is, because he's become high or intoxicated.

I've also seen professionals do this and I've always felt they were defeating their purpose, as well as cheating both themselves and the audience out of a good performance.

I know that having a drink can be relaxing and can give one the feeling of being uninhibited. But it truly is a waste of time and effort because, for the most part, the artist won't remember what he or she did or whether they were good or bad. In fact, they'll probably think they were great and if they were video taped, they would be in for a rude awakening!

So I highly recommend that you go on stage as you truly are. Believe me, it's better to go up there in a state of excited alertness so that you'll be able to remember the stimulating experience. That's the fun part of it! As I said before, the "natural high" you get from connecting with an audience is one of the greatest feelings in the world! I'll discuss this topic further in Chapter 9, "Moving Up the Show Biz Ladder."

Summary: Regardless of any talent show venue that aspiring artists may enter, each will have its own "sides to the bridge" or set of rules and regulations for entering and for its format.

Dear reader, I have personally used all of my foregoing rules, guidelines and suggestions in the past with great success and I hope they will help you to improve as a performer while you truck on down Highway 101 pursuing your dreams. Just hold on to the sides of the bridge while you are having a swinging good time crossing from one performance level to another.

Incidentally, these guidelines and suggestions weren't too hard to swallow, were they? I guess a little honey goes a long way.

Chapter 8

Yearning to Win...Learning to Lose!

"I was playing very few gigs in Bakersfield when I decided to enter a talent show on a dare at the Rainbow Gardens. After I got through, the backup band's fiddle player, Jelly Sanders, asked me if I was interested in getting any jobs. Although I came in 2nd at the talent show, it led to many gigs for me around town."
-MERLE HAGGARD, CMA Hall of Fame, 1994; ACM Pioneer Award, 1996

"In 1950, I entered a talent show and placed 2nd to none other than 'Faron Young,' who never let me forget it! I've judged many talent contests on the 'Charlie Daniels' Talent Roundup' shows on TNN. I don't know why, but the winners, in most cases, never made the big leap to major labels. But I do know of many who came in 2nd or 3rd and went on to become big stars. That's show biz!"
-MERLE KILGORE, Artist/ Songwriter/Manager of Hank Williams, Jr.

"It's always a thrill to see the faces of new talent when we tell them they have been selected to appear on national television. It's a golden opportunity, and they know - win or lose - that the experience and exposure is the most important thing."
-SAM RIDDLE, Producer - "Star Search" and "From Hawaii...Destination Stardom"

In my previous chapters, I've been on my "yes, you can" soap box and now I can hear you say, "Learning to lose! But I want to win! What does he mean by that, anyway?" Well, I'm not being negative when I say "learning to lose," and I hope to enlighten you about these two fickle imposters - winning and losing.

Aside from the invaluable hands-on stage experience that you'll be getting in talent shows and all that encompasses the territory of performing, you'll also be learning to win and lose. Or should I rephrase it and say, *"you'll be yearning to win and learning to lose."*

I'm point-blank saying this to you for a reason, because every area of show business can be one tough cookie to crack, which includes winning a talent show contest. I don't care who you are, you are probably going to lose a few times. If you do, remember this: you may have lost the battle, but you haven't lost the war. So develop an attitude towards these two fickle imposters.

But before I continue on with this subject matter, I want to briefly discuss two elements that are interrelated to winning and losing.

AND THE WINNER IS...: There are several ways a winner is chosen and every talent show will have its own procedure. In some cases, it's decided by the applause of the audience. (There are those who have won not because they were better than the other contestants were, they just had more friends in the audience.)

In other cases, it's a panel of two or three judges who make the decision (and never forget that it's only someone's opinion).

Many times, it's a combination of both the audience's applause and the decisions of the judges. Regardless of the method, each performer and his entourage will anxiously be awaiting the results.

Prizes: Whenever prize money is involved, it can be an enticing motivator that beckons people to enter contests, and many of them will be disappointed when they don't win.

These cash prizes will vary according to what the show's producers, sponsors or nightclub managers feel they can afford, which would depend on the money they made from talent shows in the past, especially if it's a weekly event.

Whether it's a local nightclub and/or a one-time talent show put on by a community organization, first place could be anywhere from twenty-five to fifty dollars. The second place winner could get a twenty dollar gift certificate to a local Western clothing store; and whoever comes in third could get a CD that was donated by a music store. Since the Palomino had a weekly talent show, I always gave a free ticket to both the second and third place contestants so that they could enter next week's contest and have another crack at first place.

Big time show prizes: There can be more alluring prizes other than money. Since I hope you'll continue taking advantage of what talent contests have to offer, I'd like to briefly discuss what some of the bigger talent shows might offer as a grand prize when money is no object.

Being interested in talent shows all my life, I've always enjoyed watching them on television and cable. Their grand prizes as well as the exposure that an artist can get on these televised talent shows are priceless. But to get on them, a contestant has to have experience in order to win out over the others who are trying to get on the show. In short, he's nearing the professional status or is one already.

The bigger talent shows that you can enter (once you've had enough experience at the local level) are the ones that usually have big name sponsors. A whole slew of wonderful things can happen when there's enough money for prizes.

In the past, some of the big name sponsors for both the sports and music worlds (in this case, talent shows) have been the tobacco and alcohol industries.

About six years ago, Marlboro sponsored a statewide talent contest in various clubs throughout California. In my neck of the woods it was at the legendary Palomino club and I was one of the judges. Several months later, they held regional contests throughout the state and all the regional winners received a free trip to Nashville where the semi-finals and the finals were held. Although I don't know what Marlboro was offering as the grand prize, you can bet it was something wonderful, such as a recording contract with a small record label and/or getting the chance to perform on one of TNN's morning variety shows.

The stakes are high in big time shows like this and so is the disappointment factor if you don't win, especially if you were within striking distance of the finals. Naturally, the competition is fierce in these bigger talent contests - from the local level to the regional level and all the way up to the semis and the finals themselves. Every time you win, you usually receive some sort of a prize. Of course, the artist who wins the big enchilada obviously has had a lot of performing experience under his belt, and many of them are professional entertainers. However, remember that they were just like you at one time, for they probably got started in their local talent show in their community.

Two fickle imposters: Now that I've discussed how a winner is chosen and their potential prizes (especially the big ones that can really get your juices flowing), we can talk about these two fickle imposters - winning and losing.

As I mentioned in Chapter 2, my first exposure to talent contests occurred when I was a deejay at KIEV in Glendale. When my boss asked me if I would be one of the judges for his weekly Saturday afternoon radio talent contests, I certainly couldn't say no. Although I really enjoyed the experience, I discovered that being a judge could sometimes be a thankless job. Since there could only be one winner, it was understandable that the rest of the contestants would be disappointed. Some of them were a little bent out of shape about it, as well as a few of their friends. Of course, the listening audience at home also had their own opinions and they certainly weren't bashful about writing in and saying, "What's the matter with you? Why didn't you like that little girl who sang 'Somewhere Over the Rainbow?' I thought she was great!" So I learned how to dance around the arrows that can be shot at you when your opinion differs from others. But we judges did survive to live another day.

Years later, when I was the emcee at the Palomino's talent show, I remember how some of the contestants' friends or family would come up to me and say, "So what was wrong with Mary? She was so much better than Suzie." Being an easy going Pisces, I started critiquing the Marys of the world for a little while until I found out that wasn't the way to go because Mary would get upset and say, "What do you mean I was singing in the wrong key?" Not to mention the fact that I didn't have the time to critique every single person who appeared on the talent show. For the most part, no matter what sort of critique I gave, many of them were resistant to accepting it, which includes their parents and/or their friends. Being bias, they thought their kid and/or their friend could do no wrong. So whenever anyone would come up to me and ask what was wrong with Mary or whomever, I learned to tactfully say, "Gee, I don't know; that's just the way it happened."

In a nutshell, whenever I was a judge and/or an emcee at talent contests, I would tactfully try to cheer up and calm down the ruffled feathers of an upset artist or his entourage who felt he or she should have won. And that's okay, because I think it's wonderful to have people care enough to get excited.

One of the main things I would tell contestants, which I'll share with you, is that whenever you enter a talent show, consider yourself a winner. Why? Never forget that the number one reason you are there in the first place is to get experience working on stage in front of a live audience with a live band to back you up. You and all the other contestants are gaining invaluable experience that you can build upon if you objectively evaluate your performance and are determined to improve.

So as far as I'm concerned, everyone who gets on a stage is a winner! The losers are the ones who won't try, or if they did try and lost, they won't try again, because they're afraid of losing. My point is this: if you win, great! If you don't, so what! Tomorrow is another day, and there's always the chance that you'll win in the future.

If you end up singing professionally with a band someday, and your confidence level and entertaining skills were built on the foundational experience that you acquired from talent shows, then this is what I call being a true winner in every sense of the word.

I personally knew about fifteen people who entered the Palomino talent shows almost every week for about two or three consecutive years. They were serving their apprenticeship, so to speak. Although it took time, they continued to improve themselves by getting into the habit of memorizing new songs, wearing new outfits and learning how to sing and develop their stage presence. The improvement from the time that I first saw them to what they turned out to be a year or two later was amazing. Most of them ended up winning at one time or another, which really didn't matter to me. I was proud of all of them for what they had accomplished!

One tall young lady comes to mind, because she initially had a complex about her height, as well as her weight. However, she was determined to be a singer, and she made a personal commitment to do something about it. So she participated every week and within two years, she was a totally different performer. She had accepted her height and proudly walked tall. She lost about twenty pounds and now had a figure that caught every man's attention from the moment she walked on stage. This built up her self-esteem and contributed to making her a confident singer. After winning a few contests, she fell in love with a guitar player and they formed a band. Soon they began getting regular gigs around town, as well as a few at lounges in Las Vegas and Reno. Although she never got a major record deal and, consequently, never became a major star, she loves being an entertainer and she continues to make a good living.

Now I'd like to briefly mention a couple of major entertainers who apparently didn't do so well in talent contests, but who ended up in the big time winner's circle.

I remember watching an interview that Larry King had with Wayne Newton, one of the all-time great entertainers. Wayne was sharing some of his early show business experiences and he said that he, as well as Elvis, flunked "Ted Mack's Amateur Hour." Then he went on

56

to say to this effect, that he could do one of two things after that experience: he could either crawl in a hole somewhere and pull the dirt over his head, or he could pull himself up by his bootstraps and move on. As music history shows, Wayne pulled himself up by his bootstraps and he went on to become one of Las Vegas' most popular entertainers for decades. Of course, Elvis' stratospheric success speaks for itself.

Here's another wonderful talent show success story that multi-faceted entertainer and Nashville Songwriters Association International Hall of Fame songwriter, Bill Anderson, shares in his autobiography, *Whisperin' Bill*:

"...I also entered a talent contest while I was a student at the University of Georgia. This particular contest was broken down into different divisions, and I entered the 'Talent & Original Song' competition. I was writing a few songs by this time and even had two or three published by a small firm in Texas. I didn't figure anybody else at the University had done that and I went into the contest extremely confident.

My confidence level rose even further on the night of the performance when I saw the printed program and realized only one other person had entered this particular division. 'Wow,' I thought to myself, 'I'll win this thing hands down!'

Well, a funny thing happened on my way to pick up the trophy - I lost! The judges selected a romantic pop-styled ballad from my opponent over my plaintive little three-chord, hurtin' country song. I was embarrassed and hurt. I was so ashamed, in fact, that I cut all my classes for the next two or three days. I didn't want to show my face on campus.

But the story has a footnote that should encourage anyone who loses in a talent competition: The boy who beat me also moved to Nashville, as I did, to pursue a career in songwriting. I figured I got the last laugh when, two or three years later, I went to purchase a pair of shoes at a downtown shoe store, and the guy who had defeated me in the two-man contest was the shoe salesman. I never saw or heard of him again."

I love Bill's story, because it gets to the very heart of what I've been talking about and it should inspire you to keep on keeping on should you ever lose in a talent contest. With the right attitude, you could become a long distance winner just like Bill!

Having said all the above, I think it's only fair to tell you that one of the most repeated words you're going to hear in show business is "no," and/or "don't call us, we'll call you." For every "yes" you get, you may hear a thousand "no's." Even as connected as I am in the music industry, I've heard the "no" word many times.

So how do I handle the "no" word? Naturally, I'm disappointed, but I brush it off and I've never let it stop me from stubbornly forging ahead. Down through the years, I've had enough experience and success in all areas of the music business to know that patience, persistence, and a positive attitude will eventually pay off. Besides, when you do get the "yes" word, how sweet it is!

Since I always put a positive spin on so-called negative experiences, let me tell you of a relatively recent "don't call me, I'll call you" experience that I had.

A few months ago, an agent friend of mine telephoned and asked me if I wanted to try out for a commercial for a big name florist company. Its theme was to suggest to the television audience that whenever they wanted to send a bouquet of flowers locally or cross-country to their parents, grandparents, girlfriend, wife or whomever, this was the florist who would quickly and efficiently get the job done. This agent thought of me because they needed a distinguished grandfather type in the commercial. Ha! Ha! Well, I guess I'm an old guy physically, but I'm a young guy mentally! (It's my darlin' who keeps me feeling young!)

So for the fun of it, I went to read for them. There must have been about twenty of us there for the first cattle call. To make a long story short, they thanked all of us after the reading and said, "Don't call us. We'll call you." Well, I didn't get called back and when I talked with my agent about three weeks later, he said that they had chosen someone else.

Naturally, my ego got bruised so I sat down in my pouting chair and smoked my pipe for about an hour. Gosh, I thought I did a great job reading those lines! I was cute and charming! What more could they want? How could they pick someone else over me? So I treated myself to some chocolate chip cookies and immediately felt better about the whole thing. Well, that's the way the cookie crumbles!

Now I've shared this little story with you because no matter who you are or how successful you've been in the past, you're not always going to win or get what you want.

I've heard contestants say time and again, "I lost it," when they didn't win. No, you didn't lose it! You didn't have it to begin with so how could you lose it! If you don't win the contest or get the gig, don't worry or complain about it! After all, you had the experience of doing it. This, in itself, is another can of beans on your shelf.

Learn to laugh when things don't turn out the way you want them to. Just say to yourself, "Those people just don't have good taste."

Yes, I know it hurts! If you want to know the truth of it, I'm hurting right now. After all, they didn't call me back to be in their commercial. I guess they just don't have good taste!

Chapter 9

Moving Up the Show Biz Ladder!
Career-Building Advice

"Cliffie Stone's name is synonymous with integrity and musical vision. He was a contemporary of my father, Si, in the pioneer days of country music. Those of us traveling down the music road today owe them so much. So pay attention! His advice comes from his vast knowledge and heartfelt passion for creative people."
-SCOTT SIMAN, ACM Board Chairman/President of rpm management
Manager of Tim McGraw

If you hang in there, it's only a matter of time until you start moving up the show biz ladder. Knowledge is power! So I thought I'd pass on a few more suggestions for you to store away for future use. Whether you're still in the embryo stages or you've become a more seasoned artist who is doing occasional or regular gigs in various clubs or other venues with a band, you should find this advice most helpful.

Even if you have a backlog of experience under your belt, you may still want to enter contests whenever they crop up, especially when there's prize money involved.

Atlantic Records' recording artist, Tracy Lawrence, was on the Academy of Country Music's Board of Directors with me one year. After one of the meetings, Joan Carol and I started talking with him and we asked him if he had ever been in any talent shows. With a twinkle in his eye, he grinned and told us that he had entered many of them to help pay the bills while he was trying to get a major record deal. He said he usually won a hundred dollars each time, which I thought was just great! What a smart thing for him to do! For he was not only winning money, but he was also building continued confidence and keeping his performance level at a high competitive pitch. More importantly, there was always the chance that there could be someone in the audience who might be able to help him get a break in the music business.

Regardless what entertainment level you're at, here are a few helpful suggestions that you may want to use and/or file away in your computer brain.

Get to the gig early: I briefly talked about this in Chapter 7, "Sides to the Bridge," and this rule of thumb applies not only to talent shows but to professional gigs as well. This has been one of my main habits throughout my entire career and it's always served me well. I like to get the feel of the environment whether I'm doing a concert, appearing on either radio or television, conducting a book seminar, or whatever. It's always good to know where you are so that you can get a sense of who you are, what you are and what you're trying to accomplish.

Arriving early also applies for any type of business meeting. If you have an appointment with a potential club owner, manager, publisher or whatever, be there thirty minutes before the scheduled time even if you have to sit in the lobby. If you have an appointment at two o'clock in the afternoon, don't arrive five minutes before the meeting. You certainly won't make a good impression if you come rushing in with your hair all out of place while you're gasping for breath and appearing as though you had just run a 10K race.

Mailing list: Start accumulating a mailing list, which will do wonders for your self-esteem. You are, more or less, expected to talk with people in the audience during the break. (Although it's a different setting, the country stars usually meet, sign autographs and take pictures with fans after their concerts. Meeting with my fans after a show was and still is one of my favorite things to do.) So while you're talking with them during the break, ask them if they want to be on your mailing list. If they like your music, they'll be happy to give you their address. Then every couple of months, depending on your gig schedule, you can send out a postcard informing them of where you'll be performing. It will make a big impression on the nightclub managers when they see that you have a loyal following. These are new customers for them and they're in the business of making money in order to keep their doors open.

Your mailing list is a mini-version of what the big stars do. They have a fan club and usually send out a monthly newsletter with all kinds of interesting information about them, which includes their current gig schedule and pictures with their fans. Nowadays, of course, stars have web sites that also have this current info, but I feel that it will never take the place of the "printed word" that's sent through the U.S. snail mail. At least you know they've received it and if they're interested, they'll mark it on their calendar or have it lying around the house somewhere, which will serve as a reminder.

Gig address/telephone list: It's also a great idea to keep an address and telephone list of all the gigs where you've performed in the past, which has the name of the manager who hired you. There's a lot of competition out there and if you check back with him from time to time, he won't forget about you. Not to mention the fact that having a resume of previous and return engagements will also make a good impression on venue managers and entertainment directors of potential gigs that you're pursuing.

If you've just finished a date at a new club, casino lounge, county fair or wherever, you might want to send them a little thank you note or letter. Sincerely tell them how much you enjoyed working there and how you look forward to coming back again sometime. It will certainly increase your chances of being rebooked, especially if you've done a good job for them in the first place.

Keep up-to-date on new product and hit songs: To be successful, it's important that you keep up-to-date on new product. If you're a singer and/or a musician, be aware of the latest hit songs in your genre. If your heart belongs to country, tune into your local country station. If rock 'n' roll has your soul, flip around the dial until you find a rock station. Whatever the music genre, simply tune in to the radio station that plays them.

If you're an aspiring comic, watch the numerous comedy channels on cable. Also, there are several late night television shows that are hosted by wonderful comedians. But if you want to learn from the best, tune into Jay Leno on the "Tonight Show" on NBC. His opening monologue usually contains the current national news and topics of the day.

One of the best places you can go to truly absorb all the subtleties of comic delivery and audience reaction is your local comedy club. (These clubs have become so popular that they have sprung up in practically every town and city in the U.S.)

Do you see what I'm getting at? Know your product! And you do this by keeping up-to-date with the current happenings in whatever area of the entertainment field that you're interested in.

Trade publications and hot artists: Being aware of the hot artists goes hand in hand with knowing the current hit songs. Whether you're into country, rock, R&B, jazz or gospel, know who the number one artist is for that week and make this a habit.

One of the ways that you can do this is to subscribe to the industry trade publications, and the most widely read are *Billboard, Radio & Records* and *The Gavin Report*. (Each one of them will have their own list of current hit songs on their charts.)

However, *Billboard* is well known as the music Bible of the recording industry, so I recommend that you spend a few bucks to subscribe to it. *Billboard* always has informative articles, which will keep you up-to-date in all areas of the business. It's imperative that you know not only who the current hot artists are and their hits, but the top record producers as well. Not to mention the fact that you should be aware of what's happening with the independent and major record labels along with knowing who their respective executives are. Why? Because someday you may cut a few songs or an album and your manager or producer may be presenting it to major record labels. So you've got the edge when you know all the tidbits about the record labels and their key executives. If you should ever have a meeting with a viable music executive, you'll get immediate respect because you'll be able to schmooze about the industry.

So consider subscribing to *Billboard* as an investment in your career. After all, what are we doing here? We're talking about taking your dream to its highest potential level - possibly becoming another Reba McEntire or Garth Brooks and making millions of dollars.

But I do understand the "starving musician" situation and if this is the case, there are ways to get around it.

For instance, music videos are a big business, so tune into the cable stations that play them. If a video is a hit, then in all likelihood the record is, too. This is just another way for you to stay on top of what's currently happening in your music genre.

And let's not forget the Mother-of-all-information sources - the Internet. Most of the major stars, record companies, publishing firms and trade magazines have informative web sites. *Billboard* has a wonderful web site that lists the current top twenty songs in all music genres as well as music-related articles. It blows my mind to think that you can even listen to portions of these hits if you've downloaded the necessary real media software.

So there's really no excuse for not knowing what's happening in the industry. Where there's a will, there's a way. Stay tuned.

On-the-road gigs/local news: If you're traveling to another county, city or state, whether it's a talent show or a professional gig, here's a few things that you can do to get the audience on your side.

If you're going to do an evening show, try to get there by early afternoon. After you check into the local hotel, tune into the local television channel or buy the local newspaper and read what's happening in that particular town or county. I can hear you say, "Why would I want to do that? I'm not going to be here that long and I want to take a nap before show time." Well, I can certainly understand taking a little nap. However, do you want to make a hit with the local people in your audience or don't you? If you know what's happening in that town, you can refer to it while you're on the stage. For instance, you could kid around about the new sanitation system or the new mayor or tell a little joke about the police chief (be careful here). By doing so, you'll become special to the audience because they'll appreciate the fact that you've taken the time to know about current topics in their beloved hometown.

World news: Now let's go global with reading material and other ways to keep informed as to what is going on in the world. When you're busy on the road, it's easy to get out of touch with what's happening on the world scene. Whether you're appearing in your town, another county or in another state, the national news eventually affects every one of us because no man is an island. By knowing what's going on, you can poke a little fun about the current state-of-affairs, which certainly includes the politicians and the political news of the day (Jay Leno has a field day with this). The point I'm trying to make is for you to have topics and material to chat about between songs, which will endear you to your audience.

Obviously, you can get the world news like you do the local news, which is as near as your newspaper, television or radio (and the Internet if you have a laptop computer and you're online).

There are other avenues as well, such as magazines, which come in handy while you're in a bus, car or airplane or just sitting in your hotel room. So I suggest you read the most prominent ones, such as *Time*, *Newsweek* and *People*. I can't begin to estimate how many publications are available to the public that are also good reading.

There is a segment of society that reads the unsubstantiated and multi-magnified stories in the gossip tabloids. You know the ones I'm talking about! The ones that have outlandish headlines that stare you in the face while you're waiting in line at the grocery store to check out. For laughs, Joan Carol and I give them a quick glance once in a while, but we don't take them seriously.

On television, there are some first class magazine-formatted shows that millions of people watch, which include "Dateline" and "60 Minutes." I've been watching them for years because their subject matters are thoroughly researched and so well done.

Also, I recommend that you listen to and/or watch some of the most popular radio, television and news talk shows with wonderful hosts like Larry King, Oprah, Geraldo and many more. You could get a whole slew of ideas from the endless variety of people who call to express their feelings and viewpoints. This certainly gives you an inside look into their minds, which is a barometer as to what the general public likes and dislikes. Now that is worth money to you!

As I've said before, the Internet is a great way to get info about everything. Even when you're on the road, you can get online if you happen to have a laptop computer that's set up to do so. If you are online, you can immediately go to the web sites of any television or cable network, newspaper, magazine, etc. and get the main news topics of the day without listening to the radio or turning on television or cable - and it's basically free!

Alcohol and performing: All nightclubs are in the business of selling liquor to make money. If you're an entertainer with a steady club gig, it can be more difficult to resist alcohol. When you're on your break, people will want to buy you a drink while you're talking with them. Even when you're on stage, folks will have drinks sent up to you. As I stated in the "mailing list" section of this chapter, schmoozing with the customers goes with the territory of being an entertainer, especially in a nightclub setting. You want the customers to come back and become a part of your following. Nightclub owners and managers love this and they'll rebook you because you bring in customers, who, in turn, will spend money on liquor.

And here's a little tip for you: it would be a good idea to clue the bartender(s) in advance as to what kind of a drink you'll have. Or you may want to have him fake it with soda water and/or dilute it. That way you can gracefully appease the customers, who are merely having a good time and want you to join the party. If you do, they will think it's wonderful and they're happy.

But there are some folks who won't take "no" for an answer and may even get insulted if you don't have a drink. With all due respect, that's their problem, so never feel coerced into taking one. As I said before, the tactful and diplomatic way to get around this is to dilute it with soda water. Personally, I always ask for a Seven-up or coffee and I really don't care what anyone thinks.

I suppose having a drink or a few beers won't hurt anyone - just as long as they know their limit. But if an artist should ever get out of control with alcohol (or any other substance), the owner or manager isn't going to be very happy and may not book the artist again even though he brings in customers. In many states, the laws are pretty strict when it comes to drinking and driving and the establishment is often held responsible.

Now for one of my pet peeves: *please don't walk on the stage with a bottle of beer in one hand and a cigarette in the other.* You may think it's cool, but it's not. Leave your beer and your cigarettes backstage or at the table where you were sitting. You're being paid to entertain people, and watching someone drink beer and smoke a cigarette is not exactly the most exciting entertainment in the world!

As I've said before, one of the greatest feelings in the world is the "natural high" you can get from performing and connecting with an audience. There's nothing like it!

Narcotics/drugs: I'm not here to preach about the destructive nature of substance abuse, because everyone has to make and live with their own choices in life. However, what I've said about alcohol and performing applies double to narcotics and/or drugs.

At one time or another, I'm sure you've heard and/or read about some big time entertainers (in all music genres) who have indulged in "drug roulette." Some have died from overdoses; some continue to have an ongoing problem with it, while others have stopped and have courageously gotten their lives back on track.

What you do with your life is your decision, but I encourage you never to be persuaded by anyone into taking drugs of any kind. I also caution you to be aware of the dangers of prescription drugs, which can also become a habit.

As for me, I think it's "cool" to be square and to get a "natural high" from performing. It's harmless and it gives me continued zest for living, which I feel keeps me looking, acting and feeling younger than my physical years. It will do the same for you, too.

Summary: Knowledge is power. So stay tuned to what's happening in the music industry as well as the state-of-affairs in the world. I have successfully used all the guidelines and suggestions that I've mentioned - both for myself and for the artists that I've managed. If you choose to, you can use some or all of them as you climb up the show biz ladder - from the beginner's level to regular gigs to whatever performance level you finally attain in your life.

Chapter 10

How and Where Do I Find Talent Shows?

"When I was growing up in Waco, Texas, I used to participate in the programs at schools, churches and outdoor functions. The real boom was the "Kiddie Matinee" at the movie theater, which was preceded by a 30-minute amateur show. I used to enter them because it gave me the opportunity to perform in a professional atmosphere on stage and broadcasting on the radio..."
-HANK THOMPSON, Entertainer/Songwriter/Musician
Country Music Association Hall of Fame, 1989

How and where do you find talent shows so that you can enter one? Well, I asked myself that question for you and after giving it considerable thought, I've come up with the following suggestions, which should be food for thought.

Radio Stations: The more I thought about it, the more I realized that one of the best sources for finding out about talent shows or any kind of shows is through radio stations. Why? Because it's simply a matter of business, and the entertainment field is one of the biggest industries in the world. Radio stations are being paid to advertise various products, including nightclubs, supper clubs, theaters, county fairs, etc. (If it's a benefit or a fundraiser for a local community club or event, more likely than not, they'll advertise the event for free.)

As a young artist, one of the things Hank Thompson would do is enter talent shows at a theater in Texas, which was also broadcast on the radio. That's probably how he heard about it. Of course, country music is a thriving industry in Texas. In fact, the Texas Music Office is a division in the Office of the Governor and its Program Director is Casey Monahan. When our songwriting book was published in 1992, we sent Governor Ann Richards and Casey each a copy. I'm proud to say that Governor Richards responded by commissioning both Joan Carol and me Honorary Texans!

Recently, I spoke with a friend of mine, Dave Warner, who co-owns a store called Warner's Music City with his wife, Wanda, in that great state. Since he also manages a new artist, Dave Keys, he was telling me about the "Johnnie High Country Music Revue." I met Johnnie years ago when my deejay buddy from Shreveport, Larry Scott, introduced us at an ACM awards show.

Johnnie's music revue showcases new talent every Friday and Saturday night at a large theater called the Arlington Music Hall. His Saturday night show presents experienced performers, which is broadcast nationwide from midnight to 2 a.m. on numerous radio stations, including WBAP in Fort Worth, KVOO in Tulsa and KWKH out of Shreveport, as well as worldwide via the Internet. However, his Friday night show is geared towards beginning artists, which they have to audition for. Auditions are fun and this is how I discovered new talent for my "Hometown Jamboree" shows, which I talked about in Chapter 2. So I take my hat off to Johnnie High! The world needs more people like him, because he produces shows that give new artists the opportunity to develop and perform in a professional atmosphere, which includes radio exposure.

In the golden state of California, one of my favorite country stations is KHAY (100.7) out of Ventura. The reason I enjoy all the deejays there, especially Bonnie Campbell (who is a musician and a songwriter), is because they inform their audiences about everything that's happening in the country field in their area - from artists performing at various local venues to the annual Ventura County Fair. This, in turn, gives their listeners a sense of community.

The ACM award-winning Crazy Horse Steakhouse in Santa Ana has had top country artists performing there on Sunday, Monday and Tuesday nights for years. They are constantly advertising on KZLA-FM (93.9) - the biggest country radio station in Los Angeles. One of my favorite deejays, Jim Duncan, has been there for years.

Tommy Thomas, one of the Palomino's original owners, and I were longtime friends. During its heyday, I'd intermittently put on a c/w show or be the emcee when Tommy had special concerts starring some of country's current major stars like Willie Nelson and Bobby Bare, whom I know personally. Of course, one of the reasons why the Palomino was so popular is because of Tommy's promotional efforts, which includes radio advertising.

There are times when a radio station will sponsor a talent show at a local club or participate in a fundraiser for a worthy cause, and the station's deejays or producers will also participate in the contest.

As I mentioned in Chapter 2, my good friend, Steve Tharp, who was an engineer/producer at KLAC, asked me if I'd help him put together a talent search contest for the radio station. At the time, he was producing biweekly remotes for KLAC from popular and well-known venues such as Disneyland, Knotts Berry Farm, Magic Mountain and the Palomino club. It was a lot of "fun" work and it turned out to be an annual event for three consecutive years.

There were categories for male and female vocalists, group or duet vocals, bands, songwriters and instrumentalists. Any artist or band who was interested in competing had two weeks to submit their cassette and entry form to KLAC. We received over three hundred tapes. I was one of the six judges and each of us was responsible for one category. Mine was the songwriter's division and it took me about ten days to listen to fifty tapes and pick out the top four songs. The other judges did the same with their respective categories. Steve then scheduled a meeting at the KLAC conference room and, as a group, we listened to the four tapes from each category and eliminated it down to one winner from each division.

The first year, Steve and I did a remote from the Palomino club on a Saturday night. Being the emcee, I presented all the winners from each category. Steve would do a live mix and then hand carry it to KLAC so that it could be played on radio later that evening.

The main prize for each category winner (except the songwriter) was a recording contract with Granite Records, which I owned. The songwriter had his (or her) song published with Al Gallico, one of the most successful publishers in the business at that time.

The second and third years, Steve produced biweekly KLAC remotes from Magic Mountain, which, at that time, was presenting established country acts on weekends during the summer months. When we had the annual KLAC Talent Search, we decided that the main prize for all of our category winners would be the opportunity of being the opening acts for various major country stars who were appearing at Magic Mountain. Steve would do a live mix of the entire show, which would be played later that night on KLAC.

The next year, KLAC was sold, which I was sad to hear because their talent contests offered wonderful opportunities for aspiring artists and I wish that more radio stations would have them.

About the time that Los Angeles was in the planning stages of hosting the Olympics, I was the entertainment director at a unique outdoor arena in Santa Clarita called Rivendale for one summer. On the weekends, I hired some of the current country stars, like Merle Haggard, who was well on his way to becoming a legend. During that time, I decided to produce a "Battle of the Bands" contest, so I did radio spots on numerous stations all over Southern California. Over a hundred bands sent in their cassettes and my associates and I listened to them and finally whittled it down to about ten bands.

Then I scheduled a Saturday afternoon date and had an exciting "Battle of the Bands" contest, which started about 2 p.m. The crowd turnout was fantastic and the success of this contest was due in large part to the advertising that I had done on radio stations, as well as other promotional avenues such as poster and flyers.

Radio promotion, as well as all forms of advertising, is very instrumental to the success of any event, whether it's a talent show, concert, county fair or whatever.

So check with radio stations. If any talent shows are happening anywhere, they should know. You'll find that most of the radio personnel are happy to accommodate you.

Nightclubs/Community Organizations: Call around to the c/w nightclubs in your vicinity and outlying areas. They usually have a weekly or monthly talent show on off nights like Tuesday or Thursday, which can be a big draw, if it's properly promoted.

Naturally, there are other venues where talent shows can be successfully produced, such as your local community organizations like the Elks Club, Rotary Club or women's clubs. They may be putting on a fundraising talent show for one reason or another.

Surf the Internet: Nowadays, any venue that showcases talent, such as the "Johnnie High Country Music Revue," will have a website. Of course, television/cable talent shows will also have them. The talent competition "From Hawaii...Destination Stardom" has one, which explains in detail about its show. I salute its dynamic executive producers, Al Masini and Byron Allen (who both have terrific TV industry credentials), for the opportunities they are giving new talent.

Newspaper/Entertainment Section: Another great source is to look for ads in the entertainment section of your local newspaper.

71

Community clubs, nightclubs and various organizations will undoubtedly be advertising in them. There may also be different flyers hung up or given out to the public at various public establishments like restaurants or parks in your community.

Schools (grade schools, junior high, high schools, colleges): Many big name country acts entered talent shows in their respective schools when they were first starting out. Among the artists that I know who did are Hank Thompson, Faron Young, Merle Kilgore, Bobby Bare and Bill Anderson.

High schools and colleges generally have a multitude of entertainment classes in which you can enroll. In the smaller cities as well as the major entertainment cities of the world like Los Angeles, Nashville and New York City, they have special schools that cater to whatever your artistic soul is attracted to, such as dancing, singing, acting, producing, writing, etc.

There's a training center in Southern California called the Learning Tree University. I wanted to mention them because they have a variety of courses for almost any interest imaginable, which includes the arts, such as musical instruments, singing, acting, comedy, film, makeup, television production, and the list goes on. I don't know if they have any talent contests after the courses have been completed, but it wouldn't be a bad idea, would it?

County Fairs: I was talking to a singer/songwriter recently who had called me from Oregon. He was so excited because he was one of five artists (out of eighty potential contestants) chosen to be in his hometown's talent show at the county fair. He said that he had heard it advertised on the radio, so he sent in his audition tape. He had just gotten back from rehearsals and he was a little apprehensive about it because he was going to sing an original song and accompany himself on the guitar while the others would be singing to a Karaoke tape. I told him not to be intimidated because simplicity is the key. If he sang from his heart, he would do just fine.

So check out county fairs in your vicinity, as they'll probably have a talent contest. (If they don't, suggest to whoever is in charge that they do!) Of course, listen regularly to your favorite music station because this is one of the first places you'll hear about it.

Magazines (*Billboard*, State Music Organizations): Regardless which music genre has your interest, try to read *Billboard* or other weekly or monthly music magazines. I remember reading about the "John Lennon Songwriting Contest," which was being promoted in *Billboard*. In all likelihood, if any state or national talent shows are going to be sponsored by big time companies such as True Value, they'll probably be advertised in trade magazines such as these.

Newsletters: If you're in the country field, there are a variety of newsletters and magazines from country organizations that are sent out monthly or bimonthly. I remember some really big time talent show sponsors and many of them are large corporations like Jim Beam, True Value and Marlboro.

For instance, several years ago there was a wonderful article in one of the country newsletters called the *Country Times*. There was to be a year long, nationwide talent competition called the "Third Annual Jim Beam® Country Music Talent Search." The finals would be held at a top c/w nightclub in Nashville, and if you were talented and lucky enough to be in them, you would be performing in front of a panel of industry professionals. Since this is every aspiring artist's dream, you can imagine what kind of a response they got. As in all talent show advertisements and articles, they have an address where potential contestants could write to get the information that's needed to enter.

There was another article in the same country newsletter only it was in the dance category and it was called the "Black Velvet Smooth Steppin' Showdown!" The spokesperson for this competition was the dynamic country singer and Black Velvet Lady, Tanya Tucker. This contest was going to be the first-ever, national two-step dance competition for amateurs! The contest, itself, would have preliminary competitions in various states throughout the year and would progress through three levels: the preliminaries, the regional finals and then the national finals.

These first-rate talent contests also have wonderful prizes. In the latter contest, the first and second place winners from each regional event would receive an all-expense-paid trip to Nashville on whatever date the nationals were scheduled. To make it more exciting, one of TNN's top country shows would be telecasting the event. Naturally, the article ended with an address where interested dancers could write to get the necessary information.

I also want to mention the wonderful hardware store chain, True Value, which has been sponsoring the "True Value Country Showdown" for over fifteen years. They usually have their finals at prestigious venues like the Grand Ole Opry in Nashville.

I've cited the above examples to show you what type of talent shows and contests are out there for aspiring artists. They certainly should inspire you and give you a goal to work towards.

Summary: No matter how many seminars you've gone to or how long you've taken lessons or academic courses in music, you're going to have to find out whether or not you've got what it takes. So there comes a time when you've got to lay your cards on the table - win, lose or draw. Although the entertainment world is a fantasy world, it's a "real" fantasy world that we have to go out into and explore. Just be gentle with yourself and enjoy the journey one step at a time! If you believe you've got it, you probably do!

Chapter 11

The World Is a Stage: Know Your Part

"I sang 'The Glory of Love' in a talent show at Spirit Wood Lake, ND, and won $5.00. You'll enjoy reading Cliffie's book, because he knows whereof he speaks."
-PEGGY LEE, Legendary Pop Entertainer/Capitol Recording Star/Songwriter

"Peggy Lee once told me that she considered herself an actress when she sang. I believe that whenever anyone walks out on a stage, they are acting out a part, whether they are a singer, a musician, a comic or an actor in a play. Once you 'know your part,' act it out with all the passion in your heart!"
-CLIFFIE STONE

My first book, *Everything You Always Wanted to Know About Songwriting But Didn't Know Who to Ask,* was published in 1992. Since there will always be budding songwriters on the horizon, I gratefully say that my book continues to enjoy a long shelf life.

This was corroborated four years later, when the Barnes & Noble Booksellers store in my community of Santa Clarita asked me to speak and promote it at one of their special book signing/writer's workshop engagements, which was scheduled for September 14, 1996. To say that I was excited and thrilled is an understatement.

On the night of the event, a musician buddy of mine, Mike Ley, came with Joan Carol and me. He brought his guitar and the three of us put on a little ten-minute opening show. Then Joan Carol and I talked and answered all the people's questions and sold a lot of books, which made Barnes & Noble happy.

As we were walking to our car after the event, a young man who had been in my audience came up to me and introduced himself. He told me he had learned a lot from my songwriting book and was pleased with his writing progress and looked forward to reading my

75

talent show book. However, he surprised me with his next statement when he said, "Mr. Stone, I'm also very interested in becoming an actor and I would like to know how to go about it. I know that there are a lot of schools that I could go to, but I don't have the money. What should I do?"

Before answering him, I leaned up against my car, lit my Bing Crosby pipe (the famous one with the silver band) and thought about it. I couldn't recommend talent shows, because it really isn't the right setting for actors, since they are generally for singers, musicians, songwriters, comedians, etc. Oh, I suppose someone could get up there and recite Shakespeare if they wanted to, but the nightclub audience wouldn't be receptive to it. So I'll share with you what I told him, because the acting and singing worlds are truly intertwined.

I believe that at some point in our lives, all of us have fantasized about becoming an actor or an actress. At the beginning of my show biz career when I was young, frustrated and trying to find my place in the sun, I certainly thought about it. So I talked with my cousin, Victor Jory, one of the all-time great actors, and he gave me some solid advice. (Victor was a star on radio, stage and screen and had appeared in hundreds of movies, including *Gone with the Wind*.)

He recommended that I do several things. First, to spend a minimum of six months to a year just studying the theatrical world by going to my local library where they have a multitude of books on all phases of acting - free for the reading! He also recommended that I read famous stage plays like *Our Town* and *The Gin Game*, as well as some of the classic plays by William Shakespeare.

Secondly, Victor told me I needed acting experience and that the most important thing I could do was to join a little theater group. Since both of us lived in the Los Angeles area, he suggested I get my acting feet wet at the Pasadena Playhouse, which always presented a combination of small and large theatrical productions. So I followed all of his suggestions for the next six months with a minimum output of money.

Incidentally, if you should ever decide to join a theater group (and practically every town has one), don't be surprised if the person in charge starts you off by sweeping the stage floors, moving sets around, doing show cards for the lobby and/or selling tickets to the show. Above all, don't think it's beneath you because it's all part of the total picture, especially the evolving of you as an actor.

When I joined the Pasadena Playhouse, they didn't give me a starring role in a play, but they sure gave me one backstage! I certainly did my share of lobby show cards, selling tickets, sweeping the stage, moving sets and being an all round stagehand. Even though I wasn't in some of the show productions at first, I learned that the smoothness of the set change on the front stage is based entirely on backstage organization, which takes training, timing and hard work. It was great experience for me because I really got a feel for everything that encompasses putting together a stage play from A to Z.

After serving my backstage apprenticeship, I started getting roles in quite a few shows and had a good part in *Brother Rat* and acted my heart out. They also had a smaller stage where the students could do some original productions. Many of them would write plays, and we aspiring actors would act in them.

I learned two important things as an actor. First, to always "dress the part," because this helps you to feel and act the part (see Chapters 5 and 23). Secondly, how to memorize and to "think." As an actor, you have to memorize your lines while simultaneously thinking about body language along with knowing where and when to move and stop on the stage. But you can't adlib because there are other actors waiting to recite their lines as a reaction to your lines.

So I acted at the Pasadena Playhouse just long enough to realize that I would never become a great actor like my cousin, Victor, or make a good living from it. I was also becoming more involved in all areas of the music industry, which paid for the food on the table for my growing family, so I didn't have the time to devote to acting. Quite frankly, I really didn't feel that I had the natural ability to memorize the exact words that some great author had written. It was hard work and it didn't seem to flow for me as it did when I was adlibbing on my radio stations or when I was emceeing or performing on one of my Saturday night dances in El Monte.

A few years later, however, I realized that all the hours I put in at the Pasadena Playhouse learning various aspects of the acting and stage play trade were beneficial to me, because it became a part of my stock-and-trade for the rest of my show business career. It was unbelievable how much I had absorbed at a subconscious level. All this knowledge was used in understanding the principle elements involved in casting, programming and producing musical variety television shows as well as concerts. I am thankful to this day for all the cumulative acting experiences that I have had; it's helped me to grow in all areas. As I once jotted down in one of my notebooks that I always carried with me, *"I was not what I wanted to be, but I was better than I used to be."*

All of us are acting out various roles of our own choosing on the stage of life. You may be playing the triple roles of husband, father and whatever profession you've chosen for a living. If you're a woman, you may be playing the role of wife and mother, which encompasses a multitude of acting parts, such as a housekeeper, chef or limo driver for your kids as well as their friends.

To further embellish on this, let's use some music roles for examples. In most cases, the top music executives (or any executive regardless of profession) will have a big beautiful office, which is like a movie set on a stage. On the walls, he'll probably add a few gold albums and autographed pictures of himself with major artists. He'll definitely have a tape/CD deck that he has easy access to and probably a computer, too. This is his stage!

If someone is a songwriter, he (or she) will probably have a special room he writes in that gets him into a creative mood. This also applies to a music producer who is in his own soundproof recording studio, which has all kinds of microphones, knobs, buttons and gadgets. These are their respective stages.

In the past few years, we've had some dramatic legal cases wherein the actual court trial has taken center stage on television. The next time you're watching any of these trials, observe the demeanor and attitude of the lawyers when they give their opening and closing statements, as well as their line of questioning. Many of these lawyers have a dramatic presentation style and a flair for acting. The courtroom is their stage and their audience is the jury and everyone else in the room.

As for me, I've enjoyed wearing all the musical hats during my career, but one of my favorite roles is that of an author. I love to share my knowledge about show business principles to aspiring talent and give them a glimpse of the glamorous roles that could be available for them in the industry. Not to mention the fact that I dearly love being in front of a live audience, because once a book has been published, it brings with it numerous speaking engagements on television, radio, women's clubs, etc.

Now what do all my above comments have to do with talent shows? Well, there are many people who aren't very happy with their role in life and they'd like to find a way to change it and/or become something else. This is why amateur sports, hobbies and all aspects of the art world in general are so important. People have their needs and fantasies, which are an integral part of their lives.

For those folks who are interested in music, talent shows could very well be what the doctor ordered to get away from their humdrum existence. It allows people to get up on stage and "be" whatever it is they have imagined themselves to be.

To illustrate this point, I'd like to share with you one of my favorite talent show stories. One night I was emceeing a talent show at the Palomino and a party of fifteen people came in. It was obvious they were there to celebrate and they were catered to because a large group of people celebrating anything means the cash register will be ringing. They had their own corner and two or three waitresses who made sure they didn't lack for anything.

So I went over to the happy crowd and started a conversation with one of the ladies who told me they were there to celebrate the birthday of a very special guy (their boss). Since he always wanted to be a singer, he decided to enter the Palomino talent night show for his birthday! When she told me his name, I almost fell over, because he was the editor-in-chief of *Variety*, one of the most popular show business magazines in the industry. (*The Hollywood Reporter* is another one.)

When it was his turn, I introduced him. Now this guy was serious and well prepared, because he immediately passed out lead sheets to the band. I knew what a big deal this was to him, so I talked with him longer on stage than I normally talk with contestants and he basked in the spotlight. One of the comments that I recall him making was "I always wanted to be a singer all my life but for one reason or another, I never had the time or the chance to become one. Tonight I'm going to have that chance, and I want to sing 'My Way,' Frank Sinatra's signature song."

Although it's been years, I've never forgotten him because he made a deep impression on me about people and their innermost desires and fantasies. Think about it! Here was a man with an enviable position with a prestigious magazine who has been involved in all aspects of writing big time Hollywood articles and attending influential events. Yet, deep down, it was his secret desire to sing and perform himself.

So, for a few moments in time, this executive got to play out his fantasy role and he was terrific!

This true story absolutely touches my heart every time I think about it because it epitomizes why I'm so passionate about talent shows and their importance to aspiring talent.

One of my favorite quotes is "I know my part," which I borrowed from my songwriting buddy and music associate, Charlie Williams, who became an actor in the latter part of his life before the Lord called him home. Whenever anyone suggested doing something, the first words out of Charlie's mouth were, "I know my part."

While I'm on the subject of music people who have branched out into the acting field, take a look at how many major recording stars have included acting in their music portfolio. Several that come to mind are Johnny Cash, Willie Nelson, Dwight Yoakam, Dolly Parton, Kris Kristofferson, Reba McEntire, and Barbara Mandrell.

Most singers who are signed with a major label get a taste of acting when they make music videos for their singles. Actually, a song is a mini-story so the video is actually a mini-movie.

So there is a connecting bond shared by the acting and music worlds alike. A singer has to get "inside" the lyrics for their true meaning before he or she can interpret them. This, in turn, makes the audience feel and relate to the emotions of that song. The same thing is true with an actor. He has to get "inside" the character of the role he (or she) is playing. It may take time but you'll be more comfortable as you gain experience and knowledge while going through the process of becoming an actor or a singer as you go from stage to stage.

Summary: In the early spring of 1995, I was discussing the possibility of doing a country album with the legendary pop diva, Peggy Lee. At that time, she told Joan Carol and me that she considered herself an actress when she sang, and she was right on the money about her art. Later that summer, she made a rare appearance at the Hollywood Bowl with Mel Torme and George Shearing. Her performance was an unforgettable experience! She's a master at changing her emotions from a sad to a happy song, and she hypnotically took us, as well as her entire audience, on this emotional music journey into the soul with her.

I believe that whenever anyone walks out on a stage, they are *acting out a part*, whether they are a singer, a musician, a comic or an actor in stage play. In other words, no matter what they do on stage, it's basically a role that they are going to play out. Yes, the world is a stage and we individually play out our roles.

So I thank the young man who attended my Barnes & Noble book signing/speaking engagement for asking me about the acting profession. I feel this subject has added an important element to my book, which will help aspiring artists to be all that they can be.

To quote Charlie Williams, "I know my part." However, along with knowing your part, you also have to practice your part because you're only as good as your last performance. It's my belief that "a singer is not a singer unless he's singing. A writer is not a writer unless he's writing. A musician is not a musician unless he's playing his instrument, and so it goes with whatever role anyone chooses."

My friend, once you "know your part," act it out with all the passion in your heart!

Chapter 12

Writers: Sing Your Song for All You're Worth!

"I won my first talent show at Rockhill High School in Ohio by singing 'Shot Gun Boogie.' Talent shows are important because they give you confidence and reaffirm what you suspect about yourself - that you have talent!"
-BOBBY BARE, RCA Recording Artist/Songwriter/Publisher/TNN Host

"Talent shows give songwriters a place to showcase their songs, and sometimes you gotta write bad songs before you can write good ones. Regardless, proudly step up to the mike and sing your song for all you're worth!"
-CLIFFIE STONE

W hat a lot of people don't realize about talent shows is that they offer a wonderful opportunity for all categories of entertainers, which includes aspiring songwriters.

So if you're a writer and you have some new songs that haven't been exposed to an audience (other than singing them for your family and friends who will think they are hits), then talent shows are a place where you can showcase them. Why? Because the nightclub or venue is generally full of people who are performers. It's true that many of them are amateurs. However, from aspiring artists come the stars of tomorrow! I could name many super stars from all music genres who have participated in talent shows at the beginning of their careers, such as Frank Sinatra, Peggy Lee, Alabama, Randy Travis, Melissa Etheridge and the illustrious list goes on.

When I was the talent show emcee at Tommy Thomas' Palomino club, I had the most talented group of musicians in the house band, who called themselves the Palomino Riders! With their great playing, they could make the contestants feel like real professionals on the stage.

My regular A-team group consisted of Jay Dee Maness on steel guitar (Desert Rose Band); Steve Duncan on drums (Desert Rose Band); Skip Edwards on piano (Dwight Yoakam's band); Harry Orlove on guitar and Arnie Moore on bass. When Skip was out of town with Dwight, John Hobbs or Jim Cox would sit in for him. They were all so much fun. I'd kid and tease around with each one of them and they would always go along with me. In fact, I'd have a little routine going with them, especially when I decided I wanted to sing, which got great laughs from the audience. (Not my singing - my jokes!)

Anyway, my guys would always get their twenty-minute break every hour (as all bands do) so they could take a breather from their chores of backing up singers.

Now, if nothing is happening on stage during those twenty-minute breaks, there is a "dead mike," and a dead mike contributes to an audience dwindling down to a precious few, so it's best to try to keep their attention.

What I usually try to do during a break (especially if I have an abundance of contestants) is to put on songwriters who can sing two or three of their original tunes, which is a wonderful way for them to expose their songs to the audience. (This is what I recommend you do, too.) Hopefully, they can accompany themselves by playing a little piano, guitar, harmonica, tin pan or possibly a tape. Of course, the songwriters could also use the band when they're not on break if they've brought in sheet music for them. Even if they didn't, my guys were so talented that they could improvise or fake it if they had to.

I'd like to briefly address one of the concerns that some new songwriters seem to have, which is someone stealing their song. I've been involved in talent shows for years and, to my knowledge, I don't know of anyone who has ever stolen a song from anyone just because they sang it at a talent show. It could happen, but I really don't think so. Besides, there's a thing called "copyrights" and I recommend you read Chapter 14 in my other book, *Everything You Always Wanted to Know About Songwriting, But Didn't Know Who to Ask.* However, it's your choice as to whether you want to keep your songs in a drawer somewhere, or put them out into the world.

But let's get back to the positives of exposing your song(s) at talent shows. You'll have an edge on the other contestants if you showcase your song(s) during a break. First of all, since it's an intermission, you'll have the spotlight longer and can probably do a couple of songs, whereas the other contestants in the show are usually limited to one song.

And after you've sung each one of your songs in front of an audience, you'll be getting their immediate reaction to them. Now don't become distressed if some of the people in the audience aren't listening to you. They may be busy drinking or gabbing or both. By the same token, many of them do pay attention and those are the reactions that count. Of course, their reaction will be their own opinions as to how good or bad your song is. If it's a negative reaction, don't get discouraged. After all, you're relatively new at the game.

You see, often times *you gotta write bad songs before you can write good ones*. In other words, as a beginning or an intermediate songwriter, your songs may not be so hot when you first start to write them, even though you may think they are. Believe me, I understand the miraculous feeling you can get when you've created something out of nothing, which is hard to put into words. But do remember that the more you write and learn your craft, the better your songs will be. This is all part of the learning curve. And you'll be walking on air the first time a total stranger comes up and tells you how much they loved and identified with your song, which will inspire you to keep on writing!

Secondly, all the contestants will be hearing your material, and possibly some of them may ask if they can sing the song themselves in the next talent show they enter. If you want them to sing it, it's okay. Who knows? Maybe they'll even want to make a little demo recording of it!

Thirdly, and this is important, sometimes music publishers will go to talent shows if they're invited to go see a singer. So when it's your turn to get up on stage and sing your songs, there's always the possibility that there may be a publisher out there who may become interested in your material. If he thinks you're a diamond in the rough, he may even sign you as a writer.

This could happen, and let me give you a wonderful example. My darlin' wife, Joan Carol, wanted to join ASCAP (one of the performing rights societies), but the only way she could join as an associate member was to have one of her songs performed in a public venue such as a nightclub. So on a Tuesday night, it was sung at the Palomino's weekly talent night show, which was emceed and video taped by a friend of mine, Allen Bee. I wasn't the emcee at the time because I had another talent show gig on Thursday nights at a club called the Silverado. On Thursday night, she came over to pick up her video from Allen and he introduced us. Ironically, this was to be my last night as the emcee, because I had just been hired by Gene Autry to be the Consultant/Director of his publishing companies, which would take up all my time. So I gave her my card and told her to call me for an appointment, which she did about a month later. I met with her and her co-writer, Marc Levine, listened to their songs and published six of them.

There is a footnote to this story. After my beloved wife, Dorothy, passed on, I started dating a couple of ladies, one of them being Joan Carol, whom I eventually married. So you never know what miracles can happen as the result of participating in talent shows!

In case you're not aware of it, there are songwriting organizations in most states and they do have special events wherein a writer can perform their songs. For instance, in Southern California, we have the Los Angeles Songwriters Showcase (LASS) and it's a wonderful organization for aspiring songwriters to be associated with. In Nashville, they have the Nashville Songwriters Association, International. And you can always check with the musicians union located in your city or with performing rights societies such as BMI and ASCAP for information about songwriting organizations.

Let's move along to another aspect of songwriting. Many songwriters are also aspiring singers and during the years that I was involved in talent shows, they've asked me for advice before and after performing their songs. Usually I say, "Well, you sing your songs pretty good, but what do you want to be? Do you want to be a writer or a singer or both, because it makes a difference." A lot of them are bashful and they'll say, "I just want to write songs for somebody else." Many of the more confident ones will say, "I believe in my songs and I want to sing them myself."

The rewards are great for those who believe in themselves and dare to try! There is always the possibility that a songwriter/singer could end up as a successful recording artist some day, because some of the songs he (or she) writes may become big sellers for a major artist. This type of success story has happened time and again and they include Willie Nelson, Kris Kristofferson, Brooks & Dunn and Rodney Crowell.

Rodney, who has an incredible track record, is one of my favorite songwriters. I was so happy for him when he released an album as an artist himself about five or so years ago, which spawned four or five number one *Billboard* hits! This multi-talented artist does it all, for he's also an excellent producer.

Even a minor hit record can open the label's closed doors. Record companies are always looking for artists who can write their own tunes. This makes life a lot simpler for them, because their record label has a music publishing company and it might be part of the deal that they get publishing on the artist/songwriter's songs. So it's desirous to have a singer who can write and vice versa.

Dear songwriter/singer, take heart! The musical lotto jackpot could potentially happen to you. Some day one of the songs you write could become a hit by some other artist, which could lead you into becoming a recording artist yourself some day.

There's a sign in my office that I look at every day: "No guts, no glory!" So proudly step up to the talent show mike and "sing your song for all you're worth!"

Chapter 13

Comedians: Timing Is Everything!

"One of the things I learned to do when a joke went south on me was keep on talking and keep the show moving. If you can laugh and not take yourself so seriously, this attitude will transfer over to the audience."
-CLIFFIE STONE

"If Cliffie believed in you, you not only had his backing, but his loyalty and friendship – usually sealed with nothing more than a handshake and his word. If it hadn't been for his handshake, friendship, and the spotlight that he gave to my Dad, the world would never have heard the name Tennessee Ernie Ford."
-JEFFREY "BUCK" FORD, Producer/Writer/Executive/Actor

While I'm on the topic of discussing opportunities for different entertainer categories, I encourage all aspiring comedians who are reading this book to pursue the talent show circuit.

Like all artists, comedians need a stage to get experience before a live audience, and I firmly believe that talent shows are a perfect vehicle for them to try out their comedic wings. I'll bet that many of today's top stand-up comedians (or sit-down comedians, as I am) got their start in a talent show somewhere.

As I mentioned in the previous chapter, whenever I emceed the weekly talent show at the Palomino, I would put on a songwriter during the band's break. Likewise, it's also a perfect spot to put on a comedian, which I would do if there was one in the club that night. If I was lucky enough to have both, I'd let the songwriter perform one or two songs and then let the comic do about five minutes (or ten minutes if he was really rolling).

Top-notch comics can sure make it look effortless, but take it from me, it's not easy to be a comedian. They are a different breed of cat than singers, songwriters and musicians! I ought to know because I'm a combination of all four of them myself. There's nothing I like to do more than tell a good joke or to laugh (unless it's holding hands with my darlin'). I believe with all my heart that the only way one can get through life is to have a good sense of humor!

I first realized that I had a knack for comedy when I played bass on Stuart Hamblen's radio shows at the tender age of sixteen. Stuart loved to spontaneously make up funny stories on the air and to put the nearest people around him on the spot, which he would do to me constantly. But I discovered that I, too, had a quick wit and Stuart and I would play off each other with one one-liner after another all the time. Our radio audience just loved it, as did the other band members and radio station personnel. It was one of those rare unexplainable chemistry things, not unlike the unique chemistry that Whoopie Goldberg, Robin Williams and Billy Crystal all have with each other. It just is!

I shake my head in amazement as I look back, because I was sure one busy guy during my early years in the music business. I had this insatiable appetite to keep learning everything I could about entertaining, and I dearly loved comedy!

One of my gigs was playing bass at Ken Murray's Blackouts in 1942, which was a very popular and prestigious club in Hollywood back in those days. Whenever it was time for a comedian to take center stage, I would listen intently to how they would time their jokes, as well as watch their facial expressions and body language when they delivered the punch line. I constantly tried to learn from them and it paid off.

The timing of a joke's punch line is everything, and what better place to try out your new jokes than at a talent show. If you forget the punch line or your timing isn't quite right, so what! Sure it can be a little embarrassing when no one laughs. Goodness, that still happens to all the top comedians in show business.

For instance, Jay Leno (of NBC's "Tonight Show") spent years learning his craft by performing in small clubs and other venues across the country, which is a tough grind (just as it is for singers and musicians). He's a great comedian who has written his own material all his life, and he still works hand in hand with his staff writers. The next time you watch his NBC television show, observe how he gets himself out of it whenever he has a joke that fizzles in his opening monologue. Sometimes he'll look off to the side and say to the staff writers, "I told you that wasn't going to work," or he'll make a funny remark as he looks over at his jovial bandleader, Kevin Eubanks, who just smiles and laughs. Jay has a razor sharp mind and can come up with a humorous quip in the blink of an eye. His expressions and his adlibs are usually funnier than the joke would have been, and I laugh more just seeing his reaction to the audience's non-reaction whenever his joke falls short of the mark.

Probably the most gifted humorist and quickest wit I ever knew was my good buddy, Pat Buttram, who had a Will Rogers style of homespun humor. He had a world-renowned reputation as a humorist and emcee. *Time* magazine described him as "probably the most quoted wit in the nation," and some of his national television appearances included "The George Gobel Show," "The Ed Sullivan Show," and "The Jack Benny Show." He was also an actor and he was Gene Autry's sidekick in forty western movies as well as over a hundred television episodes of the "Gene Autry Show," which I produced for one year. Many remember him as "Mr. Haney" on CBS's "Green Acres" series with Eddie Albert and Eva Gabor.

Anyway, Pat wrote all of his own material and he could stand up before an audience either as a comedian or as an emcee and tell jokes for hours. If he forgot any of his jokes and stories, he just made them up on the spot, and he never let anyone or anything bother him when he was on stage.

But we can't all be like Pat. Yes, it can be nerve-racking when you're trying to be funny, because you never really know if the joke is going to go over. There are many factors involved, such as the timing of a punch line (and timing is everything) or maybe the joke isn't "politically correct" for some of the people in the audience or whatever. Take it from me, that momentary dead silence that occurs when no one laughs after you've delivered a punch line can make your heart skip a beat. It does take experience to be able to brush it off and to go on with the next joke as if nothing had happened.

I'm speaking from firsthand experience because I have had my share of jokes that didn't quite make it. Whenever that happens to me, it's generally because I haven't been on stage and in front of an audience for a while. So what it boils down to is I lost my timing - and it's all in the timing. As I've said before, "a singer is not a singer unless he's singing and a comedian is not a comedian unless he's telling jokes." To keep from getting rusty, all of us have to keep doing whatever it is we do.

One of the things I learned to do when a joke went south on me was to keep on talking and keep the show moving. If you can laugh and not take yourself so seriously, this attitude will transfer over to the audience. This is what all the great comedians like Jerry Lewis, Jay Leno, Robin Williams and all the others have always done.

Comedian icon, Bob Hope, is the epitome of impeccable timing and timing needs to be practiced. Whenever he did one of his shows on television, he would begin with a monologue. Now I don't know if you've ever been to a television rehearsal or a taping, but before the show starts, the producer will have someone get on stage and warm up the audience by chatting with them and telling a few jokes. And it's my understanding that Bob might practice his monologue two or three times in front of different audiences before he ever did it in front of the camera. For instance, there may be another show in rehearsal at the same television studio where he was scheduled to have his show. So Bob would come out and do his monologue in front of another television show's audience. Of course, that was an unexpected treat for the lucky audience. By doing this, he found out what jokes didn't work and what ones did and those were the ones he'd use on his own show.

Testing out jokes like this is not a weird or an uncommon thing for any comedian or comedienne to do. In fact, it's necessary and important for them to do, because they have to stay on top of their comedy game, especially if they have new material.

There was a wonderful place over in Pasadena, California, called the Ice House that had several stages, and various artists would be performing on each one of them throughout the evening. So I would go over there from time to time to catch different acts. Now, the Ice House wasn't really a talent night show. However, it was similar in nature in that there were all categories of artists (singers, musicians, comedians, magicians, etc.) on stage in front of a live audience polishing their acts.

I remember seeing actor Harry Anderson (before he became well known as the judge on the long-running television comedy series, "Night Court") do a little magic act on one of the smaller stages. I guess he loved fooling around with magic tricks because he was having a great time. I also saw a few professional comedians trying out new material for their acts and one of them was Lily Tomlin.

There's a famous club in Hollywood that's been around for over thirty years called the Improv, which is a hang out for comedians and most of the big time comics got their start there. I've heard that many of them still drop by unexpectedly and get up on stage.

Major star comedians trying out their new jokes at smaller and more intimate clubs is nothing new under the sun. Many of them do this before they take their act to big time gigs such as Las Vegas.

If you're an aspiring comic, take your cue from the big guys and practice your material wherever and whenever you can in front of live audiences, regardless of size. In a sense, you're an actor, because you've got to tell these jokes as if they were the first time you ever told them. You're only as good as your last performance.

And here's another stage for you to keep in mind: benefits or charity shows. Many entertainers (including me) will do several throughout the year. If a comedian comes out and bombs with some of his jokes, then he knows that he shouldn't be doing them on a money gig. When an artist is performing for nothing, he has a lot more freedom than he would if he were getting paid.

Usually at a paid gig, they'll give you maybe twenty minutes and that's it. This is why a lot of us comic hams like Pat Buttram and myself like to participate in benefits. We can get up there and stay on longer then we normally could anywhere else. The people running the benefit can't tell us to get off the stage because they don't want to lose their free entertainment.

Sometimes I've watched other comedians and singers at these benefits and I've heard people mumbling to one another, "He's been on a long time." Well, you can forget about trying to get him or her off! That comic or singer is having too much fun and they'll keep on doing it until they run out of material.

I'm sure you've known women (possibly your mother) who would cut out recipes and then paste them in a scrapbook. Well, that's what I did with jokes all my life (and you might want to consider doing this yourself). Whenever I heard jokes that tickled my funny bone, especially in normal conversations with Pat Buttram who would say the funniest things, or some of my other friends who could have been professional comedians had they chosen to, I would quickly make notes on a piece of paper. Later, I'd write them down in one of my special joke notebooks, so that I could refresh my memory in case I ever wanted to use them on stage someday, or whenever I needed to have a good laugh. Laughter is medicine and jokes are meant to be shared and passed on!

Speaking about sharing and passing on jokes, it reminds me of one of Jerry Lewis' yearly MS (multiple sclerosis) telethon shows when Milton Berle made an appearance. Both of them were making witty wisecracks to each other and Milton says to Jerry, "I'll tell the jokes." Jerry says, "Whose?" Milton Berle was kidded and teased about this all the time by all the great comedians.

Here's a suggestion for aspiring singers: your goal should be to develop yourself into an all round entertainer who can relate to an audience on a one-to-one basis. So it would behoove you to casually talk with the audience between songs, otherwise your act could get a little boring for them. Laughter makes everyone more relaxed so you might try throwing in a few funny lines or jokes between songs. I'm certainly not saying that you should be a full-blown comic, because your bread and butter is singing. I'm merely suggesting that you include a few funny remarks once in a while.

Multi-talented singer/songwriter/musician, Vince Gill, is a perfect example of balancing out a show with music and laughter. Have you ever seen him host any of the CMA Awards shows? His natural wit makes him a great entertainer and emcee!

Another great example is my dear buddy, the late Tennessee Ernie Ford, who was not only a great singer/entertainer, but a natural born comedian as well. When I announced him on my "Hometown Jamboree" show, he'd come out and we'd start adlibbing. Neither one of us knew what the other was going to say; however, I was usually the straight man and Ernie would come out with homespun remarks that always had the audiences in stitches. Later when he became a big star, he continued to adlib whenever he was on a concert stage or on his weekly NBC television show, and his down-home country sayings won the hearts of millions of people across-the-board worldwide. Ernie would always close his shows with *bless your pea pickin' hearts*, which was his most famous "Ernie-ism."

And the comedic baton has been passed on, for I'm happy to say that country humor is in good hands with Jeff Foxworthy. I can't help but think of Ernie whenever Jeff stands unpretentiously before an audience and starts telling his Southern redneck jokes, which are enjoyed by everyone across-the-board. He's had several top selling albums and continues to be one of country's premier comedians.

Since I'm a country guy, I would be remiss if I didn't mention the late Minnie Pearl, country's treasured CMA Hall of Fame comedienne. Whenever she and Ernie got on stage together - look out! Their homespun and natural sense of humor always rocked the walls of the Grand Ole Opry or any TNN television shows that they appeared on together. I'll never forget the limo ride that Joan Carol and I took with them when we were going to NBC studios to tape Ernie's 50th anniversary in show business for The Nashville Network. They were so hilarious, and I wish that I could have had a tape recorder turned on at that time.

Dear aspiring comedians and comediennes: Do your homework! Watch the pros perform either in nightclubs or on television (cable has their own comedy channels). Observe how they deliver a punch line as well as their facial expressions and body language, because timing is everything. Then go out and get on as many stages as you can - be it a talent show, a comedy club, benefits or wherever - and tell your jokes.

And while you're laughing your way through life (and to the bank) remember that *You Gotta Be Bad Before You Can Be Good.*

Chapter 14

Know Your Audience!
A Day in the Life of Cliffie

"I can't carry a tune in a bucket. My brand of entertainment is trick roping and riding. Every new artist needs a stage and an audience. Mine was small town rodeos where, as a youngster, I stood on a platform and gave a rope spinning exhibition while learning to smile and be at ease in front of people."
MONTIE MONTANA, World Famous Trick Roper and Cowboy

"There is nothing more gratifying then seeing, hearing and feeling an audience's love after doing a successful show where I've given my best to entertain...and as I look up at the sky, I think to myself, 'Thank you, Lord...it's a wonderful world.'"
-CLIFFIE STONE

Do you know what the most difficult thing is for artists to do? It's not doing the show - that's the stimulating and fun part! It's all the mental and physical preparation, including the time it takes to get ready for and travel to the show.

Here's an overall view of what the average entertainer and/or musician has to go through. Let's say that Johnny Singer is a fairly successful entertainer in that he not only makes a decent living from local gigs, but intermittently, he and his band have on-the-road gigs in Nevada and other Western states. So they pack their suitcases, put their equipment into two vans and drive eighteen hours for a two-week gig somewhere in Montana. Johnny gets up late the next morning, picks out the clothes he's going to wear that night, thinks about the songs he'll be singing, the order he'll be doing them and then makes out the set list for each musician. In the afternoon, they haul their equipment to the club and set up for the sound check. Later that night, they do four sets that last about forty-five minutes each, which is the gratifying part of the entire process.

Although I've curtailed my performance schedule, let me give you "a day in the life of Cliffie" and what I go through whenever I have my "Hometown Jamboree" concerts.

94

First of all, I'll start from square one - the mental preparation. When Joe Graydon (one of the sharpest agents in the business) or one of the other agents I deal with calls me about a gig, I get all the important information such as the date, time, location and gig offer. Then I tell him I'll get back with him as soon as I can.

One of my first thoughts is the audience. I've got to *know my audience*, because they're made up of different ages, interests, occupations and backgrounds, etc. So before I hire a band or any entertainers who will be on the bill with me, I think about it. Will it be a younger or an older crowd? Or will it be an admixture of both age groups? Of course, this will depend on whether my concert is at a senior citizens venue, Performing Arts Center or in a park. (The two latter venues are geared towards all age groups.)

If it's a younger crowd, then I've got to have some cool jokes they'll be able to identify with. So I look through my "young bones" joke notebook. Naturally, this younger crowd will want to hear the current country hits of today. So I'll hire a younger bandleader, and entertainers like Mikal Masters, who keeps up with the current hits.

If it's at a senior citizen venue at Leisure World, I'll tell jokes they can relate to such as health issues. For instance, I'll poke fun at myself and say, "I came to California for arthritis and sure enough, I got it." Or I'll stop in middle of my act, look at my watch and say, "It's eight o'clock - time to take your pills." As for songs, they'll want to hear the classic c/w tunes that bring back memories to them. So I'll hire older established artists who know them.

The band I hire has to be familiar with the songs in my guest artist's repertoire as well as mine. I usually hire the same multi-talented bandleaders such as Danny Michaels, Al Vescovo or Garth Phillips, who have performed with me and my guest stars for years on my concert dates all over California.

Then I give thought to the venue itself. Where is it located and how much traveling time is involved? Is it indoors at a Performing Arts Theater or at an Indian gambling casino or outdoors at an amphitheater or in a park?

What I've been doing is mentally mapping out the entire gig before I hire anyone. After I've given thought to all the above, I make up a budget and make the gig calls to my artists. After I get commitments from them, I call my agent back to confirm the deal and he sends me a contract, which I sign and mail back.

I'll use Leisure World as an example because I usually do a concert there annually. I know going in that a majority of my audience will be made up of senior citizens who probably came to my Saturday night "Hometown Jamboree" shows in El Monte and/or watched it on television four decades ago.

Once my agent gives me the date, I call one of my bandleaders and several guest artists to see if they are available at that time. This usually takes me about three days to get commitments.

So this gig has been signed, sealed and delivered about ten months in advance, because I've already hired a bandleader and several older established entertainers who have box office appeal for the Leisure World crowd. In the past, they've included Eddie Dean, Roberta Linn (Lawrence Welk's original "Champagne Lady"), Hank Thompson, Molly Bee, Sue Thompson, Billy Armstrong, Candy Carter and the legendary Western group, Riders of the Purple Sage.

A week or so before the concert, I call my show people to touch base with them and chat for awhile. Since we've all performed together many times before, it's like a family reunion for us.

A day before the gig, I'll sketch out my show's format. When show time day arrives, I go through the routine of meticulously picking out my show clothes. Usually around eleven in the morning, Joan Carol and I are packed and on our way to Leisure World, which is about a two-hour drive. While traveling, I'm thinking about the show and I go over the jokes I've written down on my notepad. Then I figure out what order I'll be scheduling each act and what I possibly may say when I present them. I'll also be singing a few songs, which always includes one or two duets with my darlin', so we have fun rehearsing them in the car as we're driving.

It's always been my life-long habit to arrive at my gigs at least three or four hours before the show starts because I like to check out the entire venue. When we hit town, we have lunch at one of the local restaurants. While there, I buy the newspaper and scan through it looking for local news events, so that I can joke around about whatever the current topic is when I'm on stage. People appreciate it because they know that I've taken the time to find out what's happening in their hometown.

After lunch, we go to the venue, unload the car and get settled in my dressing room. Though I've performed at Leisure World before, I meander out on stage so that I can familiarize myself with the surroundings, which I love because it's a wonderful outdoor theater with great sound and lighting systems - sort of a mini version of the Hollywood Bowl.

Then I usually chitchat with the agent and the concert manager. Once the other entertainers and musicians have arrived, we have a sound check, which is simply checking the microphone levels, monitors, amplifiers and the sound system in general. Joan Carol and I rehearse our songs with the band and, afterward, the band runs through the song routines of each guest star.

They have something very unique at Leisure World, which is a closed circuit TV channel that goes into everyone's home in the huge community complex; so I do a forty-minute pre-show interview for this TV channel, which includes my guest artists.

About thirty minutes before show time, Joan and I go to our private dressing room where I get into my show clothes and usually take a quick nap. I don't like to talk to anyone at this time other than Joan because it's important that I become centered within myself. About ten minutes before show time, I schmooze with the band and artists while all of us excitedly wait for the curtain to open.

The Leisure World management is adamant about the show being no longer than an hour. Of course, I agree knowing full well that there will always be encores, so it usually lasts about an hour and fifteen minutes - especially when I have the wonderful Western singer, Eddie Dean, on the show, who always gets standing ovations.

After the show, my band, guest artists and I spend about forty-five minutes to an hour meeting and talking with fans backstage, which includes signing autographs and taking pictures with them.

As I said at the beginning of this chapter, the show itself is the easiest thing to do. What can be a chore is all that other time-consuming stuff that has to be done, but I happen to love every minute of it because it goes with the territory.

Here's another "day in the life of Cliffie," which is a perfect example of how an entertainer has to be flexible and prepared for anything in order to give the audience what they want.

A group of doctors from Northern California called me a year in advance to put together a c/w show, which was to take place at an elite Palm Springs hotel. They wanted a band that knew both the standard and current country hits and also requested that I hire a cowboy dance line instructor.

So I go through my usual pre-show preparation routine. Since the doctors' families would be there, I knew the audience would be made up of all age groups. I hired Danny Michaels, who I can take anywhere because he and his band can switch music genre gears at the drop of a hat - from country to pop to blues to jazz. I also hired Sharie Penny (wife of the late Hank Penny), who was a big band singer at one time. My dance instructors were a wonderful husband and wife team, Pat and Bob Weiss.

I always negotiate hotel accommodations in the contract when I have out-of-town gigs. So Joan Carol and I left for Palm Springs the day before the performance so that we could get enough rest for the next day's show, along with getting used to the environment.

Well, I had a wonderful show planned and I had all of my "doctor" jokes ready. After I met with the group's administrator, we had a sound check at the venue, which was a large beautiful ballroom that had dinner tables set up with an allotted dance area. Everything was going smoothly and we're closing in on show time.

I started out doing the show that I had originally scheduled, but fifteen minutes into it, I realized it wasn't going to work. The audience was filled with high-energy doctors of all ages who were on vacation and they weren't interested in simply sitting at their tables watching a show, and neither were their kids. They wanted to table hop as well as dance, and their eclectic requests ranged from pop to rock to country. So we played it by ear and went into the dance band mode with Sharie and Danny singing a variety of pop and country tunes. When I put Pat and Bob on to give cowboy line dance instructions during the break, practically everyone in the audience participated, including the children and teenagers, which was literally a showstopper that lasted about forty-five minutes.

So the entire show was a success and I got the most wonderful thank you letter a week later. Even though I "knew my audience," they didn't want what I had originally planned. So I immediately switched gears on stage and simply gave them what they wanted.

Another "day in the life of me" occurred about five years ago when an old friend called and wanted me to do a little afternoon show for a senior citizen group. I actually did it as a favor to him, because it paid very little. Besides, Joan Carol and I would have the opportunity to sell our songwriting book and CDs.

Now when I say a small show, I mean a small show. The cast consisted of Joan Carol, Garth Phillips and me. Regardless of size, I care about my audience, so I spent time preparing my jokes and songs. In my mind's eye, I visualized myself performing in an air-conditioned clubhouse with my audience sitting about five feet from the stage. I would have great eye contact with them and would be able to see, hear and feel their reactions to my jokes.

However, this gig didn't turn out the way I had envisioned. The day before, they decided to have a luncheon barbecue in the park outside the clubhouse. It was a hot summer's day and the stage was cement. There was only one mike and no stool for me to sit on.

Joan Carol and I had arrived around eleven in the morning and the barbecue was going full steam ahead with smoke from burnt chicken thighs filling the air. It was one o'clock in the afternoon by the time we got on that cement stage.

The good news is the benches were all in the shade. The bad news is the chairs in front of the stage were empty because all the folks were sitting on the benches forty feet away.

Being a trouper, I got on the hot cement stage (with a big soda pop stain on the front of my shirt that a senior citizen lady had spilled on me in her excitement of getting my autograph), and started entertaining an audience that's forty feet away. I couldn't see their faces because the sun was too glaring on my sunglasses.

When one is working in an outside venue, any sound or laughter from the audience goes up and not towards the stage. So when I told my jokes, I couldn't tell if there was a reaction and I couldn't react to their reaction. Then I recalled what my buddy, the great comedian and humorist, Pat Buttram, once told me: *"Anytime you're performing in an outside arena with a bunch of people who are actually there for another reason, just do your thing and don't worry about it. Don't feel bad if they don't send up any balloons, flares or rockets. They are enjoying it, but you're kind of an opening act for whatever reason they are there for."*

So I told a few jokes and sang a few songs, which included a duet with my darlin.' And bless Garth's cool pea-pickin' heart! He went with the flow like a pro and stood on that hot cement stage with us singing and playing guitar while throwing in his Johnny Cash and John Wayne imitation routines. I had him close the show with "Sixteen Tons," which the audience loved. I sure felt better about the whole thing when Joan Carol told me that the people did laugh at my jokes even though I couldn't see or hear them.

So, the bad news is Joan Carol, Garth and I were the opening act for a television drawing the senior citizens were going to have. The good news is we sold enough books, CDs and tapes that made us smile all the way home. By golly, we even made the front page of their local newspaper the next day. Thank goodness my soda pop stain didn't show! So all's well that ends well.

I laugh affectionately whenever I think about this gig. But it also serves as an example as to what can happen to entertainers from time to time. If things don't quite work out the way you had planned, don't become unduly upset about it.

The morale of this chapter is for you to preplan your shows and it all starts with *knowing your audience*. Then be flexible enough to go with the flow so that you can give them what they want!

Chapter 15

Have Fun Producing Money-Making Talent Shows!

"It seems to me that talent shows are on the endangered species list. So I call upon aspiring producers out there. Where are you? We need more dedicated producers like Art Linkletter and Dick Clark."
-CLIFFIE STONE

"Cliffie and I became good friends when he was the executive producer of Tennessee Ernie Ford's NBC television show, and I was the MCA rep. Later, we formed our own corporation for other television production ventures. He gave more people opportunities to present their talent than anyone I ever met."
-DALE SHEETS, President of International Ventures, Inc.

Noon is approaching on this beautiful but hot 4th of July as I tape my thoughts down about producing talent shows. Tonight there will be thousands of free events that will be produced in parks and other venues across the United States for the sole purpose of having "fun" celebrations to honor our nation's birthday! Of course, we, the people, will be indirectly paying for it through our tax dollars. As the saying goes, there's no free lunch because it does take money to pay for the fireworks as well as the numerous people involved in putting on these events. Naturally, the fire department does have to be on call, along with the police department in case some folks get carried away with the festivities.

And so it goes with the responsibilities of producing and coordinating a talent show (or any show for that matter). The basic principles that I talk about in this chapter can be applied to any talent contest, whether it's held in a nightclub, school, or a community organization that's having a fundraiser.

It seems to me that talent shows are on the endangered species list, especially in nightclubs, which is probably the type of venue most professional entertainers will be performing in during their careers. But regardless of venue, I felt it was important to include a chapter in my book to inspire potential producers. You can't have a talent show without someone wearing the producer's hat.

I've thoroughly enjoyed being a producer in the past even though it can be taxing on the nervous system at times. However, to see a show come together after one's hard work of coordinating it is an accomplishment (creatively and, hopefully, financially). This incredible feeling of accomplishment can hook you into wanting to produce another show again and again - just like an entertainer gets hooked on wanting to perform over and over again. As I've said before, the basic principles that I'll be sharing here can be applied to producing any type of a show. You may start with talent shows and who knows where your production skills can take you.

Dear reader, let's assume that you want to try your hand at putting together a talent show. If it should be a first time thing for you, don't let the word *producer* frighten you, because whether or not you like it, that's what you're going to be. The word has kind of an important ring to it, doesn't it?

Now, there are certain requirements that you have to have in order to be a producer and one of them is to look and act the part. Having produced a wide variety of shows on radio, television, nightclubs and every conceivable venue imaginable during my long career, I found that having one of those folding wooden director's chairs with *producer* printed on the back immediately gets the attention and respect of people. I've also appeared as a guest on countless television shows as well as being a VIP visitor backstage, and I've noticed there is always someone scurrying around with a clipboard in hand acting as though they are in charge. Everyone goes up to them and asks them questions and they seem to have the answer. So get yourself a producer's chair, a clipboard with lots of blank paper and while you're at it, get a baseball hat that also says *producer*. Then hang around the show, sitting as much as possible in your producer's chair with your ever-present clipboard and cool baseball hat. You are now a producer!

Let's get serious here. Whether you're a manager in a nightclub or a committee member of a church, school, senior citizen group or some other community organization, you're in a perfect position to make the suggestion about putting together a talent show, which can be fun for all. They'll probably say, "Great. You're in charge!" And there you are

- immediately elevated to the rank of producer. (So get that clipboard, chair and baseball hat!)

If you're the type of person who enjoys being behind the scenes pulling all the strings, then being a producer may be very appealing to you. But I warn you that once you experience any degree of success, it could get into your blood and may be the start of a whole new career for you, especially if you can make a few bucks at it. And you do deserve to get paid for your time, even if it's not much at first! If you're volunteering your time for an organization, you'll be getting invaluable experience and you never know where the long and winding road may lead you.

A wonderful example of this is my longtime ACM Board of Directors' buddy, Gene Weed, who nicknamed me "the Legend." I remember Gene when he was a rock 'n' roll deejay who followed the beat of his own drum to become a premier TV director and producer. His elite producer/director track record includes "Golden Globes Awards," "Soap Opera Awards," "Academy of Country Music Awards Show" and TNN's "Prime Time Country." Today, he's Senior Vice President/Television of dick clark productions, inc.

Then there's my good buddy, Paul Corbin, whom I call the "hat." Paul, Dale Sheets and I were co-executive producers of three Tennessee Ernie Ford television specials for PBS (Public Broadcasting Station). He eventually moved to Nashville and went to work for The Nashville Network and ended up becoming Vice President – Music Industry Relations/CBS Cable – TNN & CMT. Although he turned in his producer's hat for a suit, look where his love for country music took him!

Now that I, hopefully, have you all fired up about producing a talent show, let's get on with it. I'll do my best to clue you in on some of the tried-and-true principles and guidelines for producing a talent show that have successfully worked for me.

First of all, I'm going to concentrate on the operation of a talent show and it doesn't matter whether it's for a school, a community club or a nightclub because its principles are adaptable.

In the big time world of business, any expenses that have to do with producing a show are referred to as "below-the-line" or as I like to refer to it, the "bottom line."

BUDGET: Naturally, the budget is of prime concern with talent shows, fundraisers or any type of show. As a producer, it's your responsibility to squeeze every penny, nickel and dollar to get the most out of it. I suggest that you keep some sort of a running total of the expenses that the budget incurs at all times so that you are aware of where you stand every day! Otherwise, you may spend more money than you take in. So be careful not to go over the budget. I can't overemphasize this enough and I'm speaking from experience. There were times in my life that I was so focused on other areas of the show that I went over budget and the extra money needed to pay bills had to come out of my own pocket.

Delegate someone to oversee your budget: If it's a small show, the person who watches the budget (whom we'll call the treasurer) will probably be you because you may not be able to afford one, unless a friend of yours volunteers (don't be afraid to ask). But if it's a fairly big show, it's best that you delegate the budget to someone who you feel is trustworthy and who is also good with figures.

The treasurer should make out all the checks; however, I suggest that these checks require a double signature. You, as producer, would be one of the signatures and the treasurer would be the second. The right hand should always know what the left hand is doing. It's kind of a checklist so that everyone knows what's happening. Otherwise, it might be "goodbye U.S.A.- hello Mexico!"

If it's a fundraiser, you might know of an accountant in your organization or in the area who might volunteer their time to oversee and handle the budget. Don't be shy about asking, because accountants do more than just play around with figures in their heads all day. They are generally community-minded and have children themselves. My CPA, Gary Condie, has been involved with the Santa Clarita Valley Boys & Girls Club for over twenty-five years, as well as serving as its president for four years.

Regardless who you delegate the authority to, he or she can take it out of your hands so that you don't have to worry unnecessarily about it. Believe me, you'll have a hundred other responsibilities to be concerned about. However, since you're the producer, I suggest that you always be aware of your budget's daily running total so that you can be on top of things. Don't put it in someone else's hands and then forget about it!

SHOW LOCATION: As they say in real estate - location, location, location: Location is everything and so is adequate parking, because both factors play a big role in the success of your show.

You need to *advertise* where your show is going to be and include simple directions on how to get there. People need to know this ahead of time, so they don't have to worry about looking at maps or stopping to ask directions at the last minute.

It would certainly be a wise decision to try to get a venue that's been previously advertised for other shows, because someone else has already paid a lot of money for advertising your future show's location. Indirectly, this is another example of the word *free*.

ADVERTISING: One of the most important things about making money for a talent show, especially if it's a fundraiser, is the *free advertising* and *free publicity* that can be available to you. This is an absolute must!

Let me give you an example when I talk about free publicity. Let's say that you're trying to raise money for a youth group, which is such a worthy cause. So check around and see if there's a photocopy business or a printer who'll either Xerox or print your tickets and flyers for nothing and/or at a discount.

Don't forget your local newspaper. Just call the editor and they'll probably have one of their staff interview you for an article in the paper, especially if it's a community event.

Radio spots vs. the printed word: I have previously emphasized the word *free*, which is important to keep at the forefront of your mind. If you're on a limited budget and you start buying advertising, whether it's on radio or an ad in the paper, you're probably never going make it.

Most radio spots (which are usually thirty seconds long) can be quite costly - even the inexpensive ones can run into a lot of money! Hypothetically speaking, if your radio spots cost ten dollars and they run five of them a day, that's fifty dollars. If they run ten a day, that's a hundred dollars. Although I don't know what today's going rate is, I would venture to guess that most radio spots are well over one hundred dollars, which would equal five hundred dollars if it's run five times a day. If it's within your budget range, great! Go for it! Naturally, radio advertising can be instrumental to the success of any type of show, but the thing to remember is that listeners hear it for thirty seconds and bang - it's gone.

This is why I personally recommend as much printed advertising that you can get. Be sure to include on your flyers the important *eye-catching facts,* such as the date, time, location, judges, sponsors and simple directions to the show.

If you have a weekly talent contest at a nightclub, give those flyers out to the contestants on the evening of the show. This not only helps to bring them back, but they'll probably be handing them out to their friends as well.

PERMITS, LICENSES, LIABILITY INSURANCE AND SECURITY:
I'd like to forewarn you about some of the things that can "sneak" up on you and bite you on the foot, such as permits, licenses, liability insurance and security, which go with the territory. If you forget or neglect to check them out, you could be in deep trouble, especially when you find out you've only got one day to straighten it out or it's a no go with your show.

First and foremost, check out the situation on the liability insurance! Goodness, what if someone fell off the stage and broke their arm? Nightclubs, of course, will have liability insurance. However, ask about it anyway just to cover yourself.

For those of you who are new to the producing game, you do have to get a permit if it's in a park or an out-of-doors venue somewhere! Without the proper permits, the proper security and the proper liability insurance, you shouldn't put on a show.

If it's in a building, the fire department will probably be paying you a little visit before your show opens. They have definite rules and regulations about any enclosure that's used for a public gathering. They'll certainly be checking out the exits in case of a fire, as well as making sure that your seating capacity is not over the appropriate limit. Of course, it's to your advantage if the show is outdoors somewhere (for instance, in a park) because you won't have to be that concerned about the fire department. Regardless, you must have the proper permits and liability insurance.

Any one of the aforementioned details that you forget to check on or didn't know you were supposed to have can become a migraine headache or even close the show before it opens unless it has been addressed. This last minute emergency stuff can take all the fun out of producing, and being stressed out about it isn't going to make your day.

"FUN" FUNDRAISERS: If you need to raise money, talent shows can be great fundraisers. Please notice that the first three letters of fundraisers (as well as its sound) formulates the word "fun."

It's taken me a long time to realize that nothing is worth doing unless you're having fun doing it. Life is too short! When we're younger, we have the pressure (whether it's self-inflicted or from our peers) of making money and being successful, especially if there is a family at home with little mouths to feed.

I certainly felt the pressure, which is why I had three and four gigs going on all at the same time for many years. If I hadn't been so motivated, I wouldn't have had all the accomplishments that I've been lucky to attain in my career. Of course, it was something that I loved doing. Regardless, in my later years I decided that I would never put myself under any undo stress again unless I thought it was going to be fun.

This is why show business can get into your blood, because after you've gone through all the hassles of getting the gig, the fun part comes when you perform, which is the big payoff. So whatever purpose that your group or organization has to raise money for via a talent show, if you have the right attitude, fun will follow as night the day. After the expenses of putting on the show have been paid, the rest of the proceeds can go towards the fundraising project.

CREATIVE WAYS TO MAKE MONEY: There are no two ways about it. The bottom line for your talent show success is to make money, and rightfully so. You have bills to pay and if you've made a profit, you'll be able to produce another show. If you don't, you won't. It's simple economics.

Now, there are different ways that you can make money via your show, which will help to keep your budget in the black.

Entry fees and ticket sales: The contestants' entry fee could be one price and general admission for the public another (many of them will probably be the contestants' family and friends).

Since my talent shows were in a nightclub setting, I would charge anywhere from three to five dollars. Of course, this was years ago. Still, I didn't want to charge too much because many of them were regular customers. These people came regardless of whether or not there was a talent show and they spent enough money as it was buying drinks and various snack foods that were available.

However, you'll have to make your own determination relative to your show's venue situation and who you think will be making up a good portion of the audience. If you charge too much, people won't pay. If you don't charge enough, you may come up with the short end of the stick and be left with a bunch of unpaid bills in your hand. So be fair to the people, as well as to yourself.

Obviously, ticket sales to the talent show are very important because it's one of the main ways you make money, and here is where proper advertising plays a large role. You may have to spend money on advertising to make money on ticket sales because the contestants, as well as the public, have to know about it. Once again, I encourage you to get all the free advertising that's available to you, because you'll be saving money indirectly.

Food/vendors: Naturally, we human beings have to eat to live so selling food is another great way to make money. The type of food you sell will depend on your particular venue's kitchen facilities to handle it. If you have an Italian or a country-style buffet, you may need a larger kitchen. For the most part, I recommend hot dogs, hamburgers, tacos or any kind of food that keeps well and doesn't spoil easily. (Be careful with chicken.)

If any vending companies are involved, you can probably make a deal with them and they'll give you a percentage of the money they make from selling their product at your event.

Coffee vendors are a perfect example. There are a lot of us "coffee drinkers" in the world and money is certainly made from selling it. I don't know what it costs per cup to make coffee, but let's say that it costs the vendor ten cents a cup and he sells it for one dollar. Now that's a hefty return on his money.

I've always had success in persuading a woman's group or club to become involved in making and selling coffee. They could also have a homemade cake or cookie sale, which is always popular.

Drawings: Generally, you wouldn't have drawings at regular talent shows, but they're wonderful for fundraisers or benefits.

I think lotteries are illegal in most states unless they are state operated, but you certainly could sell raffle tickets. It's another great way to bring in revenue for your fundraiser or benefit event, and it would create a little excitement for the audience.

As for the raffle prizes, I suggest that you or your assistant contact some of your local merchants. Most of them are usually happy to cooperate because it would be good publicity for their business and it's a tax write off as well.

These prizes certainly don't have to be expensive items. Maybe a portable radio from an electronics store or five CDs from one of the local record stores or possibly a cowboy hat or shirt from your local country/western clothing store. If your talent show is rock 'n' roll oriented, maybe you could get a household goods merchant to donate some new pots and pans for the heavy metal enthusiasts to beat on. (Just having a little fun here, folks.)

I recommend that you keep the raffle ticket prices minimal. Maybe a dollar a piece or four dollars for five tickets, etc. After all, the prizes are being donated to begin with, so this is all profit, which can be quite substantial if you sell enough tickets.

Be creative in thinking of ways to sell these tickets because, as I said before, it's a good way to make money for your organization. For example, get three or four ladies with great personalities (and good looks don't hurt either) who relate well with people. You could have a table set up by the door, so that people would be aware of the raffle tickets when they first come in. Later in the evening, you could have the ladies walking to different tables and casually asking the people if they'd like to buy more tickets. When someone has had a few drinks, it loosens up their pocketbook.

Maybe you could get some of the waitresses from a local restaurant chain to volunteer their time at your show. They usually have great personalities and certainly know how to deal with people. In fact, they could mention the event to their customers in a casual way before the actual show date in order to get more folks interested in coming. However, the main idea is to get ticket sellers who know how to kid around and talk with the public.

I once heard of a big fundraising event wherein one of the airlines volunteered the time of four or five of their flight attendants who wore their uniforms while selling the tickets. They really charmed the folks and sold a lot of tickets, not to mention the fact that they did a wonderful public relations job for their company.

With regard to the drawing itself, I feel it's best to have a couple of them at various times throughout the show. Don't do it all at once because it takes too much time and it's boring to people who aren't winning. Maybe half way through the fundraiser, you could have the drawing for the main prize and have the winner come up on stage to collect it. Then move on with the show. Later, have a couple of other drawings and so forth. The important thing is to space them apart during the evening in order to keep the audience's interest.

Donations: If it's a charity or fundraising talent show, you may want to consider writing a letter or contacting various businesses or people for donations. Community-minded people are happy to make generous contributions. They're in a benevolent frame of mind and are willing to spend more money than they normally would because it's for a good cause (and it's also a tax write off).

Capitalize on your celebrity emcee/special guests: Another way to increase revenue is to sell a printed program for fifty cents or a dollar a piece. I always had a booklet or a flyer of some sort made up for any shows that I ever produced or performed in. Since I was the emcee and was well known in the music industry, especially on the West Coast, I'd have my picture on it. If I had celebrity guests on the bill such as a well known television personality, a local deejay or an artist who has had a recording contract and a few hit songs in the past, I always included their photographs. People love to buy these souvenir programs and many of them will have the celebrities (and even the contestants) autograph them.

If it's a celebrity artist, he or she can sing two or three songs, which will certainly be inspirational to the aspiring talent. Some of the contestants may be thinking to themselves, "Wow, she's such a professional! Maybe I can be just like her some day!" Or "he moves so well while he's singing and he's really got a good sense of humor. I think I'll try that the next time I'm on stage."

110

These are the types of special guests that you could have on your show because they are true professionals and they pull the people in, which means you can charge more money for the show tickets.

THE BOTTOM LINE SUMMARY: As the producer, one of the important things for you to remember is this: you have to make money to cover all the expenses of putting on this talent show.

If it's in a nightclub setting, it's to make money for the club, which in turn helps to pay for the club's expenses to open its doors, pay for the electric bill, producer's fee, etc.

If it's a fundraiser for the American Legion Hall or for the Rotary Club wherein they want the funds to buy a new television set for their recreation room, your goal is to raise the cash in order to do so.

In other words, everything that I've talked about so far is relative to the bottom line, which is to make money so that you can pay the bills and still have enough left over to finance another show.

THE TALENT SHOW: Now, let's discuss various aspects of the talent show itself, and I want to say something that I hope you'll keep in the back of your mind. Don't get upset if the caliber of talent isn't the quality of a future Reba McEntire or George Strait. Oh, once in a while you might come across someone with potential star quality. However, no matter how talented someone may be, it will depend on how much desire they have, because I believe it's anybody's ball game. Who knows what someone can become if they work hard and stay focused on their objectives. They could be a potential star in the making, which isn't apparent at this stage of the game. But whether there is or not, you, as producer, are contributing to their development regardless what level they ever attain.

Talent shows come in sundry packages and part of its success will depend on the area or location of where it's being held. As I've already said several times throughout this book, I'll be using the nightclub venue as the talent show setting.

For example, the legendary Palomino club is less than fifteen minutes from Hollywood. Since Hollywood has always attracted young talented hopefuls in all areas of show biz, we always had very professionally oriented people entering the contest. In fact, some of them were professionals who entered just to keep their skills sharp.

At one time, there were talent shows happening throughout most of the clubs in outlying communities such as San Bernardino, Orange Country, Riverside and Long Beach. Many of the contestants who participated in these other shows were made up of a totally different crowd and they were, for the most part, beginners compared to the Hollywood crowd who'd come to the Palomino.

However, many of the contestants from the Palomino talent show circuit would take the time to drive clear out to a nightclub in San Bernardino, which is about seventy miles away, to participate in the show, especially if there were cash prizes.

Needless to say, you, as producer, have a lot of responsibilities to oversee in your show, and many people will be asking you about this or that. I personally think it's great being the center of attention, but it can get to be a little too much at times. So to make things easier for you, there are some things I'll be discussing to help you to alleviate repetitive questions.

"Sides to the Bridge" (Chapter 7): So that you're aware of where the aspiring artists are coming from and their goals, I suggest that you read Chapter 7 carefully. I will be reiterating some of the things that I wrote in that chapter because many of the show's rules and protocol will have emanated from you, the producer, in the first place. They are important to the format of the event, because they can be a determining factor on whether or not the actual show is run smoothly, which is one of your main objectives.

Printed Outline/Talent show protocol and rules: I'll share the simple rules or guidelines that have worked for me when I produced and emceed the Palomino talent shows. However, its rules, protocol or guidelines are easily adaptable to other talent contest venues, too.

In order to have a show that's moving smoothly all evening, as well as insuring that everyone who enters will get on stage, *have a typed outline of the show's format and rules for the contestants.* This will save everyone time. Otherwise, you or your associates will have to keep explaining, which is a waste of your valuable time.

Generally, most of the contestants will be singers. If you have a big contest that has forty contestants and thirty of them are singers, you should limit them to one song. However, if you only have twelve people and eight of them are singers, then I suggest that you let them do two or three songs because you need to fill up the time.

Entrance Fee: I've briefly discussed the cost of show tickets at the beginning of this chapter, but it was geared more towards the people who weren't contestants.

For a contestant to participate in a talent show, there's usually an entrance fee. Depending on what type of a talent show it is and its venue, the artist will either send their check through the mail along with the application form or, if it's in an informal nightclub setting, they'll pay as they come through the front door.

Naturally, this fee goes toward the various expenses of putting on the show. It's important to understand that for the beginning talent to be on a stage anywhere is a rare privilege and a wonderful thing. The aspiring talent intuitively knows this and they're going to be excited about it, so they won't mind paying to enter the contest.

The fee amount can vary, but in the final analysis, it's your decision. If it's a big time sponsored talent show, it could be twenty dollars or more. Since I'm referring to local talent shows in nightclubs, the entry fee shouldn't have such a high price tag on it.

For instance, let's say that you're doing your show at a local nightclub and you're charging the talent five or ten dollars as an entry fee. You should explain in the show's outline or guidelines that this fee helps to pay for the backup band, advertising and many other sundry expenses. The talent will understand and accept this. Just be fair in what you charge. If it's unreasonably high, you won't get an adequate number of contestants.

Show Card Information: Along with the printed guidelines of the show that you give the artists at the front door, they should also be given a pre-printed card that has blank spaces for them to write down some relevant information about themselves. On the appropriate lines, each of them should fill in their name, address, telephone, fax and/or e-mail.

Also have a "category" line on this card where they can indicate the particular category they're entering (male or female vocalist; instrumentalist; comedian; magician; or whatever). Since singing is the most popular, have another space after that category for them to write the name of the song and the key they'll be singing it in.

113

At the bottom of the card, there should be a blank space reserved to indicate what set and position number this contestant will be performing in. You'll be filling this out after all the artists have signed in for the evening so that you can program the show.

Programming your talent show: If this is a weekly talent show wherein the contestants enter on the night of the show, you'll be making up the program on the fly. Now, there are two or three ways that I would program this type of a show so that it could be as smooth running as possible.

Since my shows usually started at 8 p.m., the contestants would start arriving and signing in around 6 p.m. Whoever signs up first is usually put into the number one position and, therefore, would start off in the number one spot at 8 p.m. Whoever signed in second, would be in the number two position and so it goes. I've used this method on many occasions for it's the simplest way to do it.

However, producers must strive for a balanced variety show. Many times the aforementioned way of programming can create a problem because it all depends on the number of contestants who have signed up for each category. Hypothetically speaking, maybe the first five contestants who signed up in the first five positions were all girl singers and maybe the next five spots were all male vocalists. Possibly you had a comedian, a duet act, a magician, an instrumentalist also sign up that night. Obviously, if you tried my first programming method, you would have five girl singers in a row and then five male singers and this wouldn't be a balanced show.

As with everything in life, your program has to be open to modifications. On many occasions, I would have to reprogram the show after I looked over all the participants in the different categories. This doesn't always go over very well with some of the contestants, especially when they've been the early birds. However, I would tactfully explain to them that they would be placed in the proper position to make them look as good as possible!

What I'm about to say to you, I would never point blank say to the aspiring artist because, first of all, I wouldn't want to hurt their feelings; secondly, I was the producer and I have the last word, because I'm responsible for having a smooth running show. (I'm glad that the aspiring artists who are reading this book will now be aware of a producer's point of view.)

For example, if the first five spots were five girl vocalists, I would have no way of knowing how good they were unless they had participated before. Maybe one of them is a good singer and the other four weren't so hot. If I put them on one after the other, none of them would look or sound good.

Also, I usually liked to start my talent shows with a man who can sing an up-tempo number like "Kansas City." Since everyone (including the producer) is in an excitable or nervous state of mind at the beginning of the show, an up-tempo song usually calms everyone down and also gets the audience's attention. Then I would program a girl singer and would follow her with a duet act or possibly an instrumentalist. Next would be another girl vocalist, then another male singer and after him, I'd put on an instrumentalist or a comedian. This is the type of pattern that I'd follow in programming my show. What I'm doing here, which is what I suggest you do, is giving the audience a variety show. You've got people sitting out there and they need to be entertained, which includes the other contestants. If they're not, they may not last the evening and probably won't come back to the next talent show.

As you can see, there's an art to programming a show. Just try to balance out the different acts so you will have a variety show that makes the contestants look as good as possible while keeping the audience interested and entertained.

Talent Show Sets: Generally, your show will be anywhere from three to four hours, depending on the number of contestants. You can't have a show going on for three straight hours, because the backup band should have at least a fifteen-minute break every hour. My show sets were usually forty-five minutes each. If you work it right, you can get about ten to twelve artists in each set. If you do three sets, you're up to thirty to thirty-six people. Now that sounds like a lot of contestants and it is; however, if you keep the show moving along with a new artist, there will always be something happening on stage that will keep your audience's attention.

Also, keep in mind that when an artist is performing in any talent show, a good portion of the audience will be comprised of the other contestants and their support groups.

Master of Ceremonies: Your choice for emcee can make or break your show. He or she should have a good personality and the ability to talk personably to each contestant as well as to the audience. So whomever you have chosen to be your emcee is of the utmost importance. Maybe it'll be you, and don't be shy about it if you feel you're the best one for the job. I certainly wore both hats for many years and loved it.

A 21-Gun Salute to Dick Clark: Speaking of someone who can wear both hats, I want to mention a man I've known and admired for years, Dick Clark. As you probably know, he is an icon in the television industry and one of its premier executive producers of music award shows (and other entertainment shows), as well as a great emcee. This ageless energetic man has given of his emcee talents and ingenious production expertise for decades and still continues to do so. He more than deserves all the accolades and awards that have been bestowed on him. Not only does he surround himself with the best production personnel, such as Gene Weed and his talented son, Rac, who is making his own mark in the industry, Dick astutely oversees all aspects of his shows.

Naturally, I'm very prejudice when it comes to the Academy of Country Music Award Shows, and I've enjoyed being one of its award presenters from time to time; the success of this show is due to Dick and his company, who produce it for network television.

One of the highlights of this yearly event is Dick's enthusiastic way of interviewing each ACM award winner backstage, which is incorporated into the show as it's happening. Talk about someone who is dedicated to presenting musical talent to the world - it's Dick Clark, who, in my opinion, has done more for the promotion of all music genres than anyone I know of. He has my deepest respect and I give him a "21-gun salute" for his decades of service.

Standard of performance: Whether it's you or someone else whom you've chosen to be the emcee (such as a local disc jockey or the bandleader) have your "standard of performance" for him or her.

One of the main prerequisites for an emcee is to always treat the aspiring talent with respect and dignity. What these courageous contestants are trying to accomplish means so much to them, regardless of whether they are good or bad. Therefore, the emcee should at all times be courteous to the talent as well as giving them encouragement. Believe me, this simple act of kindness and respect will be remembered. These artists need all the pats on the back they can get at this crucial time in their fledgling careers. In turn, the audience will respect the emcee for doing this because a good portion of the audience is made up of other contestants and their support system. I feel so strongly about this subject that I'm going to embellish on it in the next captioned paragraph.

Once you've made out the evening's program, which can be hectic but quickly done once you've had experience at it, then the emcee (I'll assume it's you) should announce who will be coming up next after he introduces the current performer. In other words, you would say, "And now I'd like to present Sam McDonald, who is going to be opening the show with his version of 'Kansas City'." Then after you have introduced him, also announce that Suzy Jones will be the next contestant. By doing this, Suzy has time to get ready. She'll get up from the table where she's been sitting with her friends and go over to a designated spot by the stage. This is equivalent to the next batter in a baseball game going over to the batter's box in order to be ready for his or her turn at bat. But instead of Suzy getting a bat, she gets her guitar and makes sure it's tuned along with getting her sheet music ready to give to the band. Possibly Suzy will think, "Maybe I better go to the restroom first and make sure that my hair looks okay." Contestants will do various things like this and it's all part of the deal. But the reason for announcing the next performer is for them to get ready for their turn on center stage.

When Sam McDonald is through singing and as he exits and the applause starts to die down, you'll say, "Good job, Sam. Next we have Suzy Jones, who'll be singing 'Crazy' and after Suzy will be the Smith Brothers." This is the Smith Brothers' cue to get into the music box.

Do you see what I'm getting at here? If you didn't pre-announce like this, the artist might be sitting at the table and you'd say, "And next is Suzy Jones." Then you'd have to wait for her while she gets up from the table, finds her guitar and makes her way to the stage. Meanwhile, back at the mike, you're losing five minutes in between acts. Consequently, the audience gets bored, including the band and, more importantly, you won't have a tight professional show.

You, as the emcee/producer, are responsible for the show running as smoothly as possible, which will keep the audience's attention. Expect to be thrown a few curve balls from time to time. This is the time when you must be flexible and professional enough to go with the flow, and this is where your sense of humor will save the day.

I can't say this enough times: if you don't keep the folks in the audience interested, especially those who aren't part of the artists' support group, they may leave before it's over and never come back when you have your next talent show. It's only fair to everyone that the show moves quickly and the next artist is waiting in the wings ready to perform. This is what a professional show is all about.

Note the announcing procedure in the instruction sheet: What I've just told you about announcing and pre-announcing should also be noted in your guidance or instruction sheet that you give the artist when they enter the contest. If they know the pre-announcement drill, they can prepare themselves accordingly.

Interviewing the performer: The aforementioned is the basic guideline for the emcee. However, there's something else the emcee (you) should do. After you have announced the current performer and who will be following him or her, this is an opportune time for you to interview the current artist for a few moments before they perform. (See the "Master of Ceremonies" section in Chapter 7.)

I have always had great success doing this. I care about the talent, and I want to help train them to be natural before an audience, especially while they're being interviewed. Someday this artist may be performing on Jay Leno's "Tonight Show" or some other television show and they might as well start learning how to be themselves during an interview.

Bear in mind that personality is everything, which is another reason you're asking the contestants various questions. You want the audience to become aware of their personality as well as their talent, which is all part of whether or not the audience is going to identify with them when they perform.

If you're doing double duty as a producer/emcee, there's a million simple questions that you can ask each contestant such as: "What do you for a living?" "Where were you born?" "Why do you want to be in show business?" "What do your parents think about you wanting to be a singer?" As I've said before, this helps to relax the artist as well as letting their personality shine through.

If you're producing a weekly talent show, many of these contestants will be coming back week after week; and you can develop a relationship with them and will be able to kid around and have fun with them. I developed a little routine with some of the talent in the past, which was very entertaining for the audience.

Treat the aspiring talent with respect and dignity: It's really very simple: *"Do unto others as you would have them do onto you."* As I said before, your emcee can make or break your show, which is why you must have a "standard of performance" for him or her or you. This includes having a good personality and the ability to talk personably to each contestant as well as with the audience. This is all part of the emcee's stage presence. As far as I'm concerned, the most important prerequisite of all is for the emcee to treat the aspiring talent with respect and dignity. No matter who your emcee is, whether he's a local deejay or whomever, be aware of his attitude and make sure that he (or she) is always respectful. If they are not, on the next break or after the show tactfully but firmly tell him not to do it anymore.

If any member of the band displays a put-down attitude towards the talent at any time, have a word with him, too. The band (and the emcee) must realize they are not dealing with a professional (yet). Many times a singer won't know their key when they sign up before the show, or while they're performing they get out of tune. None of the band members should ever make any demeaning remarks or a facial expression that implies the same thing. For instance, if a band member rolls his eyes or grimaces when a singer makes a mistake, the audience sees that! Don't forget that a good percentage of the audience is made up of the contestants and their support system. If they see anyone in the band doing this, they might think, "He'll do that to me if I make a mistake!" This could make them more nervous than they already are or turn them off from ever entering another talent show.

If anyone involved with your show still has this kind of an attitude after you've previously spoken with them about it, I suggest you give them their walking papers.

Joking around with the talent in the spirit of fun: By the same token, the emcee should have the freedom of being able to joke and kid around with the talent, as long as it's done in the spirit of fun and without a demeaning attitude. This has always been my style, because it always loosened and relaxed both the artist and the audience. It also teaches aspiring artists to have fun and not to take themselves so seriously. They will be making mistakes, but it's not the end of the world or their potential careers when they do.

Don't forget that you have an audience out there! Some have paid to come in and have bought a few drinks, others are contestants and their friends. Regardless, these people have to be entertained. With all due respect to new talent, at times it can be a little tedious to watch twenty or thirty aspiring artists who really aren't very good entertainers yet. This is why the emcee must have the luxury of kidding around with and about the talent without anyone taking offense to it. Again, I stress that it must not be done with a put down attitude. It's not what you say, but how you say it.

As I said before, if the same contestants come back on a regular basis, the emcee can work out a little comedy routine with them! I always did and it went over big with both the artist and the audience. After all, the person who courageously gets up on stage and tries to do their best deserves respect - no matter how bad they may be at that point in time. They'll get better with more experience. That's why they're entering talent shows in the first place.

So treat the artists with tender loving care because without them, you've got no show. If you don't have a show, you won't sell any tickets, liquor or food, which translates into no revenue! However, money isn't the reason you treat them with dignity. It's simply a matter of respect and courtesy from one human being to another. Just "do unto others as you would have them do unto you."

Contestants with an attitude: Occasionally, an aspiring artist will have an "attitude" and after he's through singing he may make a remark such as, "The band didn't know my song" or "They didn't play it fast enough" or "They played it in the wrong key."

Now, I don't intend to get into a psychological discussion here. However, I've always considered the source because when I do come across an amateur like this, I know he's basically insecure and has to blame someone for his mistakes. Because of his inexperience or nervousness, he's the one who probably went off key or off tempo.

If an artist does this on any of your shows, it's best not to feed fuel to the fire, so ignore him. However, if he gets too obnoxious or insulting to the band, you might want to pull him over to the side and tactfully have a few words with him.

By the same token, maybe it was the band's fault because they weren't familiar with the song or maybe the sheet music that was given to them was inadequate. The artist can come back next week and the band will probably know the song. They're professionals and it won't be long before they get it right.

Just remember that if you have a weekly talent show, it's these beginning artists who come back week after week who will keep it going. In due time they'll learn the ropes. After all, it is a talent show so let them get up there and make mistakes.

Let the emcee entertain: Those of you who know something about me will chuckle at this statement. Let's face it: I'll get up on stage anytime anywhere to speak, sing, tell jokes, and play the bass or whatever. It's a passion with me and I love it!

That's the way it is with all entertainers who have show biz in their blood. An emcee has to be a ham who loves the spotlight or he wouldn't be up there in the first place. So for goodness sakes, if he wants to tell a few jokes, play an instrument or sing a song, let him! It will endear him to the audience.

I would usually open the show by welcoming the audience and the contestants and give a little rundown on the importance of talent shows. Then I'd tell a few jokes, sing a couple of songs or play my bass. As I said in Chapter 12, I had the best musicians in the business as my regular backup band - Skip Edwards, Harry Orlove, Jay Dee Maness, Steve Duncan and Arnie Moore, as well as others that I'd use from time to time, like John Hobbs, Ronnie Mack or Billy Block. They all knew all my songs and I had a regular ongoing routine with them. I would purposely start singing my song in the wrong key. Then I'd stop, turn around and look at Skip who was playing the piano, and act as if it was his fault and make a few humorous comments. This was all part of my act and it always got great laughs from the aspiring talent and the audience. It was also my indirect way of teaching the contestants that if they did go off key or forget the lyrics when they were performing, it's no big deal!

121

So give your emcee the green light if he wants to tell a joke or sing a song at the beginning of the show to warm up the audience. However, don't let him compete with the performers. Your emcee's main job is to present the talent. He's the pointer! He's the guy who points and says, "And now here's Cliffie Stone!"

Hook the talent into coming back: If you want your talent show to be successful, you want the contestants (and the audience) to come back again. So give the second and third place winners a free ticket, which is a cute little hook.

I usually gave the second and third place runner-ups a ticket for next week's show. Upon occasion, I would give every one who performed a ticket because it made them feel important, which they are. However, I'd like to stress that you just give them *one ticket* - not two! Generally, an artist will bring a couple of friends and these folks have to pay a small admission fee to get in. Once they're in, they'll buy drinks or food, which means revenue towards the expenses involved in producing the show.

On most weekly talent shows, there will be five or six people who are so interested in performing that they will show up every week. They'll come back with a new song, a new outfit or a new idea. Bless their hearts! They work hard all week long to learn a new song or try something new. When you give them a free ticket, it encourages them to come back to your show again and again.

Never say, "Well, I've already had this person on the show so I can't present him or her anymore." I've never done that, because talent shows are their training ground. This is their internship, which is why it's the most important stage in the world! It's one of the few places where they can practice and develop their talent.

Many of these beginning professionals work the talent show circuit. For instance, if there are other nightclubs in your general area and outlying counties who also have weekly or biweekly talent shows, your contestants will probably enter them, too. Maybe one of the clubs will have one on Tuesday nights and another club across town will have one on Thursday nights.

Many of the contestants know a lot of other artists whom they've met at other talent shows. They'll talk to each other and say, "Listen, that talent show over at the American Legion Hall on Thursday nights is terrific. They've got a good band, good sound equipment and a wonderful crowd." Through word-of-mouth, other artists start showing up to get in on the action!

So once you've got a credible talent show happening, word will spread like wild fire and you'll be surprised at the number of people who will be showing up. Your show could get such an excellent reputation that you'll get so many folks wanting to enter that you may have to turn some of them down. Should you be lucky enough to be in this position, give them a free ticket for next week. It makes them feel good and it's great promotion!

Your talent show name: What's in a name? Everything! So think about it and be sure it's catchy so people will remember it!

There are hundreds of good names that you can come up with. Years ago, there was a talent show on one of the local television stations in Southern California called "Hollywood Opportunities," and another was called "Stairway to Stardom." I remember one that was on the radio called "Stairway to Fame." Recently, I thought of a good name, "Star Trip," which means you're on a trip to becoming a star.

Once you have decided on your name, refer to it as many times as possible whenever you're on stage or advertising or just talking about it in general. You could even invest some money in T-shirts and/or baseball hats with your show's name on it. By doing so, you're not only making a small profit, but you're also getting "free" advertising as well.

Choosing the winner: I briefly discussed this aspect of the talent show in Chapter 8, "Yearning to Win...Learning to Lose." As far as I am concerned, every person who enters a talent contest is a winner and the invaluable experience they get should be their main goal regardless of whether they win, place or show.

However, whether it's sports, business or a talent show, people are competitors at heart. When they compete with others (or against themselves when going for their personal best), it makes them "stretch" and go beyond what they think they can do, which will help them to be all that they can be. When one has the right attitude, it's downright challenging and fun!

However, there has to be a winner and if you have enough prizes, you can also have second and third place, which is still thrilling for the contestants. Now, there are two or three ways that a winner can be determined:

1. *Judges:* First, you could have two or three judges. They could be a deejay, a music executive, an entertainer who has known some degree of success or some other important person in the community, such as the mayor.

These judges will use a one to ten point rating system when they evaluate each contestant's performance and they write it down on a piece of paper. Maybe one judge will give Sam McDonald a "two," which isn't very good. Another judge may give Suzy Jones a "ten," which is the highest mark. This is how they evaluate each performer. At the end of the show, the judges will give their papers to either the emcee or the producer, at which time all the points are added for each performer. Naturally, the winner is the one with the most points. The one with the second highest points comes in second and so it goes. I suggest you have second and third place winners for it boosts their confidence and motivates them to come back.

2. *Audience applause:* This is a good way to do it because it means that people will have to stay to applaud for their favorites, especially if they're family and friends. The longer the people stay, the more money they'll spend on snacks or drinks.

But there is one drawback to the audience applause method. If one of the artists brings in a ton load of people, they'll have the edge on winning even if they aren't the best performers! However, there's nothing you or anyone can do about it so just accept it.

More often than not, especially in local talent shows, audience applause will be the method you'll be using to determine the winner. So let's talk about how you go about it, and I suggest you do it the tried-and-true old-fashioned way.

At the end of the evening, line up all your contestants in a row on the stage. Before proceeding any further, tell the audience how the applause rules work. This in itself is very simple because all you do is say each artist's name while you place your hand over their head and the audience voices their opinion through applause. The artist who gets the most applause wins. Be sure to request that they don't scream or whistle, because this makes it difficult to figure out who received the most applause.

124

For instance, you walk behind the first contestant, hold your hand over her head and say, "And now, Suzy Jones." There will be applause and you thank them and let the clapping fade away. Then you go to the next artist and say, "Sam McDonald" and there will be applause. Then you let that slowly fade away, too. This is what you do with all the contestants one by one.

Even though you requested that the audience refrain from whistling and screaming, they may do it anyway. There's really no way you can control them. They are enthusiastic, which adds vitality to the show. So if they whistle and scream, try to block it out and concentrate on the applause. Good luck!

3. *Combination of judges and audience applause:* A third way to do it is with the combination of the above two ways that I've just mentioned. The judges could be seventy-five percent of the vote and the audience applause could be the other twenty-five percent, etc. As the producer, the decision is yours.

Once again, you run the risk of an average singer bringing in fifty people who are going to jump up and down and applaud loudly for him. So the audience applause will go to him. That's the way it goes and, hopefully, the judges' opinion and vote will balance it out.

Prizes: One of the most important elements of the talent show that will pull in the contestants will be the prizes, and if you've got good ones, be sure to publicize it. They can be cash or items such as a radio, guitar, CD or Vince Gill concert tickets. Of course, cash prizes are always the contestants' number one preference. (I refer you to Chapter 8: "Yearning to Win...Learning to Lose.")

I recall how nice the people were in the hundreds of talent shows that I emceed. It was just wonderful to see how serious they were about performing. These contestants really wanted to have a credible talent night show with finals that paid cash, which seemed to be so important to many of them.

If the prizes are cash, the amount is determined by the show's budget and/or how well last week's show went. Often times the cash prizes at some of the talent shows at smaller clubs where I emceed wasn't very much. The winner would get twenty dollars; second place, ten dollars; and third place, five dollars. However, it was enough to make them feel good.

Likewise, some of the contests had higher stakes with first prize being seventy-five dollars, fifty dollars for second place and twenty-five dollars for third. Naturally, the contestants were always more excited whenever the money was in the higher bracket.

So if you're opting for prize money, the dollar amount will vary. There's no two ways about it; it will depend on your budget. Once you've established an amount, it will be entirely your call as to how much the winner and two runner-ups should be awarded.

If it's an ongoing weekly show, the second and third place runner-ups could be invited back to showcase themselves and possibly be paid ten or twenty dollars apiece. And it's important that everyone else who performs that week also be invited back.

If you have a merchandising and promotional mind, you might want to give away a free T-shirt to each contestant, which is a cute as well as a smart thing to do. It only costs you about five dollars per shirt, but they'll be wearing it, which means free advertising. Or you could sell it for a minimal amount and not only make a small profit but have the promotional angle going as well.

When I was a judge for a national talent show that Marlboro sponsored, they gave everyone who was involved with the show a quality sports windbreaker and T-shirt with Marlboro on it. I loved mine and constantly wore them. So take your cue from the big guys.

Prizes more valuable than money: I can hear some of you say, "What could be more valuable than money?" As you've probably noticed, I talk a lot about singers because more contestants seem to enter that category than any other, and there are prizes that can be more appealing to them than cash.

For instance, if you know of a recording studio in your locality, ask the owner if he would donate three hours of free studio time to the winning artist. It would be wonderful publicity for his studio and he just might get himself another client out of it someday. If the artist has never recorded before, it would be an unforgettable experience for him and he'll probably get hooked on it. I don't know of any singer who doesn't like to hear their voice on tape (unless they're not good singers). So they may personally book another three hours or cut a few sides or do a record project in the future.

126

Also, check with your local music store or any companies in your area that manufacture instruments and related items (guitars, strings or amplifiers). These items also make great prizes. I've always found them to be very cooperative in donating some of their products for a wholesome activity such as a talent show (especially if it's a fundraiser). To have a name brand guitar listed as a grand prize on your publicity flyer will attract potential contestants.

The point is there are prizes that can be more important to the winner than money, and getting three free hours in a recording studio or a name brand guitar are just a couple of them.

Offer encouragement to the prizeless contestants: You, as producer/emcee will be in a position to offer encouragement to many of those who don't win. This is where the altruistic value of producing or emceeing a talent show comes into play. Every time you put a positive spin on the so-called losing experience or you give them a soft shoulder to cry on for a moment, you're giving of yourself, which is a priceless gift in itself.

Although winning is cool and can be a huge boost to their self-confidence, it's imperative they understand that it's not the end of the world if they don't! One of the most important elements of this talent show adventure is each time an artist performs on stage, they are building a firm foundation of experience for their potential career if they have that inner desire to patiently stick with it. You, as emcee/producer, can remind them of that whenever you can.

Extended talent contests: Having an extended contest can build up excitement for the artists and your community.

For example, have a weekly talent show that lasts for three months. Thus, you'd have one winner a week and at the end of three months, there would be a total of twelve winners. Then have one gala talent show – the finals – with these twelve winners, and whoever comes in first place would win the grand prize, such as a free trip to Nashville or a free guitar or five hours of free studio time, etc.

If you really want to make the finals an interesting event, you may want to consider having second place consolation finals, which would also be a total of twelve. Then you could have the first place finals as the grand finale.

You see, if you just have the twelve first place winners, you're cutting out other contestants who have been in the entire event and they won't come because they're not in it (and they bring friends). By having second place consolation finals, you could really have a packed house and make it an exciting as well as profitable event.

Dance craze and talent shows: Dancing will always be in style, but as of this hot but beautiful 4th of July, the dance craze is upon us, and many of the clubs are catering to the dancers. But they could also have a talent night show by working in the dancers throughout the evening, whether it's a weekly or monthly show.

So what I suggest you do when you're dealing with club or other venue managers is to "show them how" they could integrate the talent show and the dancers all in the same evening.

Since most clubs give lessons around 7 p.m., which usually lasts forty minutes, this time slot would be reserved for the dancers. Then it's the talent show's turn, which could run from 8 p.m. to 8:40 p.m. When the band takes their twenty-minute break, let the dancers two-step or waltz to records. The next talent show set would be at 9 p.m. and you keep alternating like this throughout the evening.

Here's another sales pitch you can make to the club managers to convince them of the value of having a weekly talent show. You see, the dyed-in-the-wool dancers aren't necessarily a drinking crowd, which means less revenue for the club. They are there to dance. Whereas having a talent show can being in people who like to sit around and be entertained who will spend more money.

Another great idea would be getting the dancers interested in participating in the contest. It would certainly add variety to the show. In fact, you may want to consider a talent show strictly made up of dance contestants and they would love it. I've already mentioned the popularity of national dance contests in Chapter 10.

But getting back to a regular type of talent show, the contestants do bring in family and friends who will buy drinks or food. I can't imagine the managers objecting when they're in the business of catering to whatever brings customers into their club.

Here's something else for you to be aware of. Many times I've seen the dancers get up and start dancing during a talent show, which is distracting because it takes the attention away from the contestant who is trying to perform. When that happens, don't get upset because there's really nothing you can do about it.

These creative comments are food for thought so that you can stay in the game until the dance craze cycle cools off a bit.

Band break: It doesn't matter whether it's a talent show or a regular band gig at a local club. When the band takes a break, you need to have something happening in order to keep the audience's attention. If it's a regular band gig, the club will usually play records while the band is on a break so that the audience can dance if they want to. If it's a talent show, your goal is to keep the momentum going and the last thing you want is a dead mike.

One of your options is to fill the break with a songwriter/singer who could also be in the competition if they didn't need the band's services. They could do their original songs and accompany themselves if they play guitar or keyboard or possibly a Karaoke tape. (I refer you to Chapter 12.)

The break is also a great time to put on comedians, magicians or someone who does imitations. Any one of these self-contained contestants will add a change of pace and variety to the show while the band is taking their allotted fifteen or twenty minute break.

If I didn't have anyone to entertain during the break, I would tell a few jokes, which is one of the reasons I loved doing talent shows and concerts. This is why the break is an especially a good spot for comedians. There are so many of them around now who want and need the experience of doing standup comedy. So let them get up and do their thing. (I refer you to Chapter 13.)

When you advertise, be sure to emphasize that standup comics are welcome, because it's a great spot to work in the comedian contenders. If you are lucky enough to end up with two or three comics, you could let each one do ten minutes.

I have done the above not only at talent shows, but also when I have any type of show, such as my free annual country/western concert at Hart Park for my hometown community of Santa Clarita, which I've produced for over twenty years. It's a great way to fill in the twenty-minute break, which will keep the audience interested so they don't wander off and, in all likelihood, not come back.

"Battle-of-the Bands": This is another contest category that's so popular! Now I don't mean the big bands of the Glenn Miller era, but smaller bands (country, blue grass and rock) that are comprised of four or five members. They compete on stage as an entire unit.

If you're going to get involved in producing a "Battle-of-the Bands" contest, you will need to make a few changes in your show's format that differs slightly from an individual performer contest. Basically, you'll be using the same guidelines, which I've already given you in this chapter.

I highly recommend that you or your assistant personally tell each bandleader - as well as make a special notation on the format rules and outlines - the importance of everyone's cooperation when they set up and break down after their performance. Each one of them must do their part as efficiently and quickly as possible. This is crucial to keeping the contest moving along smoothly without any time gaps, which could lose the audience's attention.

The main difference between an individual contest and a band contest is each group is allowed to perform about five or six songs, which would make it about twenty-five minutes. This makes it worth all the time and effort it's taken them to cart their instruments and equipment to the club as well as all the work it takes to set up and break down. As I said before, after they are through performing, they must break down their equipment quickly so that the next band can set up. Hopefully, this will take less than fifteen minutes.

In a perfect world, it would be nice if the bands would all use the same amplifiers, the same drums, etc. However, their instruments and equipment are expensive as well as being very *personal* to them. (Many of the musicians even have names for their instruments.)

Since the drums take the most time to set up and break down, I would recommend that you pay the extra money to have one of the drummers leave his set on stage during the evening until the show is over. You'll save a lot of time (and stress) and things will run more smoothly during the set up/break down phase of the contest. (This twenty-minute set up/break down spot would be a perfect time to have a comedian or a singer/songwriter perform.)

Producing a "Battle-of-the-Bands" contest can really hook you! What's so great about them is each band member will usually bring in two or three friends apiece as well as people who are in their respective fan clubs. If a band has been around a while and has had experience in promoting themselves, they will have notified everyone on their mailing list about the event. So you can imagine what a packed house this could be, which means more tickets will be sold as well as drinks and food.

I personally know of several nightclubs in Southern California that have had band contests, which would be an ongoing thing for about three months. It culminated with each week's winning band in a semifinal and then a final band contest showdown.

Rivendale: As I discussed in Chapter 10, I was the Entertainment Director of a wonderful venue called Rivendale. And I'd like to use this venue as an example to reiterate some of the key points I've just discussed for a "Battle of the Bands" contest.

There was easy access from the freeway to get to Rivendale, which also had ample parking for everyone. It was a twenty-acre Western style property in the county of Santa Clarita where I lived. They had a huge area that was a natural outdoor amphitheater, so we had bleachers installed and it became an all-round arena. We had a variety of activities such as rodeos, live stock and horse shows and, of course, c/w concerts. I hired established country acts like Merle Haggard to perform there. Since this was a first class operation, I had a budget that could afford advertising on key country radio stations throughout Southern California, so all the events were successful.

One day, I got a great idea of producing a "Battle of the Bands" contest, so I advertised on numerous radio stations - locally as well as outlying counties. Other promotional avenues included ads in various newspapers, posters and flyers.

In the Los Angeles and Orange county areas, I, personally, did a number of interviews on radio stations as well as newspapers. So it was well advertised.

I also had my staff mail out flyers to all the country/western nightclubs and had large posters made for various businesses in the community to display in their windows.

The response was incredible. Over a hundred bands sent in their entry forms and cassettes, which was a prerequisite.

Since I had several assistants who were country music savvy, each one of us took home tapes and individually listened to them. Through the process of elimination, we ended up with a combined total of about forty tapes. Then we had a meeting and all three of us listened to these tapes together and finally narrowed the contestants down to about ten or twelve bands.

On a hot Saturday afternoon, I had the "Battle-of-the Bands" contest and it was a blast for all involved. Since each band had four or five members, they all brought family and friends so the bleachers were packed. Food, drinks, T-shirts, programs and other venue related items were sold throughout the day and evening. One of the biggest c/w radio stations in Los Angeles came out with its mobile unit to interview me and also the winning band. I had great promotion, which turned the event into a big success!

Of course, the Rivendale venue was a unique and big time operation, which is why the response to the contest was overwhelming. However, you could use the same principles when you have one in a nightclub, which I've previously discussed.

By the way, you may find that some of the band members are playing in two or three different groups. This is another matter that you'll have to contend with and you'll have to make your own rules for this beforehand. I personally didn't mind it, because I knew how difficult it could be for them to make a decent living as a musician. Besides, it gave them more of a chance to win the contest. Kind of like buying three raffle tickets instead of one.

SUMMARY: The foregoing production guidelines in this chapter are just some of the secrets I've learned along the way, which have successfully worked for me. I feel they can also be helpful to you regardless what type of a talent show you're producing.

As with all enterprises, one of your main objectives is to make money so that you can pay the bills you've incurred in producing the show in the first place, as well as making some profit.

In order to do this, get as many people involved as you possibly can. If you're too exclusive, you're not going to have a big crowd, which means the contest may end up operating in the red. If it's produced properly, there's no reason why you can't make money on talent shows, as well as having a good time while you're doing it.

As I've said in my Introduction, the most important stage in our business is the talent show stage. This is the stage where many stars of yesterday and today have tried their wings. And this where the potential stars of tomorrow (as well as musicians, comedians and producers) can also be free to make mistakes and learn from them.

I wish you good luck with your production efforts, which may be the start of a whole new career for you. Believe me, it's worth all the work, because talent shows are exciting and so much fun.

As a producer, you are contributing to something wonderful, because it brings joy to people. Music is soul stuff and it takes all of us out of our mundane lives. Just remember that you, like aspiring artists, gotta be bad before you can be good.

Chapter 16

Produce a Family Sunday Country Talent Show

"Cliffie always presented local talent on his annual c/w concerts that he'd have for the community. I was proud to participate in inducting him in Santa Clarita's Walk of Western Stars that honors great Westerners."
-JO ANNE DARCY, Mayor of Santa Clarita

"I grew up listening to Cliffie Stone. Later I had the opportunity of becoming his friend, and he became my supporter when I was elected L.A. County Supervisor..."
-MICHAEL D. ANTONOVICH, Supervisor 5th District
Los Angeles County Board of Supervisors

"As much as I enjoyed Cliffie's music, I admire him most for his dedication to his family and to his community, which made the Santa Clarita area a better place..."
-HOWARD P. "BUCK" McKEON, United States Representative
25th District of California, Santa Clarita

Although I've been around a long time, I still consider myself a young man mentally, in spite of the fact that sometimes when I try to get up from a chair, my arthritic knees say, "Who? Me?" But, oh, how I love life! I just love it!

Lately, whenever I turn on the evening news, I shake my head in disbelief at what is occurring in today's society and how it's having a negative effect on our children, who are our future. It's scary with what is happening with guns in our schools and in public areas as well. It seems as though it's not safe to go anywhere anymore.

Now I'm not going to get into a heavy-duty discussion about the woes of our society and its problems and what to do about them. However, it's my opinion that there is a lack of quality time for family-oriented activities. This is probably due to the fact that both husbands and wives are working in order to have enough money to raise their children and live the good life.

I feel that one of the things that could be done is to make time for family events amid our busy lives and work schedules. This is why I suggest a wonderful old-fashioned family activity, which is relative to the subject matter of this book.

Dear producers, nightclub and restaurant managers, as well as various community organizations: I suggest a Family Sunday Country Talent Show, because this is a place where the entire family could go for good food and have a great time together! It's an idea and an activity that will forever bind the family with memories of love, laughter and respect.

You can produce a Family Sunday Country Talent Show by using the same guidelines as you would for a regular talent show, which I've discussed in the previous chapter regarding your budget, advertising, emcee, contestant guidelines, prizes, etc. However, I do have some additional comments to make about the show's format and performers.

Entertainment: In order for this event to have more drawing power, the entertainment would differ slightly than it does for a regular talent show in that it would have a main show with professional entertainment, which normally would be a forty-five minute set. So you'll have to hire a popular local band that you can also use later to backup the contestants in the talent show set. As for emcee suggestions, I refer you to Chapter 15.

If it's within your budget, you could hire an established artist for the main show. Now I don't mean the current high-priced stars of today. Rather, there are older established name acts such as Buck Owens, Merle Haggard, Bobby Bare, Riders of the Purple Sage, Hank Thompson, Molly Bee and Bill Anderson and the list is endless. These older established name acts have put Branson, Missouri on the map, because there was a huge segment of the older country fan population who were being neglected. These wonderful artists are still out in the world doing it and they are known for their traditional country entertainment. Adding their names to your Family Sunday Country Talent Show would really attract a large audience.

However, chances are that even they may not be within your budget at this point in time. So I suggest that you start off small with your local band as the main act. As your weekly or biweekly Family Sunday Country Talent Show grows in popularity, you may be able to hire one of the older artists in the future.

Band/Children's songs: Now that we've established that your local band will be the main entertainment as a starting point, I have a suggestion for some of the songs they could perform. Since there are many wonderful children's songs that also appeal to grownups, get together with the bandleader and/or one of the singers beforehand and arrange to have them perform a couple of them.

There's an album that was released on Disney's "Spotlight Artist Series" that's a wonderful example of the type of songs I'm talking about. The album title is *Country Music for Kids* and a country star lineup of artists perform on it, which includes Buck Owens, Merle Haggard, Glen Campbell, Patty Loveless, Mary-Chapin Carpenter, Emmylou Harris and the Oakridge Boys, to name a few. A good friend and talented music associate of mine, Herb Pedersen (who was a member of the Desert Rose Band about five years ago, and who is also on the A-team for his vocal/banjo skills), produced this album with Jay Levy. So I suggest you buy the CD and have your band learn some of these songs. None of these tunes "talk down" to the kids and they, as well as the adults, will enjoy them.

Talent show set: As for the talent show set, it will depend on how many contestants enter. It may have to be a condensed version of what you normally would have in a regular show. Through word of mouth, it could grow and you may have to cut down on the main show, which would be a wonderful problem to have.

These talent shows should be open to all age groups, which certainly includes children and teenagers. Without a doubt, they'll steal the show and will probably win, which will do nothing for the grownup's ego. But that's all part of the fun.

In fact, you may even want to produce a talent show for just children contestants once in a while. It's a good idea to get the young ones started early. This certainly would be added incentive for parents to bring their children and other family members, including the grandparents. A packed house spells success and means that you'll be able to continue producing these talent shows.

Another great idea would be to encourage family members to perform as an act together, which could be a great draw. To validate the popularity of family acts, let me give you a few examples. In the pop field, there were the Carpenters (brother/sister act); in R&B, Michael Jackson and his brothers, who were known as the Jackson Five; in country - the Bellamy Brothers, the Everly Brothers, and later, the Judds, a dynamic mother/daughter duo.

All of the aforementioned became major acts in their music genres. Talk about a fun family activity that turned lucrative!

And I recently read about a couple of new country family acts that have been signed to major labels such as the Kinleys (sisters) and the Wilkinsons, which consists of a father, son and daughter. It'll be interesting to see what happens with their careers.

Comedians: I've already discussed comics in Chapter 13 and what a good idea it would be to put them on during the band's break. However, with your Family Sunday Country Talent Show, I think it might be wise to hire a professional comedian who can relate to both the grown ups and children as well as teenagers.

Songwriter/singers: Once again, songwriters, like comedians, are good to put on during the band's intermission. (See Chapter 12.)

Magician: There is nothing like magic tricks to keep people's attention. In regular talent shows, it's good to have aspiring magicians who can take the spotlight during the band's break. However, at your Family Sunday Country Talent Show, it would be a great idea to hire a professional magician. He could either perform on center stage or personally go from table to table, which would captivate both the grown ups and children alike. How you work him into the show is your decision.

Juggler: I don't have to tell you how much fun it is to have a juggler around to entertain the kids. Both the magician and juggler could also double as costumed characters during the afternoon and they can run around and socialize with the crowd. Kids love animals and having their picture taken with them. The costumes could be a mouse, bear, dogs, birds, etc. However, their costumes should cover their entire body and face so they won't be recognized.

Miscellaneous entertainment suggestions: A colorful Mexican piñata would add so much to the festivities. It could be filled with candies and inexpensive toys for the youngsters to have as souvenirs. However, don't break it until the latter part of the day. Having it hang from the ceiling most of the afternoon will keep the kids interested in staying at the show.

Food: Using the same tactic the Las Vegas hotels use to lure the people into their casinos, I suggest you consider having an afternoon buffet. However, I recommend that you hire a chef or someone who is experienced not only at cooking, but the budget as well. Otherwise, the food venture portion of this event could eat (excuse the pun) away at any profits you might otherwise have had.

But let's think positive here. Since Sunday is usually the day the family can spend quality time together by going to church and then to brunch or dinner later in the day, a buffet or various individual fast-food items would certainly be instrumental in attracting them to the show itself. Then they could not only eat together, but also have some wholesome fun with all the show's entertainers and activities.

If you go the buffet route, you could have a few main selections such as roast beef, chicken, ham, as well as hamburgers and hot dogs for the kid in all of us. Your salads could include lettuce, baked beans, corn or baked potatoes and some sort of a Jell-O dish with fruit in it. Of course, you can't go wrong with cookies, ice cream and cake for dessert.

As far as what to charge for the buffet, that would have to be carefully calculated so that you don't lose money. If your venue doesn't have the facilities to accommodate a buffet, you could sell fast-food items, which are always popular. But whatever you sell, it should be competitive with the local fast-food places or restaurants.

Once again, hire someone who has a track record with food budgets, because you want to be able to cover the food costs as well as make a profit.

Drinks: It goes without saying that coffee, milk and popular drinks like Seven-up, root beer and other diet drinks should be available for purchase.

With regard to alcohol, it's your decision as to whether or not you'll be selling any at a family-oriented event. If you do, I suggest that only beer and wine be sold, but there has to be a license for it. If your show is held in a nightclub or restaurant, they probably have a liquor license. But if it's being held at a community center or another facility, be sure to check out the alcohol license permit.

Cover charge: You want to have a reasonable cover charge per person that would cover the costs of hiring a band and special guests, as well as the show's costs such as advertising, etc. (If you sold food and made a profit, this also goes toward the show's costs.) I do feel that

138

children under ten years of age should be admitted in free, or at least one-half the price.

Likewise, you may decide to have one cover charge that would include the whole package. This may take a balancing act on your part because you don't want to go over budget and then have to dip into your personal funds to cover expenses, which would certainly insure that you'll never have another Sunday Country Talent Show.

Once you establish a competitive ticket price, you could advertise that the whole family could go out to dinner, see a show and all at an affordable cost, for example, of less than fifteen dollars apiece. That's pretty inexpensive when you compare it to other family-oriented, tourist-seeking entertainment facilities.

"Country Showdown": Quite frankly, the idea for this Family Sunday Country Talent Show came from the success of a family-oriented show that I put together about fifteen or so years ago. For three consecutive summers, I produced my "Country Showdown" shows on the weekends at a large family-oriented venue called Alpine Village in Torrance, California.

My show was a family affair because my late first wife, Dorothy, was very supportive, and one of my grandchildren, Mandy, also participated in these shows, doing a variety of things, such as selling tickets. My house band, the Electric Cowboy Band, had top-of-the-line musicians and the bandleader was my son, Curtis.

With respect to budget, promotion, advertising, flyers, show clothes, etc., I used many of the guidelines and premises that I've shared with you in previous chapters.

Since this show concept was close in nature to my successful "Hometown Jamboree" musical variety television show that I had years ago, the audiences I drew were always family-oriented people who faithfully came down on the weekends.

I presented some of the finest entertainers in Southern California. I always had special guest stars, many of whom were established older entertainers. They included comedian Pat Buttram, Molly Bee, the great Western singer, Eddie Dean, and my dear buddy, Bobby Bare, who is a great entertainer.

They had a wonderful German restaurant on the facilities, and I saw the drawing power it had, because many people in my audience would have a bite to eat there before coming to my show or would go there afterwards (including me). Since it was a big facility, they also had a bar and served alcohol.

Although my "Country Showdown" was not a talent contest, I was always hiring and presenting aspiring new artists, such as Vince Gill (who is now one of country music's classiest superstars), who occasionally sang with my son's band. Not to mention the fact that two members of the Electric Cowboy Band, Curtis and his buddy, Jack Daniels, would be part of the future CMA and ACM award-winning group, Highway 101.

Around this time period, I was also involved with the annual KCLA Talent Search radio contest, which had about five categories. One year, I remember presenting the winning songwriter as well as the winning male and female vocalists.

This is why I feel the Family Sunday Country Talent Show can be successful. Where there's a will, there's a way. Yes, it's an old-fashioned idea, but where there's passion, you can make it happen.

If you choose to produce a family-oriented show of this type or another show similar in nature, you'll be contributing to the very essence of society itself - family unity - and I salute you for it.

"The Cliffie"

THE ACADEMY OF COUNTRY & WESTERN MUSIC

PIONEER OF COUNTRY MUSIC

CLIFFIE STONE
1972

"I, along with Cliffie's children - Stephen, Linda, Curtis and Jonathan - give our heartfelt thanks to the Academy of Country Music's Board of Directors for designating the ACM Pioneer Award as 'The Cliffie' on their May 5, 1999 awards show on CBS." —JOAN CAROL STONE

Photo by Ron Wolfson/Courtesy of the Academy of Country Music

"It was my longtime ACM Board of Directors' buddy, Gene Weed, who nicknamed me 'The Legend.' I remember Gene when he was a rock 'n' roll deejay who followed the beat of his own drum to become a premier TV director and producer." –Cliffie (Chapter 15, "Have Fun Producing Money-Making Talent Shows")

Photo by Joan Stone

Spotlighting the devoted ACM staff, headed by Fran Boyd, Executive Director. Top L to R: Marge Meoli, David Young. Bottom L to R: Fran Boyd, "The Cliffie," and Linda Zandstra. A million thank you's for always being there for us! (Starfest/Pomona Fairgrounds - 1995)

Cliffie with executive producer, Dick Clark, at the 29th ACM Awards show. "Dick Clark has done more for the promotion of all music genres than anyone I know of, and I give him a '21-gun Salute' for his decades of service." —Cliffie (Chapter 15, "Have Fun Producing Money-Making Talent Shows")

Joan Carol (Mrs. Cliffie) with Glen Campbell, first recipient of "The Cliffie."

Photo by J. R. Boyd

Photo by Joan Stone

Cliffie with dear friend, Jo Walker-Meader (Executive Director/retired of the Country Music Association), by his CMA Hall of Fame plaque at the Country Music Foundation's museum in Nashville, TN. Jo was inducted into the CMA Hall of Fame in 1995.

Standing L to R: Jonathan Stone, Steve Stone, Pat Buttram, Eddie Dean, Gene Autry, Linda Stone-Hyde, Curtis Stone. Kneeling L to R: Johnny Grant, Cliffie Stone and Bill Welch.

Cliffie proudly with family and friends while receiving his Hollywood Walk of Fame "STAR" on Sunset and Vine on March 1, 1989.

"My lifelong penchant for discovering and presenting new artists took root during my 13-year musical variety TV show, 'Hometown Jamboree.' Here I am encouraging a talented youngster to sing." —Cliffie (Chapter 2: "Hometown Jamboree: My Talent Show Experiences")

L to R: Cliffie (wagon), Billy Liebert, Harold Hensley, Herman "the Hermit," Ernie Ford, Speedy West, Bucky Tibbs, Les Anderson, Gene O'Quinn, Eddie Kirk. "The countless hours that I spent as an actor at the Pasadena Playhouse learning all aspects of the stage play trade was later used in producing, programming, casting and directing my 'Hometown Jamboree' TV shows." –Cliffie (Chapter 11, "The World is a Stage: Know Your Part")

Cliffie performing on stage as an actor at the Pasadena Playhouse. "As an actor, one of the most important things I learned was to 'dress the part.' When you dress the part, it will help you to feel and act the part." –Cliffie (Chapter 11, "The World is a Stage: Know Your Part")

L to R: Cliffie, Merle Travis, Eddie Kirk, Hank Thompson, Tennessee Ernie Ford. "Meeting with the fans after a show is one of my favorite things to do." –Cliffie (Chapter 9: "Career-Building Advice")

Cliffie performing with his good buddy, Buck Owens, on TNN's "Hee Haw." (1984) Many of Buck's early hits were published by Cliffie's Central Songs. In 1988, Buck received the ACM Pioneer Award, and in 1996 he was inducted into the CMA Hall of Fame.

Cliffie jamming and trading quips with multi-talented Roy Clark on "Hee Haw" in 1983. Among the numerous ACM awards Roy has received is the Pioneer Award in 1996.

L to R: Frances Preston, Bryon Hill, Sam Trust, Cliffie, Gerry Teifer, Del Bryant. (1980s) Cliffie was head of the Country Division for ATV Music Group. "I'm Just An Old Chunk of Coal" is one of many BMI awards they received. (See Publisher-Affiliated BMI/ASCAP Award-Winning Songs)

Cliffie and Ernie Ford performing for the Vintage Invitational in Indian Wells, CA (1981). "Ernie was not only a great singer, but a natural born comedian, too. His country adlibs won the hearts of millions of people. He'd always close his NBC shows with 'bless your pea pickin' hearts.'" –Cliffie (Chapter 13, "Comedians")

Photo by Cliffie Stone

Joan Carol with George Strait after he won the CMA Entertainer of the Year Award in 1990. "George is the Frank Sinatra of the country field and I know some day he'll be inducted into the CMA Hall of Fame." –Cliffie (Chapter 18: "Great Management Is Equally as Important as Great Talent!")

Cliffie and I backstage with Peggy Lee at the Hollywood Bowl in 1995. "The legendary pop diva, Peggy Lee, once told Joan Carol and me that she considered herself an actress when she sang." –Cliffie (Chapter 11, "The World is a Stage")

Joan Carol, Willie Nelson and Cliffie. "Willie wrote 'Crazy' years ago, and I know for a fact that it's a winner because it has won more talent shows than any other song I know of." –Cliffie (Chapter 5: "The Key to Success")

Eddie Dean, Cliffie and Montie Montana at Santa Clarita's Walk of Western Stars banquet (1993). Both have appeared many times on Cliffie's "Hometown Jamboree Today" shows – Eddie doing the singing and Montie twirling his lariat!

Cliffie believed that talented country singer, Faith Hill, has long-term staying power. He enjoyed meeting her at an ASCAP awards banquet, which was held at the Opryland Hotel in Nashville.

With Alan Jackson around, traditional country music is alive and well! Here's a photo that Cliffie took of Alan and me at the Grand Ole Opry during the 1989 CMA rehearsals.

Photo by Joan Stone

Mark Kriski (of Los Angeles' popular "KTLA Morning News" TV show), Cliffie and his son, Curtis (Highway 101) after 101 performed at an Orange County fair. (Chapter 26, "Dreams Do Come True")

Cliffie with Vince Gill, who had just won the CMA award for Single of the Year (1990). Vince performed a number of times with Curtis' band on Cliffie's "Country Showdown" years ago. (Chapter 16: "...Family Talent Show")

Cliffie and me with Clint Black and his wife, Lisa Hartman-Black, at an ACM media event. Clint and Lisa were married two years after we were and they, too, have a very special love for each other. It was a joy talking with them.

Cliffie and me with the "Poet of the Common Man," Merle Haggard, at the 1994 rehearsals for the ACM Awards show. "Whenever I was in the studio while Merle was recording, that song became a hit. So he started calling me his good luck charm." –Cliffie (Chapter 5, "The Key to Success...")

Photo by Joan Stone

Cliffie proudly by his Hometown Heroes' wall at Applebee's in Santa Clarita, CA, with dear friend, Mayor Jo Anne Darcy. "Cliffie was everyone's hero! But there aren't many people who are lucky enough to marry their hero. I did!" –Joan Carol Stone

Cliffie with good friend, Michael D. Antonovich (Supervisor, Fifth District, Los Angeles County Board of Supervisors) at the Golden Boots Awards. Michael and Jo Anne are devoted to bringing a sense of community to a large county.

Photo by Joan Stone

Photo by Joan Stone

Cliffie felt that Lorianne Crook (of TNN's "Crook & Chase") was one of the most beautiful and charming TV hosts ever! He had so much fun promoting our songwriting book on her show in 1992. Here they are saying hello backstage at the ACM Awards show in 1994.

Photo by Joan Stone

"Barbara Mandrell performed on the 'Hometown Jamboree' show a few times at the beginning of her career. She was the CMA Entertainer of the Year in 1980 and 1981. She proves that big talent comes in small packages, and she's my Entertainer of the Year forever." –Cliffie (Chapter 5, "The Key to Success...")

Cliffie in emcee action at the Palomino club with two of the Palomino Riders, Arnie Moore (left) and Jay Dee Maness (right). "With their great playing, my A-team band made the contestants feel like real professionals on the stage." –Cliffie (Chapter 12, "Writers: Sing Your Song for All You're Worth!")

Many country stars had concerts at the legendary Palomino, and Cliffie usually emceed. Here's Cliffie with his good buddy, Bobby Bare, at the Palomino having a good laugh as he takes over the emcee chores.

"I've gotten to know Kenny Chesney since he's been on the ACM's Board of Directors with me. It takes time to develop as an artist and he's well positioned to handle success, which I believe will happen for him." –Cliffie (Chapter 18, "Great Management...")

"The first time I ever saw LeAnn perform was at the Hacienda Hotel in Las Vegas, where she sang at a state country music organization competition when she was about 12 years old. Since then, I watched how she handles herself on network television shows and I'm so proud of her. She is respectful, has a great attitude, and she's a wonderful representative of country music." –Cliffie (Chapter 22, "Star School")

Cliffie speaking at Barnes & Noble's "Writers' Workshop" in Santa Clarita. (1996) "I've performed for audiences at various venues all my life. But it was a whole new ball game for me to speak at book clubs, women's clubs and book stores, like Barnes & Noble. My first appearance at Barnes & Noble was a combination of a book signing and writers' workshop, and the turnout was fantastic." –CS (Chapter 21, "Talent Night at Barnes & Noble!")

Cliffie diligently at work taping his notes for his book. "This book has had an incubation period of over five years, for that's how long I've been thinking about it, and recording my thoughts on tape." —Cliffie ("Introduction")

Joan and Cliffie at their book distributor's booth with Barrie Edwards, President of Music Sales, which was held at North American Music Merchants (NAMM) at the Anaheim Convention Center in January 1992.

We had fun promoting our songwriting book on radio stations, which included Larry King's syndicated radio talk show; WYNY (Del de Moncho); KWKH (Larry Scott); KIEV (George Putnam); KZLA (Stoney Richards); and KABC (Ray Breim).

Photo by Joan Stone

We spoke at an elite So. California book club called "Round Table West," which was founded and hosted by Margaret Burke and Marylin Hudson. Here's Cliffie with Dr. Robert Schuller (TV's "Hour of Power" ministry), who was also one of the authors at the event.

"My friend, it's my desire that my book will help guide you to the realization of your dreams. But you don't need to become 'world famous' to be a bona fide entertainer, because fame, at best, is nothing but the flicker of a firefly on a hot summer's night. It's my belief that the most important thing for anyone is to *be all that they can be,* regardless what level they finally attain. Simply live each day to the max and maintain your sense of humor. Welcome to my world!" – Cliffie ("Introduction")

Baby Cliffie sharing the spotlight with puppies. "It begins when we are babies ...there's this click and flash that seems to go off every day. Maybe this is where baby starts to develop a love affair with a camera and gets his first taste of being a celebrity." –Cliffie (Chapter 23, "Look at Me! Applause, Applause!")

Cliffie with his proud parents, Nina Belle and Clifford. "When I graduated from Burbank High School, I had to choose between a football college scholarship and music. I chose to follow my heart because I had this need to perform." –Cliffie (Chapter 23, "Look at Me! Applause, Applause!")

Photo by Joan Stone

"Oh, how I love life! I just love it!" –Cliffie

Cliffie loved to drive his tractor around his Rolling Stone Ranch. Sons Steve and Jonathan are in the background. "The garden that I've had on my ranch all these years has always been a place of refuge for me where I could go to get away from the pressures of the music world." –Cliffie

"Cliffie was a great thinker as well as a doer. Here's one of my favorite photographs of him at the beach in Santa Barbara, which reflects his meditative side." - Joan Carol Stone

Chapel of the Bells
"If I Had Never Loved You"

Words and Music by Joan Carol Stone

If I had never loved you, if you had never loved me
We wouldn't have known Love's glory and all that love can be!
The day I take my last breath, I'll thank the Lord above
For giving me the gift of you, for I have loved!

"The Cliffie"

*"God gave you a gift, and what you do with it is
your gift to God!"*
–Cliffie Stone

Chapter 17

Show Me the Money! Artist Financing

"Sponsoring an artist is not a new thing, because it goes way back to the days of Beethoven and Bach. These guys had 'patrons-of-the-arts' who financed their music careers. I'm not a lawyer or an accountant, so my knowledge is limited, but I will share some basic thoughts about some legitimate financing deals that I've observed, which have worked in the past for various artists and investors."
-CLIFFIE STONE

During the years that I emceed the popular Palomino club's weekly talent show, it was inevitable that some of the veteran contestants would bring up the question of artist/album financing.

This same question has also been asked of me many times by professional singers who have regular gigs around town. Recently, one artist called me and said, "I know a guy who has some money and he's been coming into the club and making noises about financing an album for me. How should I go about it?"

I hope to address some of these questions so that any aspiring artist, as well as any potential investor who is reading this book, will have some idea of how to go about this. However, I'm not a lawyer, a banker or an accountant and I want to make it crystal clear that my knowledge is limited on this subject. I really don't know anything about loans except that when I borrow money from people or banks, I have to pay it back with interest. Or when I loan money to people, I have to worry about them paying me back. So what I'll be sharing with you are my opinions and basic thoughts about some legitimate financing deals that I've observed, which have worked in the past for various artists and investors.

Patrons-of-the-arts: Now, in the context that I'm using "patron," it means that someone with money will invest in an artist's album project. Sponsoring or backing an artist is not a new thing, because it goes way back to the days of Beethoven and Bach. Those talented guys had "Patrons of the Arts" who financed their careers. In modern times, we call them sponsors, backers, investors or venture capitalists and there are

141

potentially a lot of them out there. They could be personal friends, a relative, a company or someone in the audience who has seen you perform.

There could be any number of reasons why they may want to be involved. There are many well-to-do people who are enamored with show biz and investing in you is a way for them to be a part of it. Possibly it's a well-connected music publisher or producer who will want the publishing on the original songs. Or maybe the investor is enamored with you personally, and likewise. But the bottom line is they believe in your project and hope to make a good return from their investment.

Artist financing is a business: As an artist, you shouldn't be shy or tentative with regard to someone financing your album or your career in general, because it can be a good business deal. You bring to the table your talent and they bring to the table the money to jumpstart you towards a new career level. If the two of you can work it out, then everyone has a chance of making a few bucks while having a good time doing it.

Being an artist and a musician, I know what it's like to live solely in a creative world. But when I saw opportunities in the business end of it, I decided to become an executive, too. You certainly don't have to become a music executive like I did, but I recommend that you approach artist financing from a business perspective and become aware of some basic music financing principles. Anything less than that is not going to fly with any potential investor because, for the most part, he (or she) will have had experience in the business world, even though he may have limited knowledge about the music industry. (If he becomes an investor, he can have fun learning about it as the project progresses.)

I have fond memories of various businessmen who invested in artists and of how excited they were when they came down to the studio to observe the recording process. They were like little boys, and they had the time of their lives!

Doing business as (d/b/a): One of the ways you can approach your musical career from a business perspective is to consider starting a business entity in which you'll be "doing business as." There are different business entities that are recognized by the Internal Revenue Service, such as "Sole Proprietorship," "Partnership," "Corporations,"

"S Corporations" or a "Limited Liability Company." I suggest you seek the advice of your income tax man or a Certified Public Accountant (CPA), because he can fill you in on each entity's advantages and disadvantages.

"Sole Proprietorship" is the easiest business entity to form and organize. Best of all, the owner is free to make all the business decisions. When you have your own company with your name listed as president on your letterhead stationery as well as business cards, it will impress prospective club owners and potential investors.

Let's not forget about banks, as well, should you ever need to apply for an equity loan or a line of credit. You're talking their business language when you tell them that you're president of XYZ Music Company, where you've been the sole proprietor for five years or however long it's been open.

How does one go about opening up a d/b/a? First of all, call one of the newspapers in the county where your business is going to be established, which will probably be where you reside. Ask their legal clerk how much it will cost to have a d/b/a. Whatever amount she specifies will go towards the recording and publishing fee. If you decide to form a company, then go to the newspaper office, fill out a one-page form and pay them whatever the fee may be.

The first thing the newspaper people will do is record it with the county, which can take anywhere from three to four weeks. Once it's been recorded, the newspaper publishes all the pertinent information about your company in a special section of their paper. They do this so that it can become public knowledge that you are conducting business under this name. In business, it's always good to have a post office box and I suggest you open one.

Once you get the d/b/a/ newspaper clipping, etc., then you'll be able to open up a business bank account.

The big picture: Before I begin to talk about the overall view of artist financing, I'd like to say a few things that are relevant to this subject matter, which should give you and your potential investor incentive to work out a deal.

First of all, reach for the stars, because that's what they are there for. Let your imagination take flight and in your mind's eye look at *the big picture*. As an artist, your ultimate goal is to become a successful entertainer with hit albums that will sell into the millions. This in turn could get you guest spots on television shows like Rosie O'Donnell or Jay Leno. If you do become a superstar, you could end up with your own television special like Garth Brooks did on NBC or HBO. All this exposure means you'll probably have sold out concerts all over the world wherever you go. (This reminds me of something amusing that the late songwriter/artist Roger Miller ("King of the Road") once said: "Funny thing is that no matter where I go, I'm always appearing there!" Don't ask me why I think that's a funny line. I'm just throwing it in; otherwise, this artist funding stuff would be much too serious for me.)

At this point, it's conceivable that you could be grossing ten million dollars a year. How does that sound? All those big bucks rolling in like a broken-down slot machine that doesn't know when to stop. What a delicious sound and thought!

It's a horse race: Speaking of slot machines, I'd like to say a few words to potential investors. Basically, this is what this whole artist financing thing is about - gambling. Needless to say, most people love to gamble. The horse races, stock market, lottery, sports events and casinos, which are worldwide, all corroborate that fact.

Naturally, when you gamble, you risk! However, there are different degrees of risk. For instance, take the stock market. One of the indexes, Standard & Poor's 500 (S&P 500), has a risk rating system they call *Beta*. Beta measures the risk of the specific stock, mutual funds, etc. to the relativity of the stock market. The average Beta is *one*. Anything that is above one is considered more risky because it will yield higher returns. Anything that is lower than one, is considered less risky and, therefore, possibly a safer investment.

When you get down to it, no matter what we do in life, we're taking a risk. Just getting out of bed in the morning, you could trip over the dog and break your hip. There's an element of risk every time we get into a car or an airplane. Statistics prove that flying in a commercial airplane is safer than driving in a car. But try telling that to someone who is afraid of flying. As far as they are concerned, it's riskier to fly than to drive. Statistics mean nothing to them!

So our emotional makeup plays a big factor in the risk level we allow ourselves to be exposed to. Therefore, only you can determine what you personally think the risk level is when you're considering putting up the funds for an artist's album.

Regardless of whether you're a family member, a close friend, a professional investor or whatever, what I'm about to say applies to all of you across the board. If you have a rosy financial picture, you didn't get that way by throwing your money around. So I'll assume that you are a businessman or woman and that you're aware that "risk is a given" regardless what type of investment you make. In short, you could lose it! That's possible, right? So the bottom line is don't invest unless you can afford to lose it. In other words, if you lost your investment, it wouldn't be a hardship or encumber your lifestyle in any way.

And I'd like to say something to family members and close friends. I know that you believe in your beloved relative and/or friend and you want to help him (or her) to get his chance at the brass ring. But don't take out a loan on your house or cash in your life insurance or retirement funds in order to finance his album. As I said before and it bears repeating - don't invest any funds that would encumber your lifestyle should you never see that money again. Sometimes loaning money to family and friends can affect the relationship. So consider all angles and if you make the decision to invest, do it from a business perspective.

Having said all the above, maybe you're the type of person who is thinking, "I've got fifty thousand dollars sitting in the bank and it's only making four percent interest. At the end of the year, the interest is only two thousand dollars and I'm going to have to claim it on my income tax - not to mention that three percent has already been eaten up by inflation. So if I invest in Dave's album, maybe it's a potential way for me to earn more money! It certainly sounds like more fun and besides, I've always wanted to be involved in show business." If you're of this mindset and you're thinking about sponsoring an artist, it's your decision.

Regardless what the industry is, you always hear people say, "It's so competitive" and you get the feeling as though you're in a race against others. Well, that's the nature of free enterprise and I guess you could say it was a race. Maybe you could make this more fun by looking upon your artist investment as an excursion to the Kentucky Derby and both of you are in this deal together - win, place or show. However, you're coming from a business perspective, so you have a much better chance at making your money back with the artist, because you have a certain amount of control in the matter as opposed to the horseracing odds. (And don't you just love it when a long shot wins or places or shows, thereby beating all the odds?)

Speaking of odds, my dad used to say, "If you go to Las Vegas, take only enough money along that you can afford to lose. If you lose it, get in the car and head for California! For goodness sakes, don't hock the car or the guitar in order to stay there in the hopes of making it back!"

Investing in an artist can be an exciting adventure in capitalism and one that you'll never forget, but you must feel comfortable with your investment. It's your call.

INCENTIVES FOR ARTIST FINANCING

Once you know the "why," you'll want to know the "how." So I'll give you a few reasons "why" it would behoove you to record an album, which may be an incentive for you and your potential investor to work out a deal.

CDs are a great promotional tool: As a singer and an entertainer, the best way for you to make progressive strides in your career would be to record an album. If you have a quality album product that is attractively packaged, you could be using it as a promotional tool in a variety of ways.

First of all, your producer or manager could shop it to the major labels. Secondly, you could be sending your album out to various booking agents or club managers for potential gigs. Thirdly, you could be selling it off the bandstand to build your invaluable fan base as well as helping to recoup your backer's initial investment. Fourthly, there could be an opportunity for you to enter a national talent contest and/or a television talent show. Since they can't personally audition the hundreds of people who want to enter, most of the time it's a requirement to include a cassette along with the entry form; and you would already have a quality one that would increase your chances of becoming one of the contestants.

In any of the aforementioned scenarios, the music executives, club managers, booking agents or talent contest producers would have the opportunity of hearing you sing with a band. Therefore, they'll get an idea of what you can do vocally. Not to mention the fact that a picture is worth a thousand words and they'll see a great photo of you on the front of the CD. They'll also see your name, which, hopefully, will be impressed upon their minds as well as being able to read your bio and linear notes on the inside of the j-card. In other words, all the important things about you are succinctly and conveniently contained on and in the CD and/or cassette package. This is why it's a great promotional tool!

Since it's important that you approach your career from a business perspective, you will need to know the answers to some of the basic questions that will be asked of you by anyone interested in investing in your album and career.

HOW MUCH WILL AN ALBUM AND A VIDEO COST?

Estimated album cost: One of the first questions will be, "How much will an album cost?" The cost per song and/or an entire album is not black and white. It's a gray area because there are a lot of *variables.* In the context I'm going to be using the word "variable," it basically means that unforeseen circumstances could arise, which could change or vary the song or album cost factors.

Relatively speaking, you really don't have to spend a fortune on an album because the bottom line is the "song" itself and the way the artist vocally and emotionally interprets its lyrics. Nobody buys an album because Cliffie Stone plays bass on it (except Cliffie Stone, of course).

To have an adequate answer, a "per song" budget should be drafted by someone in the know, like a producer or an engineer. He would list each entity and its estimated and/or variable cost. However, these costs will depend on the quality of the product that you're going for so you will have to take into consideration the answers to some essential factors and questions, which have a variable undertone to them.

Producer: First of all, let's consider the producer, who is the head honcho responsible for the entire recording project. His duties include putting together a projected budget and keeping on top of it as the project progresses; song selection; hiring the engineer, musicians and backup singers; selecting the studio that has the latest state-of-the art equipment; laying down tracks; sweetening; overdubbing; mixing and mastering the final product. He may also be shopping it as well. Therefore, some relevant questions need to be asked. What is your producer's track record? What kind of connections does he have in the industry? Does he intend to shop your product? What will he charge you per hour or per song?

Engineer: In all likelihood, the engineer will be the producer's choice, but it's good to know something about him because the three of you will be like three peas in a pod before this project is finished. What does he charge per hour? What is his track record?

One of the best as well as one of the fastest engineers that I've ever worked with was Brian Friedman, who constantly amazed me with the way he worked all those knobs and buttons, along with having great ears and creative music suggestions. He can do in one hour what it takes most engineers three hours to do.

Musicians: Regarding the caliber of musicians, are they a bar band or the top-of-the-line studio recording musicians? Believe me, you save money by hiring studio musicians, which I call the "A" team; they can lay down a track the second or third time around.

Will you be adding extra musicians and/or harmony vocalists in the sweetening process to fill in the various spots in a song that will add to the overall professionalism and quality of the product?

Artist's recording experience: One of the most important questions has to do with you, the artist. How much experience have you had in a recording studio? It's a totally different ballgame than singing in a nightclub, and if you've had very little experience, you're going to be nervous. The mike picks up minute sounds and if you're not on pitch or on key, it stands out like a sore thumb. So it may take more studio time to get your lead vocals right so that you are in tune and on pitch. The only way to learn anything is to do it, and with experience under your belt, you'll get the hang of it. Here is where a credible and experienced producer will be worth his weight in gold because he'll know how to bring out the best in you.

I'll break these entities down and I'll give you rough estimates (as of this point in time, which are always subject to change) of what it could cost in the Los Angeles area.

Producer fees: If it's a credible producer who has an impressive track record, he may charge you anywhere from $900 - $2,000 per song. However, negotiation is the name of the game with any producer. (For your info, when a major record label hires a producer to record one of their artists, the approximate going rate is $3,000 to $4,000 per track, plus a 3 or 4-point album royalty rate.)

Engineer: Anywhere from $40 to $50 dollars an hour. (Some studios will include the engineer fees with their hourly rate.) Assuming that each song takes twelve hours of studio time, the engineer's fees would be approximately $480 to $600 per cut.

Musicians: Experienced studio musicians will be approximately $75 or $100 per person. If it's a union gig, it will be more. In any case, you'll need four to lay down the rhythm tracks - piano, bass, drums and guitar. If you're going for a master quality product, you'll need extra musicians, such as a synthesized keyboard player (for strings, electric piano, etc.), fiddle, steel guitar, etc., and they're in the same price range I've just mentioned. Depending on the number of songs, you may be able to work out a lower fee per musician.

Backup singers: This is optional. However, in the country field, harmonies are essential because they add to the overall quality and color of the songs. Usually, for $125 per song you can hire a studio backup singer who is skillful enough to do all the harmony parts, not to mention the fact that he (or she) can do the tunes in the least amount of time.

If you're capable of doing the harmonies, you could save money, as long as it doesn't take you five hours per song to get it right. In the long run, it may be cheaper to have an experienced studio singer do all the parts, as he or she can knock it out in an hour or so.

Materials: If you're recording in a 24-track studio, the 2-inch tape is $185 and it can hold three or four songs. However, technology has changed and, depending on the studio, your producer may be using digital equipment, which would eliminate this cost. But there will be charges for cassette tapes and DATS. (I suggest that you buy your own at a discount store and save the money.)

Studio rates: Depending on the quality of the studio and whether or not it has state-of-the art equipment, it could be anywhere from $65 to $75 an hour.

Estimated studio time cost per song: Approximately 12 hours at $65 an hour: $780. (Basic tracks - 2 hours; instrument overdubs -

2 hours; lead vocals - 4 hours (depends on the singer's recording skill); background vocals - 2 hours; mixing - 2 hours.)

However, it might be a good idea to allocate another 4 hours in the projected per song budget to cover the variable factors, which would bring it up to 16 hours at $65 an hour: $1,040.00.

Estimated cost per song/album: Adding all the above entities, I would say the cost per song would be approximately $3,000, give or take. Therefore, a 10-song quality album could be anywhere from $30,000 to $35,000. Incidentally, I've heard through the grapevine that the approximate album cost is around $50,000 for aspiring artists who go to Nashville of their own volition and hire an independent producer. (Note: The average album costs for major record labels are approximately $185,000.)

If your goal is a major record deal, you should give yourself every advantage. I suggest you go for a quality product because this is what the "ears of the industry" are used to hearing. It's your call.

Video costs: Needless to say, videos play a major role in the recording industry, but it's not imperative that you have one. If you have enough money in the budget, you may want to consider it, because they can be useful when you're trying to get a gig or when your manager is shopping your project to record labels.

If you are planning on entering a national talent contest and/or a television talent show, they usually request cassettes; sometimes they also request that videos be sent in with the entry form, too.

In any of the above scenarios, the powers-that-be could see how you react and perform in front of a camera. If they like the first impression, good things can happen for you.

If you and your manager decide to go the video route, then I suggest you get a professional video guy to film you. Once again, the word "variable" comes into play, because you want to go for a quality video so that you can show off your best face as well as your best sound. When you work with professionals who have state-of-the art equipment, they can easily incorporate one of your 24-track songs directly into the video.

Naturally, you should shop around and get quotes from various video companies before making a final decision. It's only common sense to ask each one of them if you could view other videos they've produced in the past in order to evaluate their overall production skills.

Once you've chosen the video guy, remember that "less is more." In other words, you don't have to have a fancy video that has all the bells and whistles in it like the ones major record labels put out. They have the funds allotted in their budget to spend countless hours filming, going on location and editing an elaborate video. However, you do want a top quality video that can hold its own in the marketplace and, relatively speaking, you don't need to spend a lot of dough doing it. Simplicity has an elegance that is priceless.

Since I'm not a video producer, I can't break down the cost factors. About six years ago, I did talk to various professional video companies, as well as some aspiring artists who had professionals do a video for them. The approximate rate at that point in time was from $7,000 to $15,000. However, that was way back into yesterday, so check around for today's going rate.

Estimated cost for an album and a video: In a perfect world, it would be great if you have an investor who is willing to go for the full enchilada (both the album and video). Conservatively speaking, I'd say that to put out a quality album and video that could compete in today's marketplace could conceivably be around $50,000, give or take a little. However, an album is the first priority.

HOW DOES THE INVESTOR GET HIS MONEY BACK?

There are several ways this could be done, but the main one is through a Master Purchase deal. So, I'll try to logically answer these questions step by step in the following paragraphs as simply as I can to give you the overall picture.

Production Agreement: If you get involved with a credible producer with a good track record who also intends to shop your product to major record labels, he will probably sign you, the artist, to a Production Agreement. If his only intention and involvement is producing the product, then he won't. You and your manager will have to do the album shopping on your own.

Since I've had experience wearing the producer's hat, I'll be the example. Generally, whenever I get involved with an artist with the intention of shopping their product, I will sign him or her to a production deal, which doesn't include the backer even though it may be his money that's paying my fees and the project's bills. (The artist and the investor have to work out their own deal, because it's my policy not to become involved.) My basic concern is getting paid for producing and my total focus will be on all the responsibilities involved in producing a quality album so that I can shop it to major record labels. If I get the artist a deal, I can negotiate a producer's album royalty rate (which is usually a 3-point deal) for myself.

There have been occasions when I've either waived my producer's fees or have taken a nominal one because there wasn't enough money in the budget. (I usually did this when I believed the artist had a good shot at getting a deal.) In those cases, my only potential compensation would be publishing on songs from my catalog as well as any original songs the artist may have written.

Should I get the artist signed to a label after I've shopped the product, I will be compensated for my production fees because the record company does a *Master Purchase* deal on all of the songs involved in the project. The backer will also be reimbursed from this Master Purchase for the total amount he has initially invested. If there is a profit, this could be applied to the backer's rate of return.

Master Purchase deal: You are probably asking, "What is a Master Purchase deal?" I'll keep it simple so that you'll get the general idea. Let's say that I'm going to pick up the tab, which means I've chosen to do it on speculation. So I've not only waived my production fees, but I'll also be paying for the entire recording costs as well as all the album shopping expenses, such as airfare, hotel, car rental, food, etc. Does this sound too good to be true? Well, Epic recording star, Collin Raye, was a recipient of this "too good to be true scenario," which I'll talk about later in the chapter.

Since I'm putting my marbles in the ring like this, you can bet the ranch on this horse race that I'll have a Production Agreement with this artist as well as publishing on all the original tunes. And after production, I'll be going full throttle in shopping the artist's album to major record companies.

To make a long story short, I've produced ten songs with an artist and I've shopped the product and got him signed with MCA. Now,

MCA will do a Master Purchase, which is simply buying all the song tracks in the project. Maybe I negotiate the deal for $38,500.

Let's say that the entire album expenses, including my waived producer's fees as well as shopping expenses, came to a total of $35,000. Therefore, the $38,500 has paid for my fees and all the expenses involved in the entire project, which leaves a profit of $3,500. Since I'm the investor, my rate of return is 10%.

Now there are two basic reasons why a label does a Master Purchase. Number one: So that there will be reimbursement for all the expenses involved in producing the album and/or cuts (hopefully, there will also be a small profit). Number two: The label will then own all the song tracks and/or masters in this project, which legally keeps these tracks that this particular artist has sung on from being released by anyone or any company in the future.

For example, maybe I produced twelve songs and the record label is only interested in using four of them on the artist's first album release. If they only did a master purchase on those four songs, that leaves eight songs that I would still legally own.

It costs the record labels approximately $500,000 to promote and break a new country act (I've heard it's twice as much in the pop/rock fields). To illustrate my point, let's pretend they released the first album and spent tons of money in promotion. The album is a smash hit and the artist becomes a big star. Legally, I could take the eight songs that I produced for this artist that the label didn't do a Master Purchase deal on and release them as an album with another company. And it didn't cost a dime for all the promotion to make him a star.

However, record companies cover all the bases, because in their recording contract there's a clause saying to the effect that there are no existing masters that the artist has recorded, which someone else owns; the artist has to agree to that before he signs his contract.

Investor's rate of return: There is no one pat answer to the investor's rate of return because, once again, the word "variable" comes into play. One has to deal with a lot of unknown factors, which are relative to the projected costs as well as projected earnings (as it does in all business industry ventures). You and your backer will have to work out the potential rate of return percentage before both of you can finalize your personal financial agreement.

This rate of return (like the backer's initial investment) could come from the Master Purchase deal if there was a profit. Or it could come from a percentage (points) of the album's royalties, which would be tied in with the artist's record royalty percentage (per the personal contract the backer and the artist had initially signed). In other words, if the artist were to get a 10% album royalty rate, he could stipulate that 3% of his 10% royalties go to his backer.

If a music publishing company was investing in the recording session and the songs were from their catalog, as well as getting the publishing on any songs in the project that the artist wrote, they would probably be shopping the product. If they got the artist signed, they could get their own album royalty deal, which could be 3-points or more.

Artist's album royalty deal: If you ever get signed to a record label, you'll need to have some understanding about how the artist's album royalty deal works, especially if you're ever in the position of discussing a potential funding agreement with a potential investor.

First of all, any expenses that are directly associated with the actual recording session of an artist's album (studio rental, producer, engineer, musicians, music coordinators, tapes, cartage, etc.) are considered *an advance against future earnings* and are charged to the artist. If there had been a Master Purchase, that amount would also be included in this advance against future earnings.

You see, the record company is also gambling and, therefore, they are taking a fairly high risk when they sign a new act. They really don't know what kind of a public response they'll get until the album's been recorded and released. So when a new artist signs with a label, they will advance the funds for the recording costs, but these costs are charged against the future payable royalties of the artist. (Labels generally do this with all the acts on their roster.)

There's a standard clause in the artist's contract to the effect that he gets an album royalty rate. (In Sidney Shemel and M. Williams Krasilovsky's book, *This Business of Music*, they have a chapter that has various standard music forms and one of them is the record label and artist agreement. I recommend that you not only review this agreement, but others in their book, which would increase your knowledge of the music business.)

154

But let's assume that this royalty rate is 10%, or a 10-point deal. The general rule of thumb is that the artist would receive a 10% royalty from the retail price that was established by the label for each CD and cassette unit that was sold. The label keeps track of how many product units are shipped to distributors and purchased, which, of course, is how they also keep track of the artist's 10% payable royalties. However, be aware that the unit prices for single releases, club sales, foreign sales, etc. also factor into the royalty rate equation in order to establish the correct payable royalties.

When it's time for the label to distribute royalty checks (which may be every six months or once a year), the artist's accumulated 10% payable royalties from the product sales in that time period are deducted from whatever the recording costs were. Once the label has recouped those recording expenses, from that point on, the artist will begin to receive his payable royalty checks.

As I said in the "Production Agreement" section, the producer generally gets a royalty deal, but it's usually on a per-song basis. (There could be several producers involved in an artist's album and each one may have produced a different song.) His payable royalties are also based on the product's unit retail prices and are subject to the same royalty deductions that I've just mentioned for the artist. (This same deduction formula also applies if an investor were to receive an album royalty deal.)

In short, the artist, producer and investor won't see one penny of their payable album royalties until the recording costs of the album has been recouped by the label.

"Paid from record one"/exceptions to the rule: It's a given that there will always be exceptions to the rule. So there will be times where the label would absorb the project's recording costs and, therefore, the artist would get *paid from record one*.

For instance, if a record label has had the opportunity to sign a big name act, they may give him or her a $300,000 bonus to sign with their company. And once anyone becomes a major artist, they can negotiate a larger royalty percentage because they have built-in sales and are, therefore, a low risk. So if the artist had a 16-point album royalty deal, they would immediately start accumulating their payable royalties from the very first CD and cassettes that are sold. In other words, they would be *paid from record one*.

Collin Raye's lucky break: In an article I read about ten years ago, Frank Sinatra made a statement to the effect that there were thousands of actors/artists who were just as talented as he was but they never got a lucky break. Well, I differ with him on one aspect of his statement in that no one can even come close to the Chairman of the Board's one-of-a-kind talent. But Frank was certainly on target with regard to the untold thousands of extremely talented people out there who don't get a lucky break in show business.

And so it goes in the country music industry. One of these extremely talented singers is Epic recording star, Collin Raye, who got his lucky break the day Jerry Fuller flew down to Reno to see him perform in one of the casino lounges.

Now, I've known Jerry and his wonderful wife and business partner, Annette, for years. I've produced many albums in their unique Footprint recording studio, as well as having served on the Academy of Country Music's Board of Directors with Jerry. He's been a premier songwriter and producer for decades and he got his lucky break when Ricky Nelson recorded "Travelin' Man," which hit the top of the charts and sold six million copies. (Jerry's songs have also been recorded by major artists in all music genres, which include Gary Puckett and the Union Gap, Reba McEntire, Glen Campbell, Al Wilson, Andy Williams, Tom Jones, Johnny Mathis, John Anderson, and the list goes on. Since his notable musical track record is too numerous to mention, if you're ever surfing the Internet, check out his web site.)

Meanwhile, back at one of Reno's casino lounges, when Jerry heard and saw Collin perform, his gut instinct told him that Collin had a good chance of getting a record deal. So Jerry decided to roll the dice when he took Collin under his wing and signed him to a production deal. Jerry not only invested his time, his enormous musical know-how and his meticulous production expertise, but he picked up the studio tab as well. He brought keyboard genius, John Hobbs, into the picture, and together, they co-produced five tracks.

Jerry hit the jackpot when he shopped Collin's product in Nashville. Collin was signed to a record deal at Epic and all five cuts were purchased via a Master Purchase deal. So Jerry and John were reimbursed for their producing efforts, as well as the other expenses involved in the project. (One of the songs from that album was "Love

Me," which became Collin's career song and the first of many hits in his wonderful career, which is still going strong.)

Record companies in the country field will re-cut the songs in the Master Purchase if they feel the quality can be improved upon. By the same token, the record label may decide to release some of the original masters that were brought to them.

And so it was in another project that Jerry was involved in with my son, Jonathan, who is the General Manager of a highly-successful publishing company, Windswept Pacific. To make a long story short, Jerry and his co-producer, Bob Montgomery, recorded fourteen songs with a dynamic entertainer by the name of Eddie Dunbar and they got him a deal with Giant. Although Giant did a Master Purchase on all fourteen cuts, they decided to use only six of the fourteen songs on the album. Out of those six songs, they used two of the original masters and re-recorded the rest. As the old saying goes, "don't fix something if it ain't broke."

ARTIST-FUNDING FORMULAS AND EXAMPLES

Be your own "venture capitalist": As an artist, you've freely invested thousands of hours learning to sing and/or to play your instrument. Many of you paid money for lessons; some of you didn't. Then you spent the necessary time to learn the art of performing on stage.

Now you feel it's time to move onward and upward toward your ultimate goals - one of them being an album, which could be the catalyst to getting you a major record deal. So far, there hasn't been an investor on the horizon and you're getting impatient, especially after you found a few gray hairs on your head the other day.

But where there's a will, there's a way. One of the ways is for you to be your own venture capitalist; in other words, invest your own money into your recording project. After all, you've freely invested all this time in yourself learning your craft and time is money in the business world. So why stop now? One of the positive things about investing in your own album is that you don't have to account to anyone about the project and its progress. This in itself frees up the creativity element. Several of the acts that Joan Carol and I became involved with did just that!

Jumpin' Boots: One of these acts is the Jumpin' Boots band - one of the most popular country groups in Nevada's gambling resort areas (they have about a thousand people on their local mailing list). Their versatility included the pop and rock genres, which enabled them to survive the country droughts that can occur.

So I signed the band to a Production Agreement and it was my plan to shop them to major record labels. It was a total delight to work with this talented group, which consisted of Charlie Lesink (bandleader), Van Dunson, Michael Moore, Mark Miller and John Garcia. Since they were excellent musicians, as well as harmony singers, money was saved in those areas of the project's budget. Each of them gladly invested their share of the money towards their recording project, which they had wanted to do for years.

Riders of the Purple Sage: This legendary Western group was a contemporary of the Sons of the Pioneers. One of their biggest million sellers was "Ghost Riders in the Sky." Buck Page (aka Don Duffy) was the original founder of the Riders of the Purple Sage and it does me proud to see him out there still doing it. The other two members, Mike Ley and JB (Joe Boemecke), have their own distinguished musical track records.

Being a legendary Western act, they are in demand throughout the Western states for county fairs, rodeos, concerts, and prestigious Western events, such as the annual Golden Boots Awards in Hollywood.

Their gig profits (which include other RPS albums, T-shirts and photographs they sell off the bandstand) go into their company bank account and they invested these profits in their latest album, *Drifting Clouds*, which I produced. Through promotion in all areas, including the Internet, they not only made their initial investment back, but are seeing a good profit and will continue to do so for as long as they are out there sharing their brand of music with the world.

An equity or personal line of credit: One must have equity in a piece of property, such as a home, in order to qualify for an equity line of credit, which secures the loan.

With regard to qualifying for a personal line of credit, some of the prerequisites for an applicant and his or her mate are to have good jobs for a reasonable amount of time that pay a substantial income, as well as having a good credit record. The latter is how one artist, Mark Burnes, raised the money to invest in his album.

158

Mark is a professional entertainer who has been in constant demand at prestigious nightclubs and hotels in elite beach areas along the beautiful California coast for years. Therefore, Mark (having a good musical job resume), and his wife, Tami (who had an excellent employment record of her own), had a good credit profile, which enabled them to get a personal line of credit. After giving it thought, the two of them made the decision that they would invest monies from this personal line of credit in Mark's album. Mark believed in himself and, with his wife by his side, they willingly put their money on the line - win, lose or draw. Since Joan Carol and I also believed in his talent, we signed him to a production deal. Then as a team, the four of us were off to the races.

I realize that most artists and musicians have a difficult time as it is trying to make ends meet; the local nightclub scene isn't what it used to be and gigs are harder to come by. So qualifying for a personal line of credit in order to finance an album isn't an option for many artists. But I'm mentioning it here to make you aware that there are many ways to slice a pie and it's certainly food for thought. If it's out of reach for you, take heart because you never know when your "patron-of-the arts" angel may appear out of the blue.

Family investors: As I mentioned at the beginning of this chapter, family members can also be potential investors. This was the case with a very talented religious singer/musician by the name of Deborah McConnaughy, who was funded by her parents, because they could afford to do so without encumbering their lifestyle.

Since she was a little girl, Debbie has performed at countless church events in Southern California, as well as numerous concerts for various organizations, such as the "Sons of Norway." Since her father was her number one fan, it was always his dream, as well as hers, that she would record a religious album someday.

A few years after I met this unique family, Debbie's parents, Henry and Mildred Schnathorst, decided to make this dream a reality. It was a true family undertaking because Debbie's husband, Will, wrote the album title, "A Chance to Say." Debbie's parents, her husband and their children sang on several of the tracks, which made for precious memories.

After the album was released, Debbie appeared and sang on Dale Evans' religious show on the Trinity Broadcast Network. The feedback via letters and telephone calls that have been received from numerous people whose lives were inspired by this religious album deeply touched the entire family, especially Hank. Although he prospered through numerous business dealings all his life, he felt that Debbie's album was one of the best investments he ever made.

You see, the motivation behind this album went far beyond any monetary rewards that it might reap. It was recorded by Debbie and financed by her parents as their personal offering to the Glory of God. What could be greater than that?

After all expenses are paid/fifty percent share of your album royalties: The foregoing statement is just one of many creative ways your backer could be repaid for his initial investment in your album. For instance, if you were signed to a record deal, the label would do a Master Purchase deal for whatever amount your producer and/or manager negotiates with them, which is usually more than what was initially invested.

There may be sundry expenses other than those involved in the recording project. For instance, if the producer had previously been paid for his services up front, you may have agreed to pay him a bonus if he gets you a record deal (which would be stipulated in your Production Agreement with him). But "after all expenses are paid," there should still be enough to reimburse your backer for his initial investment and possibly his rate of return (which you and your backer agreed to in your personal contract).

Now, to give the backer every opportunity to get his rate of return, you could give him a 50% share of the artist's album royalties. In other words, if you get a 10-point royalty deal, you could give your investor 5% of your 10%. Are you following me? It's actually very simple, and I hope I'm explaining it so that it's clear to you.

You are probably asking, "How long does this go on?" Look, you are only talking about this one particular album. You are not talking about your income from live concerts, radio, TV or anything else that you may have going on in your career.

So let the investor get his money back and then let him get a percentage from your royalty share of this particular album for perpetuity. "Perpetuity" in this context means that the royalties on this album are payable forever, and that's okay. Your backer deserves it because if it weren't for him, you may not have recorded this album in the first place and, consequently, may not have had the chance to go for the musical brass ring.

Two for one: Although I don't get involved in artist/investor agreements, sometimes an artist will share some of the particulars of a deal in passing, and so it was with the "two for one" deal.

This particular backer was one of the regular customers at the club where the artist had a steady gig. They would talk during the breaks and through the passage of time, they became good friends. Somewhere down the line, they started talking about albums, etc. Since the backer respected my career achievements as well as believing this particular artist had what it takes to become a star, he offered to put up the money for six cuts. He and the artist discussed the terms at length and finally came up with a formula that was agreeable to both of them.

In a nutshell, the backer was to get two dollars for every dollar he invested in the project (which would be a 100% rate of return).

Now if the artist got signed, the backer would be reimbursed for his initial investment from the Master Purchase. If there was a profit (after all sundry expenses were paid), the remainder would go towards his rate of return. If the backer still wasn't fully compensated, they came to the agreement that he would get 2% of the artist's record royalties from this particular album.

Fifty percent (50%) of your entire net profit for five years: Another way to go is for the investor to get 50% of your net profit from your income for the next five years. This would include personal appearances, artist record royalties, concessions and anything else you do in show business. The key words here are "net profit." You see, there are a lot of things you can write off before the net profit is there. Again, it all depends on the agreement that you and your backer have.

I heard through the music grapevine years ago that this fifty/fifty split across the board was the type of deal that Colonel Parker had with Elvis Presley during his entire career. I'm sure Elvis could have re-negotiated that deal or even changed managers if he had wanted to when he became a superstar. However, Elvis was committed to the Colonel and his astute knowledge of the business. (I've always believed that great management is equally as important as great talent!)

A word of advice: no matter what route you choose to finance your

161

career or your various record projects, I suggest that you and your investor get it in writing.

Corporations/overview: As you know by now, there are a number of creative ways to fund an artist, such as the various scenarios I've just mentioned. Every deal is a little different, depending on the unique situation of the artist and his investor.

Now you could either have some type of written agreement or the two of you can actually form a business entity. As I stated in my "Doing Business As" segment, there are different entities that are recognized by the Internal Revenue Service.

Regardless of whether it's a written agreement or if you've formed a business entity, some day there will be either a profit and/or a loss, which should be disclosed by you and/or your backer when income tax time rolls around.

Funding a recording project is a speculative investment or, as I like to think of it, an exciting adventure in capitalism. Since no income is likely to be generated for a while, people will probably go the written agreement route instead of a business entity.

However, I have always leaned towards corporations, which you and your backer may want to look into eventually. After all, there could always be a clause in your agreement to the effect that if the artist is signed to a major record label, a corporation is to be formed.

Obviously, I don't know how much you know about corporations. Although I have had various corporations down through the years, as well as being on the board of directors of others, this is certainly not my field of expertise. However, I will share with you some of the standard basic principles that encompass a corporation, which should shed some light on the subject.

There is a regular corporation (also known as a "C" corporation) and there's also an optional offshoot, which is known as an "S" corporation. Briefly, the "S" corporation is basically set up like a "C" corporation is; however, it has its advantages and disadvantages over a "C" corporation and vice versa.

To tease your curiosity a wee bit here, one of the advantages to an "S" corporation is that it avoids double taxation of profits (which could happen with a "C" corporation). Another advantage is any profits passed through an "S" corporation are not subject to a self-employment tax as it is in a partnership entity. Now I don't want to confuse you (or myself) with all the complexities of taxation and wages, but if the day comes when you are seriously thinking about going the corporation route, I suggest you contact a lawyer and a Certified Public Accountant. They can go over your particular financial situation and then recommend the one that would fit your needs.

It does cost money to form and maintain a corporation. In some states, such as California, you have to pay in advance an annual minimum amount of money to the Franchise Tax Board regardless of whether or not there is any income. There is also a specified dollar amount minimum to open a corporate bank account. So you should have adequate cash flow in order to maintain a corporation.

Here are three real life privately held corporation scenarios that you may be able to identify with that could open your mind to forming one someday when your particular situation warrants it.

First scenario: Being actively involved in all areas of the music business all these years, it has always been to my advantage to have a corporation. When Joan Carol and I were married, we formed one.

Being the only two shareholders with equal shares of stock, we unanimously elected ourselves to be on the board of directors and then we appointed ourselves president and treasurer, respectively. Thus, we operate and oversee the entire organization (which includes me emptying the ashtrays while Joan Carol does the windows). Any music-related expenses or income, such as producer's fees, songwriting and publishing royalties, concert performance fees, product purchases (such as books, CDs or cassettes), are processed through our corporation.

Second scenario: My son, Curtis, is one of the original members of Highway 101, and I've devoted an entire chapter to them because I believe they serve as an inspirational example to all aspiring artists. (See Chapter 26, "Keep Trucking Down Highway 101.")

As you will read in that chapter, an enterprising manager, Chuck Morris, had the unique idea of putting together a country/rock band with a country lead singer by the name of Paulette Carlson. He had them record a few songs in Los Angeles, and then he shopped their product in Nashville and they signed with Warner Bros.

After Highway 101 got their record deal, the group members (Curtis Stone, Cactus Mosure, Jack Daniels and Paulette Carlson) decided to form a corporation because it would be advantageous to their particular

163

situation. It turned out to be a wise decision because in 1986, their first out-of-the-box album had four *Billboard* Top 5 hits and two of them went to number one, "Somewhere Tonight" and "Cry, Cry, Cry."

For the next four or five years, they joined the jet set in a whirlwind tour of concerts, recording sessions, videos, media interviews, and all that goes with being a hot hit act.

As with all corporations, anything that had to do with money, such as payrolls (manager, road manager, extra musicians, etc.), concert income, album royalties, concessions, income taxes or any music-related costs (such as touring expenses), would be processed through their corporation. So it was financially beneficial for all the members of the group to form one.

Third scenario: About nine years ago, I produced an album with Larry Keyes, a country artist who had a large fan club base in a town in mid-California. Wherever he and his band played, his friends, fans and family were always there to support him at his local club gigs, as well as any out-of-town engagements, such as Reno.

When Larry decided to do an album, he and his wife, Melva, formed a corporation, and many members of his fan club, close friends and family bought stock. The board of directors was established and Larry became its president and Melva its treasurer.

Since I don't get involved in artist funding, I have no idea how many shares of stock they sold, its price per share, or how many stockholders they ended up having on their corporate books. But I was so impressed because they not only had enough money for an album, but a video as well. And one of their up-tempo tunes, "Barroom Romeos," really warranted it because this was around 1990 and the country-dance craze was building up steam. A good friend of theirs was a dance instructor and he created an original country-dance sequence to this song. The video was filmed at a very unique cowboy nightclub in their area and it turned out great!

They also had a monthly newsletter that was filled with information as to where they were performing, how the album project was coming along (it took a year to produce), and other personalized articles and photographs - just like the country stars send out to members of their fan clubs!

After we finished the album and had the cassettes and CDs

manufactured, they had a well-publicized album party, which had a tremendous turn out. Joan Carol and I attended and we were so taken with the enthusiasm that their stockholder friends, fans and family had. They all believed in their product (Larry) and felt that he deserved to have a shot at getting a major record deal. It was obvious how much pride they had in participating in the corporation as well as all the fun they were having being involved in Larry's show biz career. The corporation also invested in T-shirts and sold them at the gigs along with the CDs, cassettes and videos.

Melva kept an eagle eye on the budget and the success of their corporation was due to teamwork and cooperation by all involved.

Whether you're an aspiring artist or a potential investor, I think this corporation scenario serves as a wonderful example of artist financing, which is one of the ways you can choose to go.

Do-A-Deal, Inc.: I thought I'd give you a thumbnail sketch of a corporation's protocol and/or general rules and regulations. So let's make it interesting by hypothetically forming one.

It doesn't matter whether it's just you and a couple of other people or whether it's a Larry Keyes' type of corporate scenario, the standard basic protocol and regulations are applicable.

You've decided to record an album for several reasons. First of all, you want your chance at doing a deal with a major record label; secondly, numerous people at local as well as out-of-town gigs have asked you if you've got a CD or cassette they could purchase.

Let's say that you need to raise forty thousand dollars for an album, and your manager, as well as another close friend, wants to invest twenty thousand dollars in the project. Since you've got a mailing list of loyal fans, many of whom have expressed an interest in participating, you decide to form a corporation called Do-A-Deal in order to raise the other twenty thousand dollars.

The first thing I suggest you do is to meet with a reputable attorney in order to properly set this whole thing up. At that time, he can answer any legal questions you may have. However, if there are any income tax or accounting questions, he'll probably suggest that you ask a credible CPA.

You certainly don't need to go to one of the world's top lawyers to do this because he'll charge you an arm and a leg. Besides, that's like going to a heart specialist for a headache when all you need is the family doctor who will tell you to take two aspirin, go home and get some rest. There's a handbook that any attorney can read on how to form a corporation and it spells out all the procedures.

Naturally, any attorney will cost you money. So taking into consideration his approximate fees to form a corporation, as well as sundry expenses that would include items such as a corporate book and stamp, I would estimate the total cost would be about two or three thousand dollars. In short, your lawyer makes out the necessary incorporation papers for Do-A-Deal, as required by state laws, and then files it with the Secretary of State. In a month or so, they'll mail your corporate charter and by-laws to you. After you receive them, you can open up a corporation account at a bank and Do-A-Deal becomes a reality.

Now you need to raise capital to the tune of forty thousand dollars to finance your album (and possibly a music video). To acquire these funds, you can sell shares of stock to various people for any dollar amount you decide upon.

First of all, Do-A-Deal's product is you, and its sole business is to make you a star. Now why would anyone want to buy stock in you? Because they believe that you (the product) have what it takes to become a recording star and, therefore, they think there's a good possibility that they could make money from their investment sometime in the future. They also are aware that it's a gamble and, therefore, it has a risk factor, which goes with the territory of any investment. But since it's not their mortgage payment or grocery money that they're putting up, they've chosen to invest in you.

Each person who owns a share of stock is part owner of Do-A-Deal. For instance, if you issued 40 shares of stock for $1,000 a piece, then each person would own 1/40 of Do-A-Deal. But it's difficult to find people to cough up that kind of dough for one share of stock. However, people can spare $50 or $100 for a share, not to mention the fact that if they ever wanted to sell it, it would be easier to get a buyer at this affordable price. So it would be wiser for you to sell 4,000 shares of stock for $10 dollars apiece. Therefore, if someone buys one share of Do-A-Deal stock, then he owns 1/4000 of the company. The more shares that any one person purchases, the bigger portion of the corporate pie he or she will own.

When you sell stock, you have to issue a stock certificate to each stockholder that shows the date the shares were bought, the number of shares and what they paid for each share. The lawyer who set up Do-A-Deal will be able to advise you on this matter.

Now, once the corporation is set up and once you have stockholders, you could bargain with these investors (remember, each of them are part owners of this corporation) that you be allowed to acquire stock interest in the company at no cost to you and/or very little cost to you (particularly since you are the product). Once again, contact your lawyer; he (or she) should be able to advise you on how to do this.

Since I want to keep this hypothetical example simple, let's say that you own fifty-one percent of the stock, and the other forty-nine percent was issued to various stockholders. This makes you in control of your career and other people who are financing it.

The stockholders elect a board of directors who will handle the company operations and they, as a whole, are responsible for managing Do-A-Deal. If it's a small corporation, it could include you, your wife, your father, etc. Regardless, once people have been elected to the board, they can elect their own chairman.

Most board members are unable to give their full time to operating Do-A-Deal, so they chose a president, vice president, treasurer, etc. who will be in charge of the company operations.

As a rule, every three months, the officers will report to the board of directors on the progress of Do-A-Deal's business affairs. Once a year the board will have a meeting that's open to all the stockholders wherein the office managers will make their annual report, a copy of which should be given to all stockholders whether or not they are present.

Any stockholder can speak up if he isn't happy with the way things are going, and he can make a motion to adopt a new procedure. Consequently, the shareholders vote on the motion, etc.

Let's talk briefly about dividends. Hypothetically speaking, let's say that you didn't get a major record deal, so you've released your album on a smaller independent label. Since you have a large fan base, you sell your CDs and cassette tapes and you've made a reasonable amount of money. After you've paid all the outstanding bills, taxes, etc., you discover that you and your stockholders have made a nice profit.

So what do you do with that profit? This will be the board of director's decision. They can do one of three things: number one, they could vote to pay out that profit to all the stockholders, which is known as a *dividend*; number two, they could vote to keep it in the corporate bank account and re-invest it to manufacture more CDs or cassette tapes for future sales and/or you could record a new album; number three, they could split the difference by paying out half the profit to the stockholders and putting the other half back into Do-A-Deal. Doing the latter is known as *retained earnings*. Regardless, whenever there's a net profit, the stock increases in value.

I don't want to go any further into this because my knowledge is limited, and I don't want to inadvertently misguide or confuse you in any way. You've got enough information that should give you a rough idea of what happens at these meetings and what you and your stockholders' role is in the corporate scheme of things, which includes a brief glimpse at the dividend and profit picture.

Just remember that the important thing about any company is its earning power and its growth potential. As the artist, you're the product, and you'll be carrying a lot of responsibilities on your shoulders, which you'd have to carry anyway whether or not you have a corporation.

Let me give you several reasons why the corporation route may be the best road to travel if you have adequate cash flow. Let's say you did get signed to a major label and your first album has spawned several hits, which makes you in demand for concerts.

Now, concert dates are where you can really make the bucks. However, the corporation owns the money. But as the artist, you could also establish a weekly or monthly salary for yourself to be systematically withdrawn from the corporate bank account. Hopefully, there will be enough money in there for you to draw upon to pay for your living expenses and maybe get a new Lexus every couple of years.

But don't get too crazy with your money. Remember, you've got enormous overhead expenses when you're on tour, such as band payroll, instrument cartage, airfare, bus rental, food, hotels, and the list goes on. I would venture to say that at least half of what you make for a night's performance would have to go towards paying these overhead costs. Try to keep track of it by calling your CPA or bookkeeper at least once a month for a complete update.

Nowadays, it seems as though people tend to sue each other at the drop of a hat. When one is a celebrity of sorts, this tendency is enhanced because they automatically think the celebrity has all kinds of money.

For example, let's say that you have a payroll problem with the musicians. If they want to take legal action for whatever reason, they will have to go after the corporation. They can't nail you personally. In other words, they can't take your home, your guitar, your cowboy hat, sequinned suit or your gold belt buckle that's worth a half a million dollars by now. So liability protection is one of the reasons and benefits of forming a corporation in the first place.

Let's have some fun and project five or seven years into the future. Maybe you've become the new Elvis or Reba of your era and Do-A-Deal's stock value has increased a hundred times over. Since you've got all the money in the world, you decide you want to own Do-A-Deal completely.

When you're a superstar, a top-of-the line entertainment attorney is part of your inner circle; and he undoubtedly advised you to establish a *favorite nation's clause*, which I'll explain shortly.

So you hold a stockholders' meeting and you say, "Listen, I'd like to own all the shares of Do-A-Deal. You have forty-nine percent of the shares and I'd like to buy them all back from you. I'll pay you twenty times what you initially invested in each share of stock."

If you have a *favorite nation's clause*, you've eliminated a lot of potential problems, because all the investors would get the same deal for their shares of stock. No one gets any more or less than anyone else. If you didn't have this clause, you would have to negotiate with each individual stockholder and you'd probably end up having to give one stockholder more money than the other.

For the most part, stockholders will be happy to get their money back, especially if there's a big time rate of return. Life being life, maybe some of the original stockholders have passed away and their daughter or someone else has inherited all their shares.

I Don't Know Anyone With That Kind Of Money: I can hear some of you saying, "That's all fine and good, Cliffie. But I don't know anyone with that kind of money!" Dear reader, please finish that sentence with the word "yet." Life is full of surprises and you never know when or where someone may show up with the money.

As I've said before, there are many different sources from which artist funding can come. But the most likely source will probably be an individual who has seen you perform on stage.

You socialize with the customers during the breaks because this goes with the territory of being an entertainer, which is how you build a fan base. Some day either a well-connected music person or someone with money could say, "You're as talented as any performer I've ever seen. Why aren't you a star?" And comments like these naturally segue into an artist financing conversation. Since you know a little something about it, you may have yourself a "patron of the arts" or a "venture capitalist."

What if your major record deal isn't in the cards? I've saved this for last because I wanted this chapter and this book to be written with a positive attitude. I firmly believe that the power of positive thinking plays a major role in the success of any endeavor.

However, I also realize that one must have a realistic approach to life. I feel that if someone can accept the worst that could possibly happen, then they will be free to pursue the best that could happen.

So let's give in to "what if" for a moment. What if you gave it your best shot and your album was turned down by most of the major record labels? Well, you would be in good company because this has happened to many major acts.

One of the things you can do is hang in there like so many other acts have done when they were first turned down. Executive roulette is alive and well. Maybe next year there will be new executives at the same label, or a new independent label will open its doors.

But let's go back to square one, the record project itself. The entire process from song selection to the final master mix could possibly take six months to a year, if not longer. However, it's worth the time and effort to get a quality product.

Once it's done, your manager and/or producer enter the next phase, which is the exciting but nerve-racking process of shopping your album. And shopping a project to major labels also takes time because the wheels of the music industry move slowly.

Let's say that I was shopping your product and an executive liked what he heard. Since there are a countless number of artists who are also trying to get a deal, it takes time for him to run it past "the committee," which is made up of other executives from various areas of the company who are involved in the artist decision-making process.

It might be a month or so before I heard back from him. If they've passed on the project, then it's on to the next label.

So taking the time element into consideration, there are two things you can initially do after your songs have been mastered. Number one: you could have about ten cassettes and/or CDs made from the master mix, and this is what I'd present to the executives. Number two: if you had the funds, you could have five hundred cassette tapes and/or CD's manufactured as a finished unit, which I could also present to the label executives. In the past, I've shopped the artist's product both ways.

If I have used copies from the master mix to initially shop your product, and there's been a number of label turn downs, you and your backer may want to consider manufacturing the product. (See "CDs are a great promotional tool" section.) We could still use it to shop your product as well as promote you in other areas, which could end up being a selling point in future record label meetings.

Never ever forget that many of the major artists who have signed with big record labels were first on smaller independent record labels, which was their entrée to bigger and better things.

CD mailings/radio station promotion: If you've manufactured your product, you and your backer may want to consider doing a CD mailing to a number of AM/FM reporting country radio stations, as well as the secondary radio stations, especially in the area where you're performing or living. (Reporting stations are those stations that report their play list to trade publications such as *Billboard*, *Radio & Records* and *The Gavin Report* so that the new releases can be charted in their respective magazines. With regard to getting a list of these radio stations, check with various music organizations.)

If you did a mailing, the program director and/or one of the deejays would see your name and picture on the CD and it will make some sort of an impression on them. If they don't listen or play cuts from it on the air, it's usually because most stations are inundated with new product from major labels. It is possible that the program directors (who are usually deejays) may give your CD a listen and if he likes one of the tunes, he may play it on the air.

You see, this is a great way to start a little fire in various regions where you live and/or any out-of-town gigs where you may be performing. There is always a chance that one of the songs will grab the public's ear and heart, which could leapfrog its way to other radio stations in other regions of the state as well. This in turn can be used as a selling point for the producer while he's shopping your product. Therefore, you can see the value of putting out an album and possibly doing a radio station mailing.

Joan Carol and I used the above strategy with several of the artists that we produced. One of them was Mark Burnes, whom I've mentioned in my "Artist-Funding Formulas and Examples" section.

Since Mark had a steady club gig in the beach area where he lived, we contacted radio stations throughout the area as well as adjoining coastal communities. Through radio interviews and cuts being played from his CD, his local fan base doubled.

Intermittently, Mark and his band would also perform at the Riverside Hotel in Laughlin, Nevada. To test run our product, we contacted two country radio stations in the Laughlin area - KFLG (who reports to *The Gavin Report*) in Bullhead City and KGMN in Kingman, Arizona. Since Mark has an engaging personality, the deejays from both stations loved to interview him every time he performed at the Riverside Hotel, as well as play several cuts from his CD, namely "Bops-A-Lot Boogie." The listeners kept calling in to request this song for months, which is why the deejays put it on the play list along with the current hits of the day.

The BMI royalty checks that both Mark and I received proved that our test run was successful, which I used as a selling point later when I shopped his CD to music executives.

Now, let's get back to the "not in the cards" scenario. Before you concede that a record deal isn't in the cards for you, leave no stone unturned as you pursue your musical dream and don't put a time limit on it. Events happen on God's timetable - not yours.

But if you've done everything you can and you truly feel in your heart of hearts that it's not in the cards for you to get a record deal, then you and your support team can take pride in the fact that you had the guts to try! To my way of thinking, it's more important to be a person of substance than one of fleeting fame or material success.

With regard to your backer, let's not forget that he can still recoup a good portion of the money that he initially invested (and what he doesn't get back, he can write off on his income tax). As I mentioned in the "CDs are a great promotional tool" section, you can sell your CDs and cassettes off the bandstand. (You should get a percentage for each unit sold since you're the artist and you're also doing the sales work.) Although it may take three or four years, it can be done, because I personally know of artists who have done so in the past. However, this will depend on your promotional skills, salesmanship and long term persistence.

Regardless of whether you are a big fish in a small pond or a whale in the deep blue, you must keep your name alive before the public. Promotion is the name of the game if you want continued success at whatever entertainment level you're currently enjoying, which includes your local nightclubs and other venue gigs.

Summary: As I stated before, I'm not a lawyer, a banker or an accountant, so my knowledge is limited. What I've shared with you are my opinions and some basic thoughts about some legitimate financing deals that I've observed, which have worked in the past for various artists and investors.

You and your backer have to creatively work out your own deal that fits your particular situation. Should either of you have any questions or concerns, I suggest that both of you seek advice from someone qualified in that area, such as an entertainment lawyer and/or a Certified Public Accountant.

Artists and investors, such as the ones that I've talked about in this chapter, touch my heart and I salute them. And whether it's music, dancing, acting, painting or whatever, where would the "art world" be without artists and patrons-of-the art who dare to put themselves on the line and let the chips fall where they may?

Chapter 18

Great Management Is Equally as Important as Great Talent!

"Cliffie Stone was one of my all time heroes and role models. He was a remarkable musician, singer, songwriter, producer and manager. I had been Hank Williams, Jr.'s opening act for 21 years and when I became his manager in 1986, I looked around to see if I could extract any knowledge from someone who had experience with the business side of the industry. Cliffie was my first choice because I could relate to all the things he had done. His advice really helped me through some rough spots. I'm so glad he included a chapter about management."
-MERLE KILGORE, Artist; Manager of Hank Williams, Jr.
Hall of Fame, Nashville Songwriters Association International, 1998

Many aspiring artists, as well as professional entertainers at various stages of their performance levels and careers, have always asked me questions relative to the area of management. So I'd like to spend a little time talking about this important subject because eventually an artist is going to need a good manager, especially if he or she is within reach of getting a record deal with a major label!

The best way for me to describe the ultimate manager/artist relationship would be to equate it to a successful marriage: the artist and the manager have to respect, trust and believe in each other as well as give and take in order to make the relationship work.

I'm saying this from experience, because I spent over twenty years of my life being a manager for Tennessee Ernie Ford, as well as other artists, such as Stan Freberg, Molly Bee, Tommy Sands and Bobby Bare. Therefore, I humbly say with conviction that *great management is equally as important as great talent.*

This statement becomes even more important and downright crucial once an artist has reached a plateau in their career as an entertainer where major business decisions have to be made. Why? Because any wrong decisions can set an artist back five, six or seven years or maybe destroy their entire career as an entertainer.

But for the moment, let's start from square one and talk about aspiring artists who are getting experience in talent shows and also those entertainers who may be more advanced in their performance levels and are appearing professionally at their local nightclubs or other community venues. Whatever category you fit into presently, it will behoove you to be armed with knowledge regarding the business side of your chosen field, especially management.

At this stage of the game, you probably have someone who is helping you in some sort of a managerial way. It could be a father, brother or a friend who is in some aspect of the music field. For instance, Tanya Tucker's father, Bo Tucker, started out being her manager and continued to be when she became a big star.

Regardless of who is trying to help you, they will have their own opinions, which they believe are important to you as an entertainer and that's okay. You need to have supportive people around you, not only when you're starting out but also every step of the way as your career progresses to whatever level is finally attained. However, no matter how helpful someone is trying to be, my suggestion to you is *listen to your intuition as to what is good for you.* Someone around you may think he's a manager when in reality he really isn't. So you may have to tactfully edit out some of his (or her) opinions.

For example, let's say you met someone who believes in you and wants to invest in your album. So he puts up the cash and in the middle of the project, he starts telling you how to sing when he doesn't know the first thing about singing. Or maybe he's got a sister who wrote a song and he wants you to cut it for the album. If it's a good song, record it; if it's not, you've got to tactfully say no. Or maybe the backer will start giving his opinion on how you should act on stage. Since he's putting up the money, I suggest you listen as a matter of courtesy. But if you feel he doesn't know what he's talking about, thank him and say, "Sure, I'll try that." Then go about your business. This can be a tricky situation, to say the least. I'm candidly telling you this so that you'll be aware that these types of situations can and do occur, because it's your career.

Now let's have some fantasy fun by gazing into my crystal ball and leapfrog our way up the show biz ladder. Let's say that you've recorded four songs and a friend of yours, who is acting as your manager even though he hasn't had much experience, got them to a major label and you ended up with a record deal. Both of you are excited and you've met with various record people at your label.

While you've been in the process of listening to songs and preparing to record your first album, one of the executives suggested that you should start looking around for an established manager who has been in the business a while. Now you're torn between the loyalty of a supportive friend and the advice of an executive who appears to know what he's talking about.

First of all, I believe in loyalty with all my heart, and I'm not demeaning the capabilities of your friend or family member who was acting as your manager. However, he (or she) could be in over his head because he probably doesn't have the kind of managerial expertise or connections that it takes to properly represent you in the fast lane of the musical big leagues. With time, he can learn! Until then, he could be involved in other aspects of your career. Believe me, you'll need to have family and loyal friends around you whom you can trust and who'll be there for you no matter which way the fickle winds of fame and fortune may blow!

The point I'm trying to make is this: you may need a manager who (as the old saying goes) *knows where the bodies are buried.* In other words, someone who is well connected and knows the in's and out's of the music business.

There are exceptions to the rule, and the one I'm about to cite not only shows that a manager can *learn as he goes,* it succinctly touches upon every aspect of the manager and artist relationship that I'll be discussing throughout this chapter.

The Beatles' manager, Brian Epstein, was known as the fifth Beatle. Although he had no experience as a manager, he brought to the table his passion, belief and innate intelligence. He believed in the Beatles and fought hard to get them a deal, but every label in England turned them down. Finally, Brian got to producer, George Martin, who was in charge of a small label for EMI. He, too, became a Beatles' believer when no one else did.

After they had record success in England, Brian pursued the United States market place and was turned down by every major label. Finally a small label put out two records and when nothing happened with those tunes, the Beatles were dropped. But Brian was unrelenting and he got through to my good friend, Alan Livingston, who was the head of Capitol Records. After listening to their material, Alan signed them and put together an ingenious marketing campaign, "the Beatles are coming!" Meanwhile, Brian was determined to get them on the "Ed Sullivan Show," which he did, and they rocketed to super stardom.

During an interview one time, Brian was asked why the Beatles couldn't have done all these things for themselves since they were so bright? He commented to the effect that they were having a great time playing in the Liverpool clubs and they may not have bothered to do anything about it; and if they did, they may not have done it properly because there's so much work involved in management. Then Brian was boldly asked if the Beatles needed him now as a manager or had they gotten to the point where anyone could manage them if they had the knowledge. Brian candidly said that he didn't think they could ever be managed by anyone else.

Brian's opinion was correct. After he unexpectedly passed away, John Lennon told the media to the effect that he never had any misconceptions of doing anything other than playing music. In an interview years later, Paul McCartney said to the effect that Brian was too good of a manager and no one else would ever stack up to him because they wouldn't have had the wit, flair or intelligence. These comments show the respect they had for their great manager!

I can personally attest to the *learn as you go theory*. When Tennessee Ernie Ford's career started taking off big time with hit records and offers from prestigious Las Vegas hotels, he asked me to become his manager. I told him I didn't know the first thing about being one and he said he didn't know the first thing about being a star! So we shook hands and our word was our bond! We never had a contract! (Nowadays, I highly recommend written agreements.)

Even though I had never managed anyone before, Ernie trusted his instincts about my capabilities because I had a pretty good track record. Ernie had been a cast member on my successful radio and television shows for years. Also, I had been a Capitol Records' artist as well as a record producer, so Ernie knew first hand about my experience, dedication and love for the business. When I became his manager, I started to focus solely on his sonic superstar career because so many lifetime opportunities were happening so fast, and we had to take full advantage of them.

Another example is Kelly Brooks, Garth Brooks' brother. Joan Carol and I have been following Garth's career ever since we met him and his family backstage at the Grand Ole Opry a few days before he won his first CMA award. His original and current manager/publisher, Bob Doyle, was experienced in those areas when he took Garth under his wing.

Garth is known for his loyalty to his family, friends and business associates who supported him at the beginning of his astonishing career. His sister played bass in his band and his brother, Kelly, was helping Garth in various capacities. Both Kelly and Garth were getting a fast-forward course in learning the ins and outs of the music world as Garth was catapulting up the superstar ladder. The moral of the story: along with Bob Doyle, Kelly is now Garth's co-manager and he's earned it.

Garth is not only bright, he has a heart of gold and always takes the time to do kind acts for people. He certainly didn't get to where he is today without taking the time to participate in the business side of his career for he instinctively surrounded himself with talented business people, family and friends whom he trusted.

I admire Elizabeth Hatcher, Randy Travis' manager/wife. At the beginning of his career, Randy entered several talent shows in North Carolina. From there, he started performing at various nightclubs and, eventually, got a steady gig at a club that was managed by Ms. Hatcher. She believed he had what it took to become a star, so they moved to Nashville. She knocked on all the record label doors trying to get a record deal for him, but she was turned down. However, they didn't let that discourage them. Being a sharp businesswoman, Elizabeth learned the ins and outs of the Nashville music scene, which included the art of being a manager. Through determination and persistence, Elizabeth eventually got Randy signed to a label and his traditional country singing style has made him a major star.

Now let's get back to you and my crystal ball wherein you've gotten a deal and you're in the throes of doing your first album. Let's say that you and your friend, who has your best interests at heart, came to the decision that he'll still be involved in your career, but not as a manager at this point in time. So you're looking around for an established manager, and I'd like to discuss what you (and artists who don't have a record deal) could possibly run into.

Maybe you've got your sights on a fairly big time manager. For any number of reasons, he may not want to take you on as a client. If so, don't take it personally because you've got to understand that these great managers all have an enormous business overhead. Most managers work on a percentage of what their artists earn. So unless you're making a good income as an entertainer or unless he (or she) has foresight and believes in your talent, he may not be interested in adding you to his roster.

For example, if you're paying a manager fifteen percent and you're only making ten thousand dollars a year, that comes to fifteen hundred dollars, which isn't a lot of money. However, once you start making a hundred thousand a year, he'll be interested because the fifteen percent becomes fifteen thousand dollars. In short, as you become a bigger star, the time he invests in you will be worth it to him.

Let's look a little closer at one of these established managers. He (or she) will probably have one major star that commands big time money. The income he makes off his major artist will pay for his business overhead with a hefty sum left over for a nice profit. He can also take some of this money and apply it to other artists that he's interested in. You see, big time doors are open for these managers because of the contacts they have previously made with their major star client. So they can easily walk through that door representing a new artist on their roster.

However, there's something else you have to realize about established managers. They have to be very selective in their clients. If they have the reputation of representing great artists, the doors will always be open for them. But if they start showing up with mediocre talent, then slowly the manager will start to lose his credibility as someone who brings in exciting artists. This is why great managers have to be careful about whom they represent.

For instance, Dale Morris has been and continues to be the manager of the award-winning group, Alabama. And for some time, Dale and his management company have also been representing a fine country singer, Kenny Chesney, whom I've gotten to know since he's been on the Academy of Country Music's Board of Directors with me. Now Kenny has been in Nashville for years and has recorded three albums. You see, it takes time to develop as an artist and, as the saying goes, he is paying his dues. He's well positioned and with the guidance of Dale and his associates, he is following through on all the success building steps that are necessary to become a major star, which I believe will happen.

Let's talk about why an artist should have managerial representation. Artists are basically very sensitive and creative and it's their job to emotionally reach people through music. So it can be very difficult for an artist to fight business battles for himself while his mind and heart are focussed on the creative world of music.

For instance, an artist can't walk into an office and say, "I'm a great singer and this is what I want." Of course, there are those who have done so, but usually not at the beginning of their career. Once they become a major star, it may be a different story.

Now, I don't blame any artist for standing up for himself (or herself), especially if he thinks he's getting the shaft or isn't being treated fairly. After all, it's his career that's hanging in the balance. However, if an artist and/or his manager comes on too strong too many times, he's going to be stepping on executive toes. Then when the artist stops having hit songs, he'll be quickly dropped from the label, which, of course, can happen to any artist. However, if his manager has a reputation for being difficult to work with, the other record companies will think twice about signing him. So don't burn any bridges behind you! It's a small world and all the record executives and booking agents are closely interconnected. They know there are thousands of hungry talented artists waiting on the sidelines who are only too eager for a record deal.

Down through the years, I've heard stories about some managers who were so aggressive and annoying that they were forbidden to come into the record label's building. An artist needs an astute diplomatic manager who can negotiate and handle the thousand and one details that go with the gig. But it has to be someone who will firmly represent him without being unreasonable or overbearing.

A manager has to be available to their artist twenty-four hours a day if need be. He could get a call from him at any time of the day or night for any number of reasons. Maybe he's booked someplace and the management didn't furnish him with a dressing room or give him the advance money that he's supposed to get. Or maybe he's gotten sick and is in the hospital! Maybe he had too much to drink or got into a fight and is calling from jail for bail money! Any one of a hundred different scenarios could crop up and the manager has to take care of them.

There are endless business (and personal) decisions that have to be made on a daily basis. What songs should the artist sing? What should he (or she) say to the press? What kind of clothes should he wear? Which radio shows or television shows should he go on? Should he appear on the "Late Show" with David Letterman or would Jay Leno's "Tonight Show" give him more exposure? Most of the time, a manager has to make television show commitments four or five months ahead of time before the actual appearance.

Let's talk about the most lucrative area of all for an artist: concerts and touring. Once you and your manager make the decision on which talent agency you are going to sign with, you'll have a booking agent. Now an agent brings the gig offers to your manager and he in turn decides what jobs he should bring to you. He'll say to the agent, "Yes or no or I'll discuss it later with George." If the gig conflicts with another one on the schedule, he'll turn it down. Or maybe he'll pass on it because the gig doesn't fit your image. You see, if your manager really knows what he's doing, he'll also be advising you on what kind of an image he thinks you should have. (If the image he envisions doesn't feel right to you, speak up.)

To get my point across about image, I'll give you an off-the-wall example. Alan Jackson is a traditional country singer and if his manager was presented with a gig on the same bill with a heavy metal group, he would immediately turn it down because it wouldn't fit Alan's country image. (You would never put two acts like this together anyway because the heavy metal crowd couldn't relate to Alan's brand of music.) He has to edit out the jobs that he doesn't want his artist to be involved in. Forget about the money; it doesn't matter what it is (and this can be hard to do sometimes). However, there will be other gigs and the money will be there.

Now let's look at some of the managerial responsibilities and decisions that have to be made when international gigs enter the picture. If you're going to be touring in other countries, the manager, as well as the artist's attorney, should be involved with all the foreign contracts, which means endless long distance telephone calls, letters, fax and/or e-mail correspondence in order to negotiate the best deal for their client. Tennessee Ernie Ford performed on numerous overseas gigs when I was his manager. He once worked the London Palladium and I remember being in contract negotiations for two weeks before that deal closed.

Then there's the question of money. At least half of it should be deposited in an American bank before you even climb aboard an airplane. And exactly what are they providing you with once you've reached your destination? What are the transportation arrangements? Do they provide you with a hotel? Will it be a suite? All these details must be worked out ahead of time. It's the manager who has to make sure that his artist gets what he wants and what's due him.

After you've gotten the gig, whether it's foreign or here at home, where are you going to be placed on the program and how much time will you be allotted? For example, you might be performing with four or five other artists for the Queen of England or be on the same bill with fifteen other acts for Willie Nelson's annual Farm Aid benefit or some other humanitarian concert.

Generally, major stars are the closing act, and it sounds like a wonderful position. On the other hand, sometimes it's not. If it's an outdoor concert and people have been sitting in the hot sun consuming drinks all day, especially alcohol, they're going to be physically and emotionally tired and therefore unresponsive. Or maybe they want to go home early to beat the traffic. So this may be one of those times when it isn't advantageous to close the show. Of course, if the closing act of a long drawn out concert like I've just mentioned was George Strait or Alabama, people would wait for them. However, I just want you to be aware that there are special situations when being the closing act is not the best position on the show and your manager has to be on top of this.

With regard to the time you are allotted to perform, sometimes an act can be on too long and it gets downright boring. Generally, most artists are good for maybe twenty-five or thirty minutes. Now don't tell me about Bill Cosby, Bob Hope, George Strait, Garth Brooks, Reba McEntire or other major acts. They are in a charismatic category by themselves and can hold the audience's attention for long periods of time. What I'm talking about here is the average entertainer who does pretty well in show business, but who isn't a superstar.

This certainly applies to the aspiring artist and mediocre talent who stay on stage too long. Maybe they're great for two or three songs and then it's over - that's their act! They've done all their little tricks and the audience has heard them sing. If they do a fourth song, the audience may get restless and bored. As they say in poker, "You have to know when to hold them and when to fold them."

182

Here is where a manager comes into play because he's the guy who can say, "I think at this point in time, you shouldn't do any more than three songs" or "I don't think you should do a ballad; keep it all up tempo." You, as the artist, must have confidence in your manager so that when he (or she) suggests something, you will respectfully consider it. However, it's not wise to get involved with a manager who has a tendency to be a dictator. I have never dictated to any artist I've managed, and I don't feel other managers should do so either, because the artist will eventually resent it.

However, it's a fine line, because if the manager feels strongly about something, he should have the guts to go to the artist and say, "Look, here's what I think about you wearing an outfit like that." He should tell you why and then say, "Now, this is just my idea, but it's your career and, therefore, your final decision. But you're paying me to manage you and to give you advice. You can use it or not."

I've been involved in a number of artists' careers, and there are times when I've seen an artist turn down things that would have been great for them, but they just couldn't see themselves in that position. A sharp manager will have an instinct as to what his artist can or can't do. Sometimes an artist has no idea what he can do and if his manager has the wherewithal, he (or she) can pull something out of him that he didn't know he had.

As an example, not only did I manage Tennessee Ernie Ford, but I was also involved in all areas of his weekly NBC television show, because I was the executive producer. After the writers submitted their weekly script, Ernie and I would go over it. If I felt that something in the script was too citified and took Ernie out of his lovable country character (even if he wanted to do it), I would always find tactful ways to eliminate it and let him think it was his idea. You can take the boy out of the country, but you can't take the country out of the boy. Ernie was a natural comedian and just great at adlibbing throughout the script with his country sayings. This is what made his show so popular because he was a wonderful contrast to many of the major pop artists we booked on the show.

If you want a successful relationship, you both have to give and take while having respect for one another's feelings and opinions. Naturally, a manager isn't always going to be right and the final decision should be yours. But do be aware that he's in a position to observe you objectively, which can be a difficult thing for you to do. You may think you can, but it's a tricky thing to pull off.

I'm candidly telling you this because I've been both an artist and a manager. When I was pursuing my artistic endeavors, I found little insecurities cropping up and I was a little indecisive at times and needed the opinion of someone other than myself. Maybe I thought what I did was good when in reality it wasn't.

I never had a manager because I always seemed to be wearing three or four musical hats all at one time throughout my entire career. However, during two different seasons of my life, I always trusted the judgments of two beautiful ladies in my life. My late first wife, Dorothy, was a wonderful support system for me. Likewise, so is my second wife, Joan Carol, who is totally involved in all areas of the music business with me. I have always respected and considered both of their opinions. Sometimes it was hard for me to admit they were right (with the male ego being what it is). But I always made the final decision (or thought I did).

What I'm trying to impress upon your mind is that you should listen to your manager, especially if he (or she) has an excellent track record. Both of you may disagree at times, but work it out if you can. If you don't listen to him, then maybe you don't need him. And if your ego starts to get so big that you become too difficult to work with, there may come a time when a good manager may not want to waste his time with you. He'll just say, "Okay, you don't need me; make your own decisions; I'm out of here," and that could be your loss, which you won't realize until it's too late.

Sometimes artists who have gotten rid of their managers after they've become major stars have made some of the worst mistakes in the world. They say to themselves, "Who needs him? I know what I'm supposed to do." Well, you never really know what you're supposed to do. You may think you do, but you don't and if you ever fall into this mental mode, I wish you a lot of luck.

There are those times in an artist's career when he (or she) isn't doing so well and maybe he decides to change his manager because he thinks it's his fault. Quite possibly the manager isn't devoting enough time to him or the artist feels he can't communicate with him or doesn't trust him. If that's the case, there should be a change, and it happens all the time.

Likewise, it could also be the artist's fault. Maybe this artist has a few bad habits, like drinking too much. Maybe he's late for work or has a bad attitude or isn't as respectful to the audience as he should be. Possibly he doesn't get along with the owner or the people who are part of the organization where he's working, whether it's a radio or television station, a performing arts center, a Las Vegas show stage, a county fair or a nightclub.

Speaking of nightclubs, try to be on good terms with managers, waitresses, bartenders, security guards and bouncers. It behooves an artist to have everyone on his side when he walks on stage, and I don't care who or how big the artist is!

Having discussed the manager/artist relationship from all angles, it may appear as though I'm contradicting myself at times. However, I wanted you to be aware of all the pros and cons. This is your career and your talent is the product, but there must be teamwork between you and your manager. So respectfully listen and consider his (or her) opinion, especially if he's been around the block in the managerial field. By the same token, always stay tuned to the small still voice called instinct and intuition.

Since a manager plays such a big role in an artist's career and life, I have always wondered why the CMA and the ACM didn't have a "Manager of the Year" category. Hopefully, someone will pick up the ball and run with my suggestion. Until then, I'd like to put the spotlight on a few of these unsung heroes who, in my opinion, deserve to be in the "Manager's Hall of Fame."

Brian Epstein/the Beatles: Although I never had the pleasure of meeting or knowing Brian Epstein or the Beatles, it's beside the point. As I previously mentioned in this chapter, their unique story encompasses every aspect of the manager/artist relationship needed to become successful and it serves as an inspirational example.

Erv Woolsey/George Strait: When you've got a legend-in-the-making act like George Strait, who, deservedly, is a CMA and ACM multi-award winning entertainer, you know there has to be a great manager behind him. Well, there is and his name is Erv Woolsey, and he has been George's manager for over fifteen years. George's staying power is simple: he stays true to himself and his faithful country fans by giving them what they want to hear - traditional country music both on records and on stage, which results in one hit song after another, year after year after year. Consequently, he has sold out concerts wherever he goes!

George is the Frank Sinatra of the country field and I know that someday he'll be inducted into the CMA Hall of Fame. He certainly deserves it because he's the real deal and he keeps traditional Mother Country music alive, no matter what fad or cycle country music is currently going through! A 21-gun salute, Erv and George!

Merle Kilgore/Hank Williams, Jr.: My good buddy, Merle Kilgore, has successfully worn all the music hats.

Merle was the opening act for Hank Williams, Jr. for many years. They developed a trusting relationship and the day came when Hank asked him to be his manager. Since he had never been a manager before, Merle sought advice from me and he took to it like a duck takes to water. When a manager has been an artist, they are invaluable to their client because they've walked in their shoes.

Merle has managed him for years and they've enjoyed the fruits of their labor together when Hank, Jr. received both the ACM and CMA Entertainer-of-the-Year in 1986-88 and 1987-88, respectively.

Dale Morris/Alabama: Dale has managed the CMA and ACM multi-award winning group, Alabama, from the beginning of their fabulous career.

Many vocal groups break up after a few years of success for whatever reason, and when they learn they shouldn't mess with magic and try to make a comeback, it's often too late. But Alabama has not only stayed together as a group, they've also stayed with the person who brought them to the dance, and it's an admirable feat!

Jack McFadden/Buck Owens: Jack and I go way back to the Capitol Records' vintage days on the West Coast when he was managing the unique career of the one-and-only Buck Owens.

When he eventually moved to Nashville, he continued to shine as a top manager. One of the artists on his roster he skillfully managed was Billy Ray Cyrus ("Achy Breaky Heart"). Jack and his lovely wife, Jo, are partners in their multi-faceted music company and their doors are always open to Joan Carol and me.

And to corroborate that it's a marriage between you and your manager, I'd also like to cite a few manager/artists who have eventually gotten married as the result of their association.

186

George Richey/Tammy Wynette: Our long friendship began when he worked for my Central Songs publishing company, and he became an award-winning songwriter. Like many others before him, George became involved in other areas of the music field and became a very successful record producer and manager.

And the artist he managed was none other than the First Lady of Country Music, Tammy Wynette. Eventually, their relationship blossomed into a storybook romance, which culminated in a successful marriage for them.

Elizabeth Hatcher-Travis/Randy Travis: Although I've mentioned them elsewhere in this chapter, I'd like to make a few more comments.

After Randy became an established major star and had a great run for a number of years winning a ton of CMA and ACM awards, a new batch of artists took over the spotlight with hit songs. But with his manager/wife, Elizabeth, artfully managing his career, he not only continued to have successful concerts, he branched out and enjoyed success as an actor as well.

Cream (mixed with determination) will always rise to the top. A year or so ago, he was signed by multi-talented executive/producer, James Stroud, to a new record label, DreamWorks, and he's back on the *Billboard* charts once again big time. He, like George Strait, will always keep traditional Mother Country music alive and well!

Narval Blackstock/Reba McEntire: How can I possibly speak of a successful managerial/marriage relationship without including another ACM and CMA multi-award winning star, Reba McEntire and her husband, Narval Blackstock.

Reba, of course, is not only a great performer, but a humanitarian as well. Once, when she received one of her many awards, she paid heartfelt homage and respect to Narval by saying something to the effect that Narval was the "thinker" and she was the "doer." To me, her statement sums up the ideal successful manager/artist relationship.

In a nutshell, if you have a trustworthy personal manager, don't lose him (or her) or you will lose that bright wonderful brain that he (or she) has been devoting to you. Using the above manager/artist relationships as role models, what more can I say other than the fact that *great management is equally as important as great talent!*

Chapter 19

All the King's Men: Your Inner Circle

"Cliffie lived a life of respect. He respected the music, the artists, and the entire process (both good and bad) of the business. This is a man that stood out by opening his heart to everyone and conducted himself, always, with grace."
-LORIANNE CROOK, Premiere Television/Cable Host (TNN's "Crook & Chase")

"Fill your personal and professional inner circle with loving people who have your best interests at heart. These friendships are to be respected, nurtured and treasured, because they will make your life's journey a wonderful memory, which will warm your heart forever."
-CLIFFIE STONE

If you are participating in talent shows or have graduated in status to being a professional entertainer in clubs, you are basically doing it because you dream of becoming a major star some day, or at least taking it as far as you can go.

Should it be in the cards that your fantasy becomes a reality, you're going to need to surround yourself with various people who will be handling different aspects of your career, which is your inner circle - "All the King's Men!" After all, your talent is a product and you're the CEO of your company, so you should be aware of the inner circle structure that will comprise your business world career.

So I'll briefly touch upon some of the "King's Men" that will make up your professional inner circle:

Personal manager: I've devoted the previous chapter to the vital importance of a personal manager, and I'll succinctly sum up his responsibilities in one sentence: your personal manager basically directs and is involved in all aspects of your career.

Business Manager/Certified Public Accountant (CPA): Let's say that you've had two or three hit singles that have charted in *Billboard's* Top 10. Or maybe the album itself is in *Billboard's* Top 10. This makes you in demand on the concert tour (here is where you can really make the dough) and it appears as though you're on your way to making a fairly big name for yourself.

The money is now starting to roll in from various sources and when this happens, you'll need a business manager, and his role is different from that of a personal manager.

Being a business manager and/or a CPA is a specialized field. Generally, it's best to have both a business and a personal manager, because one can spend his time totally focussed on taking care of your money; the other can be focussed on directing your career.

However, there are those rare people who can handle both roles and John Dorris is one of them. He's a CPA as well as a personal manager; he has had artists, such as Atlantic recording star, John Michael Montgomery, under his wing for years. If you find yourself a double duty manager like John, consider yourself lucky.

Your business manager and/or CPA is responsible for advising and overseeing your entire financial picture, which includes income tax, potential investments, tax shelters and the list goes on.

Since it's important that you trust him, I recommend that you interview a number of reputable business managers or CPAs as well as check out their track records. Get the names of some of their clients and call them to see if they are satisfied with their work.

After you've made your decision, make it a habit to be on top of your financial picture. I know you have a million things on your mind, but try to have regular meetings with him at least once a month. If you can't meet with him in person because you're on the road, call him and/or have him fax or e-mail the overall figures of your finances. Get the lowdown on "where the money is coming from and going out" because financial security is important. How is he investing your money? Is it a mutual fund? If it's stocks, why is he investing it in a particular company and sector? Have him explain everything to you. You've earned your money and he's costing you a bundle as it is for his services, which will be worth it if he knows his stuff and has your best interests at heart.

If you don't take an active part in your finances, you could get in trouble with the IRS and possibly end up owing a huge sum of money. This has happened to so many celebrities. They all made big bucks, but many have ended up broke or with a small fraction of what they initially made because of a combination of things such as a high life style, unwise investments, scams, inadequate and/or sometimes dishonest business management.

For example, multi-talented country legend, Willie Nelson, has been in demand for decades. His financial picture is complex because his revenues come from song royalties, CDs/cassettes, concerts, motion pictures, etc. Like most of us, he delegated his finances to business associates, because he was on the road fulfilling his gig obligations. For whatever reason, he ended up in the "red" to the IRS, which got big time press when it happened. Since then, Willie has rectified the IRS debt, and I'll bet he makes it a priority to know the status of his financial picture now.

So no matter how much you may rely and trust someone, always be aware of what's going on in your personal financial world.

Talent agents: When you start getting a name for yourself, you will need a talent agency to represent you.

A talent agent is extremely important because concerts and tours are where you'll be making big time money. Your agent calls various venues and/or they call him. For instance, maybe your agent has a potential gig for you at the Indiana State Fair for a hundred thousand dollars. He presents it to your personal manager who thinks about it, looks over the calendar and says, "We can work that out," or "I'll get back to you after I check with George."

Do remember that the agent has to go to your personal manager, not to you. If he does attempt to go over your manager's head and comes directly to you, set him straight on the chain of command. Don't allow him to do this because you have other priorities and details to be concerned about. If you permit this to happen, then you don't need a manager and here's where you could make some big mistakes. As I've said before and it bears repeating, if you have a trustworthy personal manager, don't lose him (or her) or you will lose that bright wonderful brain that he's been devoting to you.

If you become a big star, this is when you should be represented by the powerhouse agencies, such as William Morris, Creative Artists and MCA. They have the sharpest, top-of-the line agents who can represent and negotiate deals for you in all areas of your career, such as concerts, television shows, book deals, etc.

MCA represented Tennessee Ernie Ford when he became a big star and Berle Adams was his agent. Whenever an opportunity presented itself and a deal was in the offering, Berle would bring it to me and I'd take it to Ernie. When Ernie had the opportunity to get his own NBC daily television show and later his weekly primetime show, Berle, along with Sonny Werblin, played major negotiation roles in getting the most lucrative deals for us that involved the sponsor (Ford Motor company) and NBC. These were multi-million dollar negotiations, and as Ernie's manager, I was involved in them. I had never been exposed to big deals like these before and it was a fascinating as well as a great learning experience for me.

Later, Dale Sheets took over the reins as Ernie's MCA rep and he, too, was an astute and savvy agent with great negotiating skills, who later went on to become a Vice President at MCA. After he left MCA, we joined forces and produced several Tennessee Ernie Ford television specials for PBS (Public Broadcasting). But I'll save those stories for my autobiography someday.

The important thing for you to remember is that you want a sharp talent agent who can negotiate the best deals for you - whether it's a concert, a television appearance or any other type of lucrative career opportunity. Someday, you may be fortunate enough to be in the position to make a lot of money, and you'll need an agent who is capable of negotiating major league contracts with the big boys.

Press Agent: There will come a time when you'll need a press agent. These are folks who run interference between you and the entire media. They write up press releases and advise you on what to say at media events. If need be, they are the ones who can be your spokesperson if you're not available to the media for comment.

For instance, let's say you're going to participate in the Academy of Country Music Awards show. Dick Clark, the executive producer, and the ACM usually sponsor a press conference for the media at the Country Star restaurant in Universal City. Your press agent can accompany you and be a combination of bodyguard and/or a mother hen as he (or she) maneuvers you around the media scene.

Press agents especially come in handy when there's been a newsworthy event and/or some sort of a controversy in your life. Maybe you got a ticket for drinking and driving or you've become engaged to a movie star. Maybe you're the type of entertainer who likes to be involved in politics or social causes of some sort. As I said before, if you're unavailable for comment, he (or she) can appear on television and make a statement on your behalf. Or if you're going to speak, he'll be able to help you figure out the appropriate statements you should make to the press.

In a nutshell, the press agent represents and advises you about anything that pertains to the entire media scene.

Attorney: As it is with every entertainer and celebrity, a lawyer is a "must have" in your life. For instance, if you are going to sign a record label contract, you should seek the advice of a knowledgeable entertainment lawyer and make sure your personal manager is involved so that he can keep on top of everything. Naturally, the attorney will be expensive but he will be worth it. I strongly advise you to ask questions whenever something isn't clear to you and make sure he explains it in simple layman's terms. Otherwise, you could get lost in the maze of legal jargon. You're paying big bucks for his services so get your money's worth. You certainly don't want any legal clauses to come back and bite you on the foot.

There are lawyers who also wear the manager's hat. Case in point (I'm getting legal here) is Scott Siman (Chairman of the Academy of Country Music's Board of Directors), who is president of his own corporation, rpm management. I go back a long way in the music industry with his music publisher/booking agent/deejay father, Si Siman, whose pioneering contributions to country music are enormous. Si and I both had a passionate love for music, especially country. What I was basically doing in California, Si was doing in Missouri. He was not only one of the founders of the legendary network country music show called the "Ozark Jubilee," he was also a founding member of the Country Music Association in Nashville.

Well, Si's son has done him proud! Scott spent fourteen years as an entertainment lawyer and worked his way up the show biz ladder to become a Senior Vice President of Sony Music in Nashville.

Scott is what they call "artist friendly," which means he cares and gives his all to the artists who are lucky enough to be associated with him in any way (like father, like son). He didn't hesitate when he had the opportunity to become the manager of a super hot hit act, Tim

192

McGraw, who is not only multi-talented, but one of the nicest and classiest guys in the business. Like attracts like and their association has and continues to be a highly successful one.

I guess you could say that Scott is also a manager-in-law in that Tim is married to one of the most beautiful and talented divas in the business today, Faith Hill, whom I had the pleasure of meeting at an ASCAP banquet pre-McGraw. How I love a beautiful love story and this one is it!

But getting back to the subject at hand, legalities will be coming up in all areas of your career from time to time. So it's vitally important that you have a bright trusting lawyer in your inner circle.

Summary: As I've mentioned in a previous chapter, I knew and worked for Gene Autry intermittently at different times in my life, the last one being the director/consultant of his music publishing empire.

I remember a conversation I had with Gene at one of his favorite restaurants, the Sportsmen's Lodge in Studio City. We started reminiscing about the old days and he said to me: "You know, Cliffie, practically everybody that I once had around me is now gone. Within one year, my bandleader, my beloved wife and then my secretary of forty years all passed away." My heart went out to him, for those were some of the closest people in Gene's inner circle and he dearly missed them at times. However, he was now happily married to a wonderful lady, Jackie, whose love and business acumen gave him renewed interest in life to continue on with his Angel's baseball team, publishing companies and his vast empire.

As an entertainer, you may one day have people around you like Gene had whom you can depend on as well as be a loyal friend to you. These are the people you'll be able to trust and who, hopefully, won't disclose private things about you to the outside world, such as writing an unflattering or negative book. Unfortunately, there are people who will do anything for money if the price is right - even compromise a friendship. Many family members, friends and/or employees have done this to celebrities in the past. Many celebrities will have their potential employee sign a confidentiality contract; and if they ever disclose personal things about them, there could be legal consequences. But that's the way it is and I have no other comment to make other than I respect and admire loyalty and character in people.

As you journey along in your career, you'll be meeting many new people; some will be good for you and others won't be. This certainly applies to your professional inner circle where a lot of major decisions will have to be made and you'll be relying on these people to do what's in your best interest. The test of time will certainly indicate whether or not they are trustworthy.

I cannot emphasize this enough when I say that no matter how demanding and busy your career keeps you, always be aware of what's happening in the business and financial end of it.

Regardless of the degree of success you finally attain in show business, fill your personal and professional inner circle with loving people who have your best interests at heart. These friendships are to be respected, nurtured and treasured because they will make your life's journey a wonderful memory, which will warm your heart forever.

Chapter 20

Karaoke vs. Talent Shows with Live Bands! No Contest!

"Karaoke will never replace a regular talent show as a vehicle in helping to develop potential artists to become true professionals, because it can never replace the magical vitality of performing with a live band!"
-CLIFFIE STONE

My last emcee gig for talent shows was in 1988 just before I went to work as Director of Gene Autry's publishing companies. When I began taping my thoughts for this book five years later, I thought I'd put together a list of nightclubs in Southern California that had talent contests and include them in one of the chapters.

Since I had been absent from the talent show scene, I thought I'd check with my buddy, Allen Bee, who is my eyes and ears all over Southern California. Now, there's no describing Allen, except to say that he's a loyal friend who has been involved in many of my projects, including talent shows, since 1983. Whenever I was unable to emcee any of my talent show gigs, he'd pinch hit for me. He's also an inquisitive and perceptive person who keeps me informed on the current happenings in the country music club scene.

So Allen and I got together for lunch one day. I knew, of course, that the Palomino was no longer having talent shows, and other than a unique club called the "Cowboy Palace," neither were many of the other clubs in the San Fernando Valley. When I asked him if he knew of any that were, he said, "There are no new talent night shows. After the Palomino club dropped their weekly show, the Crazy Horse Saloon in Orange County picked up the ball and it's about the only big one out here in Southern California that I know of." Since I'm an advocate of talent shows, I was rather upset and said, "Are you telling me, Allen, there are no future stars and no one wants to be an entertainer anymore?" He had a wise look in his eyes as he shook his head and said, "No that's not it. The talent is still there, but a lot of clubs have replaced talent night shows with *Karaoke* as well as deejay music." Of course, I had heard about Karaoke before but I had never taken it seriously, and I never thought it would ever replace talent shows with live bands!

Now in Japanese, *Kara* means "empty" and *Karaoke* means "empty orchestra." For those of you who aren't familiar with Karaoke, it's basically a machine that is nothing more than a CD and a cassette deck, two speakers, microphone and includes about fifty CDs and cassettes. Their cost starts at around four hundred dollars and upward, depending on the bells and whistles that are on it. The CDs and cassettes can sometimes cost you almost as much as the machine itself, which includes a booklet that has the lyrics printed on them. The more expensive units will have a monitor that feeds you the lyrics. If the machine has a recording device, you can sing along with the tracks while taping your voice, etc.

Recently, I received a Karaoke product booklet and I was just amazed! They have tracks for every music genre and artist - from standard songs to the current hits of today. It's a big time business!

Basically, here's how it works. Whether one is at a nightclub or a private party, whoever wants to sing simply picks out a song and the key they think they can sing it in. The music starts and they sing into the mike along with the tracks. It's that simple and whoever is singing can fantasize being a singer to their heart's content! It's a great way to express and release pent-up emotions!

The Karaoke principle of singing along with tapes or tracks is nothing new under the sun. This is what producers have been doing for decades in recording studios. After the musicians lay down the tracks for the vocalist in their key, the tracks are played and, as the artist sings along with them, they're being recorded.

I can remember when the first drum machine came on the music scene. The entertainer would play the guitar or keyboards while the drum machine kept time. This upset drummers because it took gigs away from them, but there was nothing they could do about it.

Actually, professional entertainers have been doing a form of Karaoke for a long time at clubs. About eighteen years ago, I decided to stay overnight at a big hotel in Orange County after one of my concerts at Leisure World. As I walked into the lobby, I heard a big band playing in the bar and the singer had a wonderful vocal group backing him up. It sounded fantastic! So I rushed in there and to my amazement it was just one guy on a little five by five-foot stage. It was just big enough for a stool, a mike and a machine. There he was playing his guitar and singing along with big band music that came out of cassettes! To his right was a big rack with several hundred cassettes and I was fascinated with the whole thing. If I had closed my eyes, I would have thought it was the Glenn Miller Band - that's how good it sounded!

Someone was celebrating a birthday so he just turned the rack around until he came to the tape with "Happy Birthday." He put it in the tape deck and sang along with this big lush band sound and included the person's name in the appropriate spot. Everybody just fell down and was tickled to death! In essence, what this entertainer was doing with cassettes was the beginning stages of Karaoke. But there was and is one "big difference," which holds true today. This was truly professional entertainment, which doesn't get boring!

I can understand why Karaoke is popular because it can be a lot of fun at private parties. However, in my professional opinion that's where it should stay.

Speaking of private parties, Joan Carol and I have been to a number of homes for various celebrations and some of them have had Karaoke entertainment. I recall this one party where there must have been about sixty people. After everybody had eaten, socialized and had a few drinks, our wonderful hostess said, "It's time for entertainment." I thought, "Oh, good!" So she opened the doors to her large den, where she had set up their Karaoke machine with big time speakers and a stack of CDs. I was disappointed that she didn't have live musicians there (outside of myself), but I watched while almost everyone took turns singing. They would pick out a song they thought they could sing and sang along with the CD. Well, you can imagine the level of entertainment. We laughed a lot and it was okay for a little while! It wasn't too long when some of the people who had been singing earlier wanted to sing again. But this time they picked out songs they didn't know as well and they couldn't hit the high notes or stay in tune. Pretty soon, people started wandering back into the kitchen where the food and bar were and they totally ignored the Karaoke entertainment.

Being a professional entertainer, I'm very partial to live bands. As much as I love people and encourage aspiring artists to wholeheartedly try their hand at singing, I'm not too keen with what's currently happening in the nightclub scene. Sadly, many clubs have done away with bands and professional entertainment for the most part. They have opted to either have a Karaoke machine and/or deejay music. (Deejay music is a guy who has a stack of CDs of various music genres and he plays them like a deejay would on the radio. Many of the nightclubs that cater to the dancers have them and they're also very popular at private parties.)

A Karaoke bar makes the audience become the performers and is, therefore, the evening's entertainment. Basically, this really sounds cool because anyone in the audience can get up and perform. There will be those folks who have always wanted to sing, but being amateurs, they usually have a couple of shots of scotch in order to summon up the courage to get on stage. If you're in the audience and the same man or woman (who continues to take a few belts of vodka all night long) gets up eight times and sings "Desperado" out of tune, it gets boring fast. Let's face it, the people in a nightclub audience who get up to sing really aren't going to be that good. Meanwhile, there are customers who don't want to sing and they're sitting there paying good money to be entertained. I'm speaking from experience when I make all these statements, because I've been to numerous clubs and I personally saw the people get up from the audience and try to sing with a machine.

So it's my opinion that Karaoke is strictly for amateurs who don't really care about singing that much. Sure, it's a hoot for them to get up and sing before an audience, but it's not part of their dream that comes from their inner most heart's desire, which is the point I'm trying to make.

Yes, nightclubs can save money as well as the time it takes to deal with hiring bands by having a Karaoke bar instead of professional entertainment. However, I predict that someday Karaoke will finally die of boredom in a club and we'll get back to bands and professional entertainers - at least I hope so!

By the same token, Karaoke does have value in the scheme of things. I can understand why a singer who is performing for a church event and/or a community function would use their Karaoke machine with its mike, speakers and tapes. It makes life simpler because they won't have to spend time or money hiring musicians, especially if they don't have the funds. In fact, I've used Karaoke singers when I had my free c/w shows for my community. I'd put them on during the break while the bands were changing.

There also have been artists who have pursued my services as a producer, and they'd send me tapes in which they sang to pre-recorded music. It sounded wonderful and it was a factor in my decision to produce an album with them.

I recently read in one of those Karaoke promotional booklets wherein they were advertising a national Karaoke singing contest. So these type of contests are available to the aspiring singer, and it's a positive thing because it helps aspiring artists to get experience in getting up on stage and performing in front of a live audience.

However, I've seen Karaoke singers try to perform with a live band and they didn't do very well. They looked so uncomfortable up there! They didn't have the natural stage presence that comes from the experience of working with a live band wherein they and the band become a living, spontaneous vibrant unit. Also, some of them have become too reliant on a monitor that feeds them the lyrics.

I don't think Karaoke will ever replace a regular talent show in a nightclub or any other venue as a vehicle in helping to develop potential artists to become true professionals! It can't replace the magical vitality of performing with a live band, especially if they're trying to make it in the big time music world.

Chapter 21

Talent Night at Barnes & Noble

"I was the guest speaker at a Barnes & Noble's workshop, which they called 'Writers' Harvest.' As I listened to these aspiring writers recite what they had written before their peers, I realized this was their 'talent night.' This was their 'show time' at Barnes & Noble!"
-CLIFFIE STONE

There are millions of bookstores all over the United States. In the midst of them is the Barnes & Noble Booksellers chain, and they are one of the classiest because they are geared to bringing back the people into their establishment again and again.

When they opened up a Barnes & Noble store in my community of Santa Clarita, California, I was as happy as a lark! Whenever Joan Carol and I can break away from our music projects, we meander over there to spend a few relaxed hours browsing through their incredible book selection. Sometimes we'll have a cup of coffee and a bite to eat at their sandwich bar. Afterwards, we sit down in their big comfortable chairs and continue to read (or take a nap). It's a great way to spend an afternoon and we always end up buying one or two books for our own personal library.

Naturally, when I saw that they had my book on their shelf, *Everything You Always Wanted to Know About Songwriting But Didn't Know Who to Ask*, I was beside myself. As an author, it's quite a thrill to see your book among thousands of others in such a prestigious bookstore like this one. No one lives forever, and long after we're gone, our words will continue to live on.

I decided to introduce myself to the manager because I wanted to thank her for having my book in their store. Being a local hometown celebrity and author, she was so gracious and said some very flattering things to me. When she invited me to speak at several of their writers' workshops, I was honored.

I've performed for audiences at various venues as well as radio and television all my life. When I wrote my songwriting book with Joan

Carol, it was old hat for me to promote it on radio and television shows. But it was a whole new ballgame for me to have speaking engagements at various organizations such as book clubs, women's clubs, the Toastmasters and now Barnes & Noble.

As I mentioned in Chapter 11, my first appearance at Barnes & Noble was a combination of a book signing and writers' workshop, which was held on September 14, 1996. Barnes & Noble promoted it and the turnout was fantastic. It started at 7:30 p.m. and lasted for several hours. I asked a good buddy of mine, Mike Ley (one of the members of the legendary Western group, Riders of the Purple Sage), to bring his guitar, and we put on a little ten-minute opening show before Joan Carol and I started discussing various chapters in the book. One of the chapters was about poetry, so we took several of her poems and showed the audience how songs could be created from them. It was a stimulating evening and the writing group asked a variety of questions and we sold quite a few books.

I was the guest speaker at another Barnes & Noble's workshop that was held a month later on October 17th, which they called "Writers' Harvest." This group of aspiring writers met here every two weeks. I was blown away with this wonderful event because I never knew Barnes & Noble had anything like this available for the public. Tonight was to be the final class for the year and all the folks who had attended all these months were asked to stand before their peers to read something they had written as a grand finale.

There must have been about twelve writers there and I sat quietly and listened to each one of them. I was not only impressed by the quality of their writing but also the selection of their material. All of their ideas were unique and different.

My favorite was a passion-filled poem entitled "Trivia," which was written by a lovely senior citizen named Ann. What she wrote was short but inspired writing that had depth and meaning. She wanted to be a writer, but she already was only she didn't know it!

As I listened to these aspiring writers recite their material, I realized this was "talent night" for them. This was their "show time" at Barnes & Noble! By standing up before an audience, they were performing and presenting their writing talent. If they made any mistakes, this was the place they could make them. This was probably the most important time they could have to explore their creative abilities. So they must give themselves TLC (tender loving care) and be aware that they are at a delicate stage and must be very careful about not letting their dream slip away.

My previous two sentences apply to all aspiring talent! Everyone is entitled to his or her dreams and fantasies! If someone dreams of becoming a writer, that's their own little box of rocks! That's what they enjoy doing. All too often, people will make one or two little efforts, and if something big or spectacular doesn't happen right away, they quit doing it. They say to themselves, "I'm no good or I shouldn't have tried that."

You (and everyone) have to understand that writing poetry or writing a song or learning to be a great singer or musician is not something you try half-heartedly, but whole-heartedly. You have to go into it with a full commitment - not whenever you feel like it.

I can hear some of you saying that you've got responsibilities such as a family, and you can only write when you have a few spare moments. I can understand that, but when I say commitment, this is what I mean. You will have to make up your mind to give yourself a fair chance at developing your talent. If you have half an hour a day to pursue writing or whatever, do it in a concentrated and disciplined way. More can be accomplished in a disciplined thirty minutes of concentration than in two hours of half-hearted effort. By giving your budding talent a chance to blossom, you are contributing to your own talent.

There are thousands upon thousands of writers' groups and classes available in schools and other facilities across America. If you have any interest in writing novels, poems or whatever, you may also want to check out your local Barnes & Noble.

And to Barnes & Noble Booksellers, I salute you!

Chapter 22

Star School: A Letter From Susie

"Dear Cliffie: Go out and perform and contact me in five years."
-JACK BENNY

"Dear Mr. Stone: I am sixteen years old and I want to enroll in your 'star school,' because I feel I'm ready to be a singing star like LeAnn and Reba."
-SUSIE

"LeAnn Rimes was six years old when she auditioned for my music revue show and she became a cast member. I remember one night when she came off the stage and a lady asked her what she wanted to be when she grew up. LeAnn looked up at her and said with conviction, 'I'm going to be a star.'"
-JOHNNIE HIGH, Producer of the "Johnnie High Country Music Revue"

Down through my sixty-plus years in the entertainment field, I have received my share of letters from fans and aspiring artists. What celebrity doesn't enjoy reading the adoring comments from their fans? This is why we perform in the first place, because we crave the spotlight, attention and applause from an audience! So I have always enjoyed my fan letters and was thrilled that I could bring happiness to people through my music and comedy.

But my favorite letters were and are the ones from aspiring talent who write and ask for advice on every conceivable aspect of the music business imaginable. This is due to the fact that my book *Everything You Always Wanted To Know About Songwriting But Didn't Know Who To Ask* is in libraries all over the United States, Canada and a few foreign countries. These letters have been a big factor in motivating me to write this book.

Recently, I received a delightful letter that I'd like to share in order to give you an idea of how youngsters think and feel out there in the world who have been bitten by the wanna-be-star bug.

Dear Mr. Stone: I'm sixteen years old and I've been singing since I've been five years old. I've sung at church events, family functions, benefits, high school plays and I won a talent contest two months ago.

203

My family and all my friends tell me that I'm really gifted.

I'm enclosing a picture from my high school yearbook, which was taken last year. I look pretty much like this today except I'm a year older and my boyfriend thinks I'm even better looking now.

I'm writing you all this because I wanted to give you an idea of how much experience I've had. I feel I'm ready to be a singing star like LeAnn and Reba, so I would like to enroll in your "star school." I'm setting aside the next few years of my life to do this and I hope to be a star by the time I'm twenty years old.

If it's not too much to ask, could you please send me your phone number so that I can call you and you can give me some advice on what I should be doing to achieve my goals?

I'm looking forward to hearing from you, Mr. Stone, and all the facts about "star school."

Sincerely, Susie

Down through the years, I've received thousands of letters that were similar in nature from the young Susie's-of-the-world who are truly interested in knowing how to proceed with their music careers. You may think she's too young, but there are a lot of young singers in Nashville who record labels are putting big bucks behind, and it takes around a half a million dollars to break an act! In today's market, Nashville's country music scene is made up of young talent that executives and producers try to mold and develop into star material (and they appear to be getting younger all the time).

LeAnn Rimes is a perfect example (which is probably what inspired Susie to write me). In Chapter 10, I mentioned the "Johnnie High Country Music Revue," and LeAnn was six years old when she auditioned for that show. Eventually, she became a regular cast member and performed there for years, which is where she obviously got her experience.

The first time Joan Carol and I ever saw LeAnn perform was at the Hacienda Hotel in Las Vegas where she sang at a state country music organization competition when she was about twelve years old. As I listened to her, it occurred to me that country music seems to be a golden stepping-stone for young girl singers, more so than any other field of music.

I remember what Mike Curb (the genius behind Curb Record's empire) said about her on one of the award shows when he joined her on stage as they picked up an award together. He said something to the effect that it was her genius that deserved all the credit. In large part, this may be true, but I believe that promotion also plays a huge factor. Mike's record company believed in her and aggressively promoted her and this, along with her precocious singing gift, has made her into a top selling recording artist.

Since then, I've watched how LeAnn handles herself on network television shows and I'm so proud of her. She is respectful, has a great attitude and she's a wonderful representative of country music.

It will be interesting to watch another up-and-coming young singer, Lila McCann, who was discovered by Mark Spiro, one of the most naturally gifted musicians and songwriters I've ever met.

At one time, Mark was in the process of buying my Rolling Stone Ranch, and he had his recording studio set up in one of my buildings on my property. Although I didn't personally meet Lila, she recorded a few tunes on my ranch, including "Down Goes A Blackbird," which helped her to get a record deal with Asylum. When her album was released, it charted on *Billboard's* Top Forty.

New artists who become superstars at a young age are rare, but not unusual. Generally, aspiring artists have to patiently earn their stripes before they make the quantum leap to stardom status.

As I shared with you in Chapter 2, when my successful "Hometown Jamboree" variety show was on television, I would announce the time, place and date for anyone who was interested in auditioning. Among the young potential star candidates was Molly Bee! She was a natural from the get-go and she gained invaluable experience during the years she was on "Hometown Jamboree." When Molly left my show in her late teens, she continued moving up the show biz ladder to become a successful recording star, nightclub entertainer and movie star. She also toured with Bob Hope for several years entertaining the troops. Not bad for a twelve-year old youngster with long braids and freckles on her face, who bravely climbed up on my "Hometown Jamboree" stage, grabbed a mike and, uninhibitedly sang her heart out, is it?

So there's nothing new about youngsters becoming stars at an early age. A few of them include Brenda Lee, Tanya Tucker, Judy Garland, Wayne Newton and the list goes on.

For the youngsters who are reading this book, I briefly gave these examples to inspire you, because what these artists attained with their talent, you can also attain. It's young people like you who pick up the music baton, which keeps the song of life moving along.

Let's get back to Susie's letter, which I feel is important. As you were reading it, you may have thought she was too naive, bold and overconfident and may have laughed a bit. However, I hope you also felt respect for her because it took courage for her to write me in the first place. Aspiring artists like her believe in their own abilities and talent; if they didn't, then how will they get anyone else to believe in them? I truly feel that the single most important attribute that artists have to have is belief in themselves, which is why I devoted a whole chapter to it in this book, "Believe and Be: It's Your Call!"

Another reason why Susie's letter touches my heart is because I can personally relate to it. Decades ago, I was a wanna-be-comedian and I, too, wrote such a letter to my favorite radio comedian, Jack Benny, whose mannerisms and style of comic delivery are still being imitated today. In my letter, I asked Mr. Benny to help me make it in show business - just like Susie asked me!

Months went by and I finally gave up on ever getting an answer. Then one beautiful day when I looked in the mailbox, I saw Jack Benny Productions on an envelope and I can't begin to tell you how excited I was. I quickly opened the letter and, with a pen, he had personally written in long hand:

"Dear Cliffie: Go out and perform and contact me in five years."

-Jack Benny

In one succinct simple sentence, Jack Benny gave me the best advice anyone could ever give, which I wholeheartedly followed. Although I never wrote back to him after five years, I appreciated the fact that he had taken the time to kindly write me.

By the way, on March 1, 1989, I was presented with my very own star on the Hollywood Walk of Fame near the corner of Sunset and Vine - just three stars away from Jack Benny! On that special day, I couldn't help but think of that letter I sent to him so many years ago nor can I begin to tell you how proud I was and still am!

Summary: In Jack Benny's note to me, did you notice the word *perform*, which I've mentioned throughout this book? That's a key word for young aspiring artists who want to try their hand at becoming a star. This is why I believe that the most important stage in the world is the talent show stage, where aspiring artists can get experience "performing" before a live audience. Money can't buy this priceless stage experience and, if you have an attitude of "gladly earning it," you'll have an edge on the competition.

Once again, I mention the "Johnnie High Country Music Revue," which is one of the stages that LeAnn Rimes performed on as she climbed up the show biz ladder. Johnnie was there one night when young LeAnn came off the stage and a lady asked her what she wanted to be when she grew up. LeAnn looked up at her and said with conviction, "I'm going to be a star."

What is wonderful about your local talent show and/or shows like Johnnie's is that it presents new talent, which is basically an inexpensive "star school." So I encourage you to enroll in your local "star school," which can be talent contests at schools, nightclubs, organizational fundraisers and/or other venues such as churches, benefits or music halls that showcase new talent. Who knows - you could graduate at the top of your "star school" class and become a star just like LeAnn, Reba or Garth!

So I say to Susie and all the aspiring artists of the world who are reading this book: simply get up and perform wherever there is a stage! Then, as Jack Benny wrote, "contact me in five years."

Chapter 23

Look at Me! Applause, Applause, Applause!

"Why do most artists have this need to be the center of attention and to hear applause? Regardless of the reason, to 'do' and to 'be' is more important than the 'why' of it. So excuse me while I go turn on my applause machine!"
-CLIFFIE STONE

Since the days of the ancient Greeks and Romans, every stage in the world has been watched over by two Gods: one of tragedy; the other comedy, and you've probably seen the famous facial masks that symbolize them. These two basic emotions influence every area of the Performing Arts.

During the creation of this book, I've become fascinated with "why" anyone would be interested in becoming an artist in order to express these two emotions and the multitude of variations in between. Maybe it's me that I want to self-analyze, because I've had this need to be on stage for as long as I can remember and I still do!

Regardless, what is this desire to be in front of an audience all about, so that he or she can hear applause, applause and more applause?

As sort of an addendum, I decided to share my thoughts about this subject because I thought you'd like to have an idea of "why" you want to be what you want to be. Besides, this need or desire can sometimes be very difficult on your relationship with your mate, which could lead to trouble in paradise. By trying to understand and accept yourself, you can honestly say, "This is what I am."

Now, I thought that I had already emptied my "smart jar" in this talent show book. However, during one of my "almost awake, almost asleep purple fogs" that I get into just before I go to sleep or as I'm waking up, my eyes opened and suddenly my right and left brain finally kicked in together. I clearly saw what that hidden element was, which I hope will hit a hot nerve to really rattle your cage as to why you have this need and desire!

Power and control: The "buzz words" that I had been searching for are *power* and *control*. Through performing, you actually have power and control over the emotions of your audience. Think about it! Every human being in the room is attentively listening and you have the power and control to make them laugh or cry with you. Possibly the show biz term might be "big time ego." If you disagree with me, that's okay. We're all entitled to our opinions.

Being a performer myself, I can tell you first hand that once you've experienced that kind of power and/or control over an audience, you crave it again and again. How I love to make people laugh and to hear them clap for me! Joan Carol knows how much I need this, so she'll spontaneously applaud me at least three times a week whenever I walk into a room, which makes me feel good and we always have a good laugh together about it. Naturally, I take a bow. What can I say? It's silly, it's fun and I love it!

Let's look at some of the one-of-a-kind superstars such as Frank Sinatra and Ms. Peggy Lee, who have incredible charisma on the stage. Both of them have spellbinding power and control over their audiences, and with the minimum of body language they can make every person in the room feel whatever emotion they are feeling, whether it's happy or sad. Of course, women are attracted to power, which Frank Sinatra has always had over women.

From the beginning of his career, Elvis Presley had hypnotic power and control over women. Of course, his body language was different from the cool and debonair Frank Sinatra in that Elvis had body language that created quite a stir with the public when he first exploded on the scene, which continued to drive females of all ages wild throughout his entire career. Every generation seems to have these charismatic heartthrobs.

The power of performing and its control over audiences can be addictive. Since an artist is merely sharing and expressing his innermost emotions that audiences identify with, I don't think there's anything wrong with it. After all, it's a gift from God in the first place and entertainers are sharing that gift with the world. Hey! I know I'm a good guy and I've had this need to be in the spotlight all my life. So let me share some of my analytical enlightenment with you, which is my opinion.

It begins when we are babies: I heard somewhere that the first six years of anyone's life are the most important because our basic personality and habit patterns are formed. That being the case, it occurred to me that from the moment we take our very first breath, we are asked to *perform* in some manner. So I made a little list of things in which a baby "performs."

Although a baby can't talk yet, he learns how to manipulate and push his parents' buttons. If he cries for any length of time, one of them (usually his mother) will come pick him up. Soon the baby begins to feel as though he is in *control*. In a sense, he's performing to fulfill some sort of a need, whether it's to be changed, cuddled, fed or loved. Talk about having *power* and *control* over people!

Soon baby notices that his mother and father will show their approval with gushy happy sounds, and these sounds occur when he's done something right. So baby thinks, "I've done something good!" This makes baby feel happy because he now knows that it's a good thing to please an audience, which are his parents. And so it begins: the habitual need for *applause*, *approval*, and possibly *power* and *control*.

As our adorable baby starts to grow and become more alert, he will learn to watch and get approval from his audience of one, two or three people. One of baby's performances, which his audience loves, is to giggle at those human beings who are tickling him and practically standing on their heads to make him laugh and smile. And there's this click and flash that seems to go off every day. For all we know, this is where baby starts to develop a love affair with a camera and gets his first taste of being a celebrity.

Then the day comes when he speaks his first words, which will probably be mommy or daddy. The coos, hugs and kisses of approval that he gets from just making that sound may be the subconscious reason he wants to sing before an audience someday.

Another historical day (or should I say hysterical day) occurs when baby starts to crawl. Then he takes his first few steps and his audience practically gives him a standing ovation. However, once he begins to walk, the initial reaction of joyous approval can be short lived. Walking soon turns into running and you better clear the coffee table - clear everything! You always knew where he was before he learned to crawl and walk. But now that he's up and about, you never know where you're going to find him and it seems as though you're always looking for him. This is the day when parents begin to notice their first few gray hairs.

When baby begins to learn how to dress himself, he gets a high approval rating from his parents. (That is, until he decides to make a fashion statement when he's sixteen and dyes his hair orange.)

Since he's been born, baby has been hearing all these raves of approval from mommy and daddy for almost every act he does and he's a happy little camper about the whole thing.

However, panic can set in when he attends his first day at pre-school or kindergarten and his umbilical cord gets its first snip, which can be a traumatic experience for both the mother and child. If baby keeps screaming for his mother, she may decide to put him in private school (only to discover he'll probably scream there, too). But once he learns to like school, it's time for more applause.

The day comes when daddy gets him a bicycle and shows him how to ride it. Once he does, there will be applause (which may wane someday if he gets a leather jacket, lets his hair grow and becomes a biker and then trips out on some records by a rock or heavy metal group).

All too soon, he's in high school. He becomes a star athlete and discovers that this is one great way of having his pick of the young ladies who adoringly applaud his performance. (This may also be one of the reasons why he chooses to be an artist or a musician!)

After he graduates, he has to decide what he wants to do with his life. Maybe he and his parents have discussed it. He wants to be in the acting or music fields, but his folks want him to get a real job or go to college.

Using myself as an example, I had a football college scholarship offered to me, which my beloved mother encouraged me to pursue (especially since she approved of my first high school sweetheart, who would be attending the same college). However, my father was a musician, so he encouraged me to pursue my music interests. By age sixteen, I was playing bass and appearing with my dad on Stuart Hamblen's "Lucky Stars" radio program. This was my first taste of applause and peer approval, which hooked me. When I graduated from Burbank High School, I had to choose between college and music. Being an only child, I was torn between the approval of my mother and my father because I loved both of them dearly. I choose to follow my heart because I had this need to perform. But all's well that ends well, because both my parents applauded my radio and "Hometown

Jamboree" television successes, which my dad was a cast member. Those years are precious memories to me!

Dressing and acting the part: It seems to me that as life goes on, there continues to be the need for approval and applause from our loved ones and peers.

Before I go on with our young man who has to choose his role in life, I want to add another element that goes hand in hand with this approval and applause craving - *dressing and acting the part.* As an actor (see Chapters 11 and 5), one of the most important things I learned was to "dress the part." When you dress the part, it will help you to act the part.

Children learn to dress and act the part at an early age, and it all begins with Halloween. If a little boy is dressed like a cowboy, he may chase his little sister around trying to lasso her (which may not get applause). If a little girl has a nurse's uniform on, she may start taking everyone's temperature and handing out aspirins. Except for the lariat act, their parents will applaud their cute performances.

Generally, whatever career our hypothetical young man chooses, he basically has to *dress and look the part.* If he's chooses to be a doctor, he wears a stethoscope that hangs down the front of his long white coat. If he's a policeman or baseball player, he wears a uniform, etc. In short, he dresses the part of the role he's playing.

Let's say that our young man has chosen to be a businessman, so he dresses in three-button suits, which is the required dress code of the company he works for. Being bright, he's climbing up the corporate ladder at a fast rate and has gotten a taste of power and control over other employees in his company. Ten years later, he's been promoted to either vice president or president and he enjoys making decisions and pulling all the strings. Although he enjoys his prestigious position and its monetary rewards, it turns him on to have the power and control that comes with it and his ego is at an all time high. However, he's a good family man and an all round good guy who has made the most of his executive gift. So our baby to manhood scenario has turned into a success story.

Summary: I've tried to make my analytical addendum somewhat amusing because heavy-duty stuff can be just that - too heavy! Quite frankly, I never gave any thought as to "why" I had this need to perform until I started writing this book.

If you've discovered that you, too, have this need and want to do something about it, I hope that your mate, relatives and friends will respect your desire and say from the bottom of their hearts, "That's great! We'll be there to support and applaud you!"

I believe that to 'do' and to 'be' is more important than the 'why' of it. In other words, it's okay! Have fun and enjoy every second of your fantasy!

Now excuse me while I go turn on my applause machine!

Chapter 24

Caution! Slippery When Snowed!
Promises, Promises!

"All my suggestions are solely directed towards legitimate ethical talent shows and other music-related projects. But be aware of scams and unscrupulous people who may try to 'snow' you with misleading statements and false promises."
-CLIFFIE STONE

At one time or another, you've seen highway signs that *caution* you of potential road hazards, such as *slippery when wet.*

Well, as you're traveling down the highway of dreams pursuing your musical fantasies, I, too, want to *caution* you of potential musical hazards - *slippery when snowed.* In other words, be aware of scams and unscrupulous people who may try to "snow" you with *misleading statements and/or false promises* about music-related events/projects (recording sessions, talent shows, showcases, etc.), which I am opposed to. They deliberately do this to make money off you, and they don't follow through on their claims or promises. Being forewarned is to be forearmed.

I am grateful to God that I've been so lucky in the music business! I've written this book with the best of intentions in order to help and encourage aspiring artists, producers and everyone who is interested in the music industry to be all that they can be. It's my way of giving back! All my suggestions and advice that I've candidly written in this book are directed solely toward ethical talent shows and other music-related events/projects.

It goes without saying that scams, shams, schemes and various ways of trying to fleece someone out of money are nothing new under the sun and they happen in every business industry imaginable. I don't want to dwell too long on this negative subject, but it does exist in the music business and I would be remiss if I didn't make some comments that should give you food for thought.

Money, of course, is one of our prime concerns because we all have to buy groceries, support families, pay bills, etc. As they say in the business world - time is money! Everyone has a right to make money. Everyone deserves to be paid for his or her time. Most people do it through honest and ethical endeavors; others don't.

In Chapter 15, "Have Fun Producing Money-Making Talent Shows," I emphasized to potential producers that the bottom line is to make money from talent contests so they can keep the show's budget on track and in the "black." Otherwise, it may end up in the "red" and the producer may have to take money out of his own pocket to pay the bills, which isn't fair to him. I candidly discussed various ways that money can be made via talent shows and also advised him to be *reasonable* and *fair* - both to the aspiring artist and to himself - when deciding the entry fee, cover charges, etc. After all, there are numerous costs involved in the entire project of putting it together, not to mention the venue's operating expenses as well. In short, if revenue isn't made, there may not be another show. It's simple economics and everyone can certainly understand and accept that premise. However, I am opposed to money being made through misleading statements and/or false promises in any type of music-related event or project at the emotional and monetary expense of aspiring artists.

Pre-sale tickets: Although my talent shows were basically country/western oriented, I had an open door to all music genres here in Southern California. Down through the years, I've known a number of struggling rock 'n' roll musicians who told me that if their band had showcases or wanted to get exposure in a nightclub, they had to buy about a hundred pre-sale tickets from the club, which is legal. Then the members could either sell or give the tickets to their friends. Naturally, the reason the clubs did this was to insure that they could make money on the night of the band's performance. The more people in the club, the more drinks and food/snacks can be sold. That's what they are in business for!

Over the years, groups have complained about it, so pre-sale tickets have taken a back seat. However, it's six of one and half dozen of the other because here is what the clubs do instead: the band has to guarantee the club that a certain number of people will come into their place on the night of their performance. Of course, there is a cover charge (which most venues have) and the club will keep a head count.

If the band doesn't bring in the approximate number of people that they said would be there, the club won't use them again. I realize that it may not be financially fair to the musicians because, in a sense, they are paying to play. What can I say, other than it's the hard cold facts of the nightclub business? (Incidentally, this is why I always felt that country bands could make a better living as musicians than their rock counterparts, as well as having longevity in the business!)

The reason I've discussed rock bands and the pre-sale ticket method is because, often times, this will be a prerequisite for contestants if they want to enter talent shows, which is legal. I'm sure some people may feel it's unfair and complain about it. But if they understand how costly it can be to put together a talent contest (or any event for that matter), they'll realize that it's just another way to make revenue to cover all the show's expenses.

As an emcee, I have always encouraged aspiring artists to bring family and friends with them whenever they appeared in talent shows. Of course, I'm a ham and I love big audiences - the more the merrier (plus the bills can get paid).

Talent shows (financially speaking): I've noticed some talent shows use the word "legitimate" in their advertisments and flyers. Because a talent show can't be described as "legitimate theatre," which refers to certain plays acted by professionals, I assume that when they say it's a "legitimate talent show," they are implying that it's a sanctioned legal show and, financially speaking, you don't have to be concerned about getting ripped off.

Now, I think the only way talent shows could put a dent in your pocketbook is to overcharge on the entry fee and/or cover charges for the public or anything else they sell at the show, such as a video of your performance. If you have concerns about any of these issues, you have the choice and the power to immediately do something about it. If you feel the entry fee is too high, don't enter. If pre-sale tickets are a prerequisite to entering a contest and you don't like that idea or feel they are too expensive, don't enter the contest and, therefore, you won't have to buy them. If pre-sale tickets aren't involved, but there's a cover charge instead that friends in your support group may feel is too high, they don't have to come to the show. If you think the drinks are too high, don't buy one (unless there is a drink minimum policy). If you feel the video is overpriced, don't order one. However, if you gave them money for a video up front, and never received it, then you do have a legal bone to pick.

Legitimate talent shows: I mentioned the phrase "legitimate talent shows" in the preceding paragraph, and I want to embellish on it because, to me, its connotation can be somewhat confusing.

Down through the years, I've heard various people say that a "talent show was legitimate on the surface but..." and to me this seemed to imply that the show had done something shady or illegal. And whenever I read advertisements in various magazines or newspapers that say "legitimate talent show," I scratch my head and wonder, "Just exactly what do they mean by that?"

So when in doubt, find a dictionary. Naturally, there were numerous definitions, but the one that seemed appropriate in context to talent shows was to the effect of *complying to acknowledged and accepted standards, rules or principles.*

In Chapters 7 and 15, I went into detail about the protocol and rules of a talent contest as well as how to go about producing one. If anyone follows my advice, guidelines and suggestions in those chapters, they will have produced a legitimate talent show.

As you know by now, I've been involved in thousands of talent shows for years - both local and big time contests, and using the above definition, they were all legitimate as well as "ethical."

Ethical talent shows: Now you're probably wondering, "What does he mean by 'ethical' talent shows?" So I checked out that word and it, too, had various definitions. The one that seemed to apply was to the effect of *complying to moral principles and/or code of conduct.* Then I looked up the key adjective in that definition, "moral," and after discerning the various definitions, the one that I felt applied in context to talent shows was to the effect of *complying to right and wrong standards of behavior.*

So the way I understand it, being in a legitimate talent show, which has a standard and generic format that's easy to follow, doesn't mean that you've entered an "ethical" one because here is where "false promises" and "misleading statements" could come into play, which segues into the next paragraph.

Advertising prominent music industry people to be in attendance: Whenever a talent show advertises that there will be prominent music industry people participating as judges, it is a big drawing card that will attract and encourage aspiring artists to enter. Why? Because these artists want to meet someone who may be able to help them get a break in the music business.

If the music industry names are listed then it's probably true. After all, if the show's producer has commitments from various prominent industry people, it's normal business practice to promotionally use the drawing power of their names and/or companies to attract potential contestants. The talent shows with big time sponsors certainly do. In my local talent shows at the Palomino, I always advertised the judges, especially if their names were well known in the community, such as a local deejay or a mayor, etc.

If meeting someone in the music business is your main priority for entering the contest in the first place, then you could always call the company on the advertisement and talk to one of its executives and/or their assistants for verification. There have been many cases where the employee was using the firm's name without permission. If this is the case, his supervisor may be glad to find out because this person is misrepresenting the firm he works for. He could possibly get fired for his unethical behavior.

If the judges' names and/or companies aren't listed in the advertisement, there may be several reasons why. Number one: maybe there's not enough room (unless it's a brochure or talent show program). Number two: maybe they don't have music industry people or any local celebrities as judges. Number three: since everything in life is relative, maybe it's a half-truth and the potential judges are in the music industry but they may be in the lower end of the prominence scale. You could find out by contacting the people who are producing the show and ask them who these music industry people are. However, if they're not being totally up-front with the public in the first place, they could easily skirt around this issue by giving you a song-and-dance routine, such as so-and-so is invited to participate as a judge but it hasn't been confirmed yet because of his busy schedule, etc.

In a nutshell, if someone involved with the talent show advertises that well know music and recording industry people will be there and they know full well that it's not true, it's a misleading statement as well

218

as a downright lie, which is wrong and, therefore, unethical.

Sadly, I have heard of talent shows that have been guilty of this. The artists will enter the show under the false assumption that they'll be exposed to some well known music industry people only to find out they are not there, which can leave the contestant with negative feelings about entering any talent shows in the future.

If you feel you are being lied to or that these are false statements, about the only thing you can personally do about it is don't enter the contest. However, you may be the type of person who takes them at their word and you don't find out who the judges are until show time. Or you simply want the experience of being in another talent show because you feel that any exposure is better than no exposure, which is certainly a wonderful attitude to have.

Music scams: Unfortunately, there are a thousand and one possible music scams that can and do occur, as they do in all industries. This includes all areas of the music business, such as publishing, songwriting, recording sessions, contracts and a real hot button issue - the illegal pirating of albums, which affects so many people in the business, especially the artists, songwriters and publishers.

Incidentally, Joan Carol and I want to acknowledge a couple of dear friends of ours - Jack and Jo McFadden (whom I've mentioned in Chapter 18, "Great Management Is Equally As Important As Great Talent"). About four years ago, Jack and Jo initiated and gave of their time to get a bill passed in Kentucky (now known as the McFadden Bill), which contained stricter enforcement laws regarding the illegal pirating of albums. The entire music industry owes them a debt of gratitude. In fact, Randy Owens, Alabama's lead singer, called Jack personally to thank him for what he did! I, too, want to give Jack and Jo a 21-gun salute! Hopefully, all the states in the union will someday have a bill like this.

I could go on and on about potential scams, but that's another book, which I don't intend to write. I choose to write positive books, which will give my readers a lifeline of hope and encouragement to hang on to.

Unethical recording session projects: However, I would like to discuss one possible hypothetical scam scenario that could occur, which is relative to talent shows, in order to caution you that things like this can happen.

For instance, maybe you entered a talent contest that could have been a "springboard" for a potential and unethical recording session scam. This talent show was advertised as being legitimate and for all practical purposes, let's say it was. The winner and the runner-ups were chosen that night by judges, and you may or may not have been one of them. Regardless, you had a great time and it turned out to be a successful performing experience before an audience for you.

Maybe in a couple of days or weeks, you are notified by mail or telephone that you're one of the lucky people in the show that is being given a recording session opportunity. They tell you that they were in the audience and were very impressed by your singing style, etc. They go on to say that you'll get fifteen hundred dollars (I'm picking a figure out of the air) off towards the cost of doing a recording session that would normally cost forty-five hundred dollars, which includes the tracks, engineer, producer, etc. The catch comes wherein they want you to send them fifteen hundred dollars up-front, and you are to pay them the other fifteen hundred dollars when the project is over. To further entice you into getting involved in this project, they tell you that this also includes the CD production (of which they'll give you ten CDs) and promise you that they'll shop it around to various record labels and/or mail it out to radio stations, etc.

Now, it's one thing to get three free hours of recording studio time as a prize (which I've previously mentioned in Chapter 15) and then if you wanted to put up your own money for any extra hours, that would be your choice. That was a cut-and-dried situation with no misleading statements or promises. But it's another thing to put out a fairly large amount of money, especially if you don't know if the guy is reputable or not.

To make a long hypothetical story short, the aspiring artist has taken the bait and has played out his role in the above recording session scenario. He goes home and happily plays one of his ten CDs for his friends and family and everybody is jazzed. Then in a couple of weeks, he phones the guy back to check on the status of the CD shopping, and he's either given various excuses or his calls are never returned. In fact, the telephone may even be disconnected. Sadly, it can have devastating effects, emotionally and monetarily, when someone realizes that they've been taken.

Unfortunately, there's really no way of stopping anyone from pulling the above hypothetical scam over and over again. Although it was unethical, the demo recording session was legitimate enough so that some people will fall for it. There are thousands upon thousands of aspiring artists who are so starry-eyed and who have a limited amount of knowledge about the business and they become easy prey for people like this.

Maybe some good can come out of any scam experience such as the above. To look on the positive side, he or she has now had some experience in a recording studio as well as becoming wiser and more cautious in the business world. And if it was a half way decent recording session with a talented singer, he (or she) may be able to use it in the future to get the interest of someone in the industry who will honestly and sincerely try to help him with his career.

The bottom line is this: before you become involved in a music scenario like the above or any others that are suspect, do your homework. Check out the guy's track record. Ask for past client references. Does he belong to any music organizations like the Country Music Association or the Academy of Country Music or a performing rights society such as BMI or ASCAP? Make a few calls to all these people and/or companies.

If you know an attorney, you may want to have him represent you from the get-go. The guy in question will think twice about pursuing the project with you if a lawyer calls him to ask for more details. It may cost you a few bucks but in the long run, the attorney may be saving you a lot of money as well as a huge blow to your self-esteem. You could also check with the Better Business Bureau in the area. Possibly this guy and/or his company may be leaving a trail of unhappy "he done me wrong" clients in his wake and they could have a file on him. Try to protect yourself as best as you can so that you don't become unnecessarily victimized.

Summary: I hope I've enlightened you somewhat with regard to legitimate and ethical talent shows as well as what to look for if someone is trying to con or scam you and what you can possibly do about it before getting involved. It happens! Being aware is being forearmed, and I don't want you to be on the short end of the stick.

Remember that the most important stage in the world is the talent show stage and the majority of legitimate talent contests are ethical. They don't cost that much to enter and you have everything to gain and nothing to lose because I feel the experience alone is priceless.

So keep participating in them because the day may come when you'll either become a professional entertainer and/or be confident enough to enter the big time legitimate and ethical talent contests. When big time sponsors such as Marlboro, Wrangler Jeans or True Value are involved, they won't be making any misleading promises or statements. You'll also have exposure to prominent industry people, and who knows what ethical opportunities could be available to you as a result of that experience.

Be cautious in all your business dealings, because your talent is a precious commodity. As I've told so many artists in the past, "God gave you a gift, and what you do with it is your gift to God." I firmly believe that good will always win out over bad, which is affirmed in Romans 8:28: "All things work together for the good to them that love God..."

Chapter 25

Make A Lemon Pie Out of Lemons!
Cliffie and the DMV!

"Roy and I were blessed to know Cliffie. We appreciated the integrity and honor that he brought to the profession. But most of all, we prized his sense of humor and what a joy he was to work with."
-DALE EVANS, MRS. ROY ROGERS - 1st Lady of the West

"Life is full of problems and they have to be solved one right after the other. So when life hands you a lemon, make a lemon pie! Above all, have your sense of humor in your hip pocket ready to use at a moment's notice!"
-CLIFFIE STONE

I've so enjoyed writing this book, and as the chapters dwindle down to a precious few, I'd like to reiterate how important it is to have a sense of humor, especially since I was so serious in my previous chapter, and rightfully so. Laughter is a gift as well as medicine for the body, mind and soul, for it can help people get through any type of problem or experience that they may encounter in their personal or professional lives.

So, with my sense of humor in hand, I'd like to further embellish about things that can happen to people, especially if they've been around a while. In short, to accept the things one can't change, especially as one grows older.

Reminds me of the time when I produced one of my annual country/western family concerts at Hart Park in Santa Clarita. After introducing an act, I slowly walked over to my car to get some pipe tobacco, and sitting under a pine tree nearby was a little five-year old boy who was wearing a pair of torn jeans and a baby western shirt. He was crying, so I walked over to him and said, "Hi, buddy! Why are you crying?" He rubbed his eyes as he looked up at me and said, "I can't do what the big boys do, so they won't let me play with them." So I sat down under the tree beside him and cried, too.

You see, I can no longer do the things I used to do, and it's been hard for me to accept at times because I still feel so young mentally.

For instance, the big boys have their brand new Mercedes and all those great things that I used to have. I still have some of them, of course, but not as many as I used to have. But it really doesn't matter, because they're only material things anyway.

The reason I've mentioned cars is because I've worked hard all my life to save enough money so that I could buy a new Lexus. I paid top dollar for it and it has everything anyone could ever want in a car. I was so proud, and I loved driving it around for a year or so.

When I got a notice from the Department of Motor Vehicles that I needed to get my driver's license renewed, I studied the rule booklet at home for a week and then I made an appointment.

Now, I don't see as well as I used to. Although I've had a detached retina in my left eye for the past few years, the DMV has been nice enough to grant me a special license wherein I could drive in the daytime. However, my right eye wasn't what it used to be, which is why I nervously went down there on the appointed day.

My first hurdle was to pass the written test and my confidence level soared when I did. The second hurdle was the eye test. Now, my right eye still works good because I can spot a pretty gal a mile away and there sure was a real cute one in charge of line number four and, like a moth to a flame, that's where I headed.

When it was my turn, she said, "Okay, Mr. Snyder, (which is my legal name), I want you to read the first line on that eye chart on the wall." And I made my first mistake when I said, "Where's the wall?" She said, "It's right behind me and I want you to read it with your left eye and then your right eye." I said, "I can't read with my left eye because I can't see out of it." She did a double take, then smiled sweetly as she proceeded to have me read it with my right eye. After making a few lucky guesses, I got through it. Then she said, "Take this piece of paper and go over to window fourteen." I said, "Is that where they're going to take my picture?" She replied, "Not yet. You have to take your driver's test first."

So I went over to that line and waited until it was my turn. She was a nice lady, too. She wrote something on the paper and then pointed to someone else's desk and told me I had to go over there. I said, "Okay, but do you want to take my picture now?" She said, "Not yet. You have to take a driver's test." So I went over to the desk and was told to bring my car up behind the DMV building and one of their drivers would take me out for a test.

I must admit that I was nervous about this third hurdle. However, I had seen a couple of pretty cute ladies there who were giving the driver's tests and I thought, "Oh, hoe! I'm gonna turn on the Cliffie charm and then have my picture taken when I get back."

So my darlin' wife, Joan Carol (who is always watching over me so that I don't hurt myself) got our car and drove it to the designated spot while I stood outside the front door and waited for one of those cute ladies to come out. Soon, one did and she had a clipboard in her hand. My daddy told me long ago that when you see someone with a clipboard, look out, because they're all business!

She walked up and asked me if I was Mr. Snyder. I said, "That's me!" She said, "Get in the car." I replied, "Yes, ma'am!" Then she told me to step on the brakes and she checked the brake lights while walking around the back of the car before getting in on the other side. She had a great figure and was very pretty, but the only thing wrong with her was that clipboard in her hand. She said, "Start the motor." So I started the motor and when she had me check my right and left hand turn signals, I thought to myself, "Boy, this is going to be easy stuff." She had me do a few other things like turn on my windshield wipers, and while she was writing on her clipboard, I thought to myself, "Boy, A+ so far. I can hardly wait to have my picture taken." Then she said, "We're going to take a little drive, and I'll be asking you to turn on certain streets. It'll be easy so don't be nervous." Well, that was easy for her to say!

When I stepped on the gas pedal, I pressed a little too hard because my car suddenly lurched forward and then backward a couple of times after I tried to compensate for it by stepping on the brakes. Of course, I apologized and she said not to worry. However, I noticed that she was holding onto the doorknob so tight that her knuckles were starting to turn white.

The upshot of it was I almost didn't see the cars that were coming on my left side a few times and it scared the lady right out of her clipboard. As for parallel parking, I didn't score high on that one, either. Hey! Who needs to parallel park anyway? As far as I'm concerned, if there's no car attendant or if you can't drive straight into a parking spot and back straight out, then forget about it!

And as she looked at me through panicky beady eyes with a glow of perspiration starting to show on her face, I begin to notice that she wasn't as beautiful as I thought she was going to be.

After we drove back to the DMV and parked, she looked at her clipboard and said, "I'm sorry, Mr. Snyder, but you really didn't do very good. Were you nervous?" I said, "No, I wasn't nervous. I was just excited." (That's the word I use instead of nervous. It works better for me.) Naturally, my heart sunk when she said, "I don't think I can approve your driving test today. If you want to try again, you'll have to make another appointment." I said, "Okay, but can I have my picture taken now." She said, "No, no, no. You've got to pass your driver's test first." Now, that was a definite answer. I guess I should have told her that my stage name was Cliffie Stone and that I was accustomed to having my picture taken!

As my sweet baby was driving me home, I wondered what was going to happen to me now, and I thought of one of Tennessee Ernie Ford's sayings: "Your get up and go has got up and gone." Well, my driver's license had got up and gone, and I wouldn't be gone very much without it. Then I thought, "I can make another appointment and try again or maybe I could talk to some heavy duty people I know who might be able to pull a few strings." When I mentioned it to Joan Carol, she gently said, "No matter who you call, they won't be able to help you see better. Besides, my darling, you certainly don't want to hurt someone or yourself if, God forbid, you should ever get into an accident. You know that I'm always here for you." Although I knew she was right, I reluctantly said, "Okay."

When I got home, I smoked my pipe a while and then laid down on my couch. Not to be able to get into my car and drive whenever or wherever I wanted to really upset me, so my knee jerk reaction was one of anger and frustration! I just couldn't believe it! A nice guy like me who hasn't had a ticket in thirty years! I was absolutely lathered into some kind of frenzy, so I put a gypsy curse on the DMV! They interfered with my freedom, didn't they, when they didn't give me another license? Here I am with a relatively brand new car and I can't drive it anymore!

Yes, I understand the DMV's point of view since I can only see out of one eye, which isn't as good as it used to be. But then what is? However, I still thought they were being picky, picky, picky.

226

Then I thought to myself, "Well, life is full of problems and they have to be solved one right after the other. So, Cliffie Stone, you can solve this one, too!"

Now, my darlin' Joan Carol and I are joined at the hip and, quite frankly, I don't like going anywhere without her. She does most of the driving anyway because she has a tendency to hyperventilate when I'm behind the wheel, and I knew that she'd willingly take me anywhere I wanted to go. But then I got to thinking, "What if she's playing tennis or has gone to visit her mother?" After all, I wanted to be able to take a break from my music work and go down to Coco's for a cup of coffee and my favorite dessert, lemon pie, whenever my sweet tooth beckoned, which is every day.

So what do I do with this lemon that I've just been handed? I then started thinking about alternatives. I could always get a taxi, but they cost nine thousand dollars to go from one corner to the other. There are buses and trains out here in Santa Clarita that run up and down all over the place. Of course, there's a little bus called Dial-A-Ride. I could phone them and they would pick me up at my home and take me anywhere in the valley for a few bucks. I also knew I could call one of my daughter-in-laws, Cathy or Ina, or one of my sons, Steve or Jonathan, because they lived nearby and were always willing to help me out whenever they could. Or I could call some friends or neighbors I knew who enjoyed my company and didn't mind driving me around.

So, in my heart of hearts, I knew I'd be all right. Looking on the bright side of things, I would be able to play tapes, smoke my pipe and enjoy the scenery more than I did then when I used to drive. Besides, I could take a nap until I got to wherever I wanted to go.

But I was sure gonna miss going down to Coco's whenever I felt like it to talk with my cronies and flirt with the waitresses while drinking coffee and eating my lemon pie.

Another one of my big deals was my weekly sojourn to the car wash. I'd drive down there and kid around with that cute lady who used to take my money. She was one of my fans and I'll bet she's gonna miss me, too! And while my car was being washed, I'd sit on a bench and wait for my Lexus to come out shiny and beautiful and talk with other folks who were also waiting. Or I'd play a little game of trying to figure out who goes with what car, and I was good at it.

My above joys might seem silly to some folks, but that's their problem. The older I get the more I love doing simple day-to-day things like this while appreciating the beautiful day, regardless whether it rains or shines. One must live each moment to the max.

And do you want to know something else? I found out later that the DMV wanted to put a black box in my car, like the Federal Aviation Agency requires of the major airlines! I wonder why?

Well, the next time I want a driver's license, I'm going to go to K-Mart and get a K-Mart driver's license and then I can have my picture taken!

My friend, I've chosen to make light of a situation that once was very upsetting to me. I'm sharing it with you in hopes that it may be somewhat inspirational to you because, regardless of your age, negative circumstances or unfair situations can also happen to you. If it's not within your power to change something, then accept it. Simply count your blessings and go with the flow.

So whenever life hands you a lemon, make a lemon pie! Above all, have your sense of humor in your hip pocket ready to use at a moment's notice.

Chapter 26

Keep Trucking Down Highway 101!
Dreams Can Come True!

"Cliffie was positive about everything! To follow a dream is a gift, and Cliffie reached beyond his dreams to create a lasting legacy. This book is that 'gift,' which may inspire you to get on stage and stand tall among the successful."
-PAUL CORBIN, Vice President/Music Industry Relations/CBS Cable-TNN/CMT

"Dreams can come true, but regardless where the yellow brick road takes you, the important thing is to enjoy each step of the journey!"
-CLIFFIE STONE

Having been in the music business for over sixty years, I know that dreams can come true. Mine certainly did! However, dreams have their own timetable! They are similar in nature to a rosebud that unfolds petal by petal until it's in full bloom, and there's nothing anyone can do to make it blossom any faster.

You, as an aspiring artist, may have to spend ten or fifteen years of your life pursuing your dream, which may or may not come true. However, I feel that everyone has a fair shot at the big time, but they have to step up on stage like others before them and take their chances.

Regardless, if you read the articles or see interviews with any of the current top artists or established major stars, most of them will say that they spent years preparing and performing. When someone supposedly makes it big overnight, it usually means that they have walked the streets of Nashville or Hollywood for eight or ten years and have played in every honky-tonk and joint in town. Although I'm not fond of this phrase, it's called "paying your dues."

My son, Curtis, and his CMA and ACM award-winning band, Highway 101, are perfect examples of dreams coming true in their own time. So let me start from square one.

My late first wife, Dorothy, and I had four children: Linda, Steve, Curtis and Jonathan. Now, being parents can sometimes be the most difficult part of a marriage. After all, you can pick your spouse and your friends, but you can't pick your relatives. You have to deal with whatever God sends along. I'm proud to say that my children all turned out great, and I love to brag about them whenever I can.

My daughter, Linda, is a speech therapist at Oralingua School in Whittier, California, which specializes in teaching hearing-impaired children from two through twelve years of age. Any humanitarian occupation such as this is the ultimate form of success!

As for my three sons, each of them is successful in his own right in the music business. Steve has held prestigious executive positions at major music companies (currently, he's with Sony Music), as well as having written songs that have charted on *Billboard's* Top Forty. Jonathan is an exceptionally talented music executive, and for the past nine years he's been the General Manager of a highly successful publishing company, Windswept Pacific. Then there's Curtis, who ended up being a songwriter, bass player and an entertainer just like his dad. I'll be using him as the example to prove that your dream to be an artist can come true!

Because of my own diversified career, all my children were exposed to every conceivable music genre, with emphasis on country and western music. Curtis was a naturally gifted musician and he truly loves performing on stage with a band. Even though I told him he could work until he was sixty if he went into the country field, he chose the rock 'n' roll genre. So I turned him loose in the universe because everyone has to chart their own course in life. Although he had a lot of fun, fame and fortune as a rock 'n' roller eluded him.

Then Curtis saw the light of day, or maybe it was that osmosis stuff finally kicking in from his youth, because he changed course and began working with local musicians in local country bands.

Among these musicians was John Hobbs, who is now one of the most sought after studio recording keyboard/piano players in Nashville. Another was Billy Joe Walker, Jr., one of the most gifted guitar players I've ever met. He, too, is on the musician's A team in Nashville and is currently making quite a name for himself as a producer. I practically adopted these two guys because they were always over at my ranch rehearsing and hanging out with Curtis. They were so much fun and I used all of them on numerous album projects.

Each of them struggled for years, and to see their individual successes and dreams come true makes me so proud!

During the urban cowboy era, Curtis met Jack Daniels, another unique guitar player. They immediately hit it off and started playing in bands together around town. Somewhere in this time frame, I had my "Country Showdown" concerts for three consecutive fun-filled summers at a venue called Alpine Village in Torrance, California. I hired Curtis and many of his buddies to be my house band. Because of their previous leanings toward rock 'n' roll, I suggested that they call themselves the Electric Cowboy Band. One of the guitar players and singers who appeared on my show with Curtis' band from time to time was Vince Gill, who (about six years later) got a record deal with MCA and became a major star, and will be for years to come.

Being a father who worries about his kids, especially if they're in the music business, I was so happy that Curtis had finally found some kind of musical direction to work towards that had a future.

Later, Curtis and Jack hooked up with a drummer by the name of Cactus Mosure, who hailed from Denver, Colorado. He, like Curtis and Jack, had also worked with many rock 'n' roll groups. A very special friendship formed between the three guys, which held them together through some pretty lean years while they honed their rhythm section that was destined to become one of the best in the country field. They played for scale (and sometimes less) in many small clubs and honky-tonks all over Southern California just to stay together as a unit. Sometimes it was barely enough to keep food on the tables for their respective families.

All aspiring artists and musicians have to have "hope" in order to keep putting their talent on the line as they pursue their dreams. And keeping hope alive when potential opportunities (the dangling carrot as I call it) often fall through can be disheartening, to say the least.

Eventually, one of those dangling carrots came through, which turned their elusive musical dreams into a reality. One day Curtis got a call from Cactus, who had just spoken on the telephone with a friend of his, Chuck Morris, manager of two successful California-based bands - the Nitty Gritty Dirt Band and the Desert Rose Band. Chuck told Cactus that he wanted to form a country band and he was looking for several musicians to work with a country lead singer by the name of Paulette Carlson.

From the get-go, Paulette and the guys just clicked. So allow me to boast about this group, which will show you the immensity of their accomplishments in the fiercely competitive music business.

Chuck got together with the four of them and had the group rehearse a few tunes. Now, it took guts as well as foresight to put a country girl singer with basically a rock 'n' roll band. With Curtis on bass, Cactus on drums and Jack on guitar, they became the future driving force and very foundation of Highway 101's great rhythm sound. Jack is probably one of the most dangerous guitar pickers in Nashville in that he plays such original guitar licks. Nobody knows what he's going to do next - not even him! I've watched Cactus doing his thing and I think he's one of the most high-energy percussionists ever to work on a stage. Curtis is not only a great bassist, he also has tremendous charisma, which is displayed every time he steps on a stage.

After Chuck heard and saw the musical chemistry between them, he fronted the money and had them record at Amigo Studios in Los Angeles. He then shopped their product in Nashville and ended up getting them a record deal with Warner Bros.

Paul Worley, one of country music's most talented ACM award-winning producers (whose impressive track record includes the Dixie Chicks), was the main producer of Highway 101's hit albums. Their debut album alone sold over five hundred thousand units, which spawned four *Billboard* Top 5 hits, including two number one's - "Somewhere Tonight" and "Cry, Cry, Cry." Their second album, *Highway 101-2*, had four *Billboard* Top 10 singles, including their number one hit "Just Say Yes." *Paint the Town* was the name of their third album, which had another *Billboard* number one hit, "Who's Lonely Now."

All these hit singles and albums catapulted them into becoming an award-winning group. For two consecutive years, 1988 and 1989, they won "Vocal Group of the Year" from both the Academy of Country Music and the Country Music Association. They were also nominated for two Grammy's in 1988: "Album of the Year" and "Single of the Year," and, although they didn't receive one, they are still winners in the big scheme of things because it's such an honor to be nominated in the first place.

Highway 101's chemistry was as dynamic on stage as it was on records, which was pretty amazing considering that the three guys had never performed with Paulette in concert until they starting touring after they had their first hits from their very first album.

Naturally, it's difficult to be objective when I talk about my son, Curtis, as well as Cactus and Jack. I'm sure you've gathered by now that I'm proud of all three of them, and I don't have the words to express my feelings when I saw them performing on prestigious showroom stages, such as Ballys in Las Vegas. What a pleasure it was to watch them having fun with their "overnight success," which couldn't have happened to a nicer group of people. They came a long way in a seemingly short period of time, but all of them, including Paulette, spent years accumulating their individual experiences before fate brought them together as a group.

The point I'm trying to make is "magic happened" when Curtis, Cactus, Jack and Paulette combined their individual talents. You see, the three guys were always sidemen who backed up singers. But with the birth of Highway 101, all three of them took center stage with Paulette (and later with their next lead singer, Nikki Nelson). Not only did they have a great rhythm section, which was the foundation of their unique music style, their individual charismatic personalities and vocal harmonies became an integral part of the act with lead singer, Paulette. You couldn't have one without the other for all the parts equaled the whole. Regardless what the fates may have in store in the future, all the members of Highway 101 will always be able to make an excellent living performing in concerts, because no one can ever take away their talent or accomplishments.

I've gone into great detail with the Highway 101 story, because I want you to understand that they didn't make it because Curtis had a celebrity father. I had nothing whatsoever to do with them getting together or getting their record deal. The guys basically made it because of their love and dedication to music - even when the future didn't look so rosy at times.

Once again, I'd like to share with you one of my heartfelt philosophies, which has become a mantra throughout this book: *"A singer is not a singer unless he (or she) sings. A musician is not a musician unless he's playing his instrument. A writer is not a writer unless he writes. A comedian is not a comedian unless he's telling jokes and so it goes with whatever it is you do in life."* You see, nobody maintains; nobody stays even. You either get better or you get worse at whatever you do. The more you perform, the better you will be. The less you perform, the worse you will be. You have to continue working to improve your skills. Never forget that you're only as good as your last performance!

Aspiring artists make their dreams come true all the time. Every year, there are new artists signed by record labels and their hit songs show up in *Billboard's* Top Forty. So don't hide your talent under a bushel. Get on a stage in front of an audience and let your light shine. You must prepare yourself so that you'll be ready when opportunities come your way.

May the Highway 101 story serve as an inspirational example that dreams can come true. Regardless where the yellow brick road takes you, the important thing is to enjoy each step of the journey! So keep on trucking down Highway 101!

My friend, welcome to my world!

Publisher Affiliated BMI/ASCAP
Award-Winning Songs

Title	Writer(s)
"Beautiful Lies"	Jack Rhodes
"Behind the Tear"	Ned Miller & Sue Miller
"Blackberry Boogie"	Tennessee Ernie Ford
"Bright Lights & Blonde Haired Women"	Eddie Kirk
"Conscience, I'm Guilty"	Jack Rhodes
"Dime a Dozen"	Harlan Howard
"Do What You Do Do Well"	Ned Miller
"Don't You Remember?"	Ace Dinning
"Five Hundred Miles"	Bobby Bare, Charlie Williams & Hedy West
"Foolin' Around"	Harlan Howard & Buck Owens
"Goin' Steady"	Faron Young
"Happy to Be Unhappy"	Bobby Bare
"He'll Have to Go"	Joe Allison & Audrey Allison
"He'll Have to Stay"	Joe Allison & Audrey Allison & Charles Grean
"I Don't Believe I'll Fall in Love Today"	Harlan Howard
"If That's the Fashion"	Tommy Collins
"If You Ain't Lovin', You Ain't Livin'"	Tommy Collins
"I'm a Truck"	Robert Stanton
"I'm Just An Old Chunk of Coal"	Billy Joe Shaver
"Invisible Tears"	Ned Miller & Sue Miller
"It's Such a Pretty World Today"	Dale Noe
"Kicking Our Hearts Around"	Wanda Jackson
"Live Fast, Love Hard, Die Young"	Joe Allison
"Loose Talk"	Freddie Hart & Ann Lucas
"May the Bird of Paradise Fly Up Your Nose"	Neal Merritt
"Milk 'Em in the Morning, Feed 'Em... Evening Blues"	Tennessee Ernie Ford
"My Baby's Gone"	Hazel Houser
"Next Time I Fall in Love"	Ned Miller
"Odds and Ends"	Harlan Howard
"Only Daddy That'll Walk the Line"	Ivy "Jimmy" Bryant
"Put Your Hand in the Hand"	Gene MacLellan
"She Called Me Baby"	Harlan Howard
"Shot Gun Boogie"	Cliffie Stone & T. Ernie Ford
"Silver Threads and Golden Needles"	Jack Rhodes & Dick Reynolds
"Snowbird"	Gene MacLellan
"Teen Age Crush"	Joe Allison & Audrey Allison
"The Gods Were Angry with Me"	B. Mackintosh, Roma Wilkinson

"The Popcorn Song"	Bob Roubian
"This Song Is Just for You"	Cecil Harris & Perk Williams
"Together Again"	Buck Owens
"Try a Little Kindness"	Curt Sapaugh & Bobby Austin
"Under the Influence of Love"	Harlan Howard & Buck Owens
"Under Your Spell Again"	Buck Owens & Dusty Rhodes
"Wait a Little Longer Please, Jesus"	Hazel Houser
"Waitin' in Your Welfare Line"	Harlan Howard & Buck Owens
"Whatcha Gonna Do Now?"	Tommy Collins
"You Better Not Do That"	Tommy Collins
"You Took Her Off My Hands"	H. Howard, W. Stewart, S. McDonald

Publisher Affiliated Songs *(includes)*

Title	Artist
"Blanket on the Ground"	Jeanne Pruett
"Bless Your Pea-Pickin' Heart"	Tennessee Ernie Ford
"Dear John"	Ferlin Husky & Jean Shepard
"Do What You Do Do Well"	Ned Miller
"Don't Go Courtin' in a Hot Rod"	Tennessee Ernie Ford & Molly Bee
"Foolin' Around"	Buck Owens
"Girl's Night Out"	The Judds
"I'm a Truck"	Red Simpson
"I'm Just an Old Chuck of Coal"	John Anderson
"John and Marsha"	Stan Freberg & Cliffie Stone's Band
"Just Beyond the Moon"	Tex Ritter
"Maggie"	Stan Freberg
"Mama, He's Crazy"	The Judds
"New Steel Guitar Rag"	Bob Wills; Bill Boyd
"Only Daddy That'll Walk the Line"	Waylon Jennings
"Put Your Hand in the Hand"	Anne Murray
"Shot Gun Boogie"	Tennessee Ernie Ford
"Silver Threads & Golden Needles"	Linda Ronstadt
"Smokey Mountain Boogie"	Tennessee Ernie Ford
"Snowbird"	Anne Murray
"Take it Any Way You Can Get It"	Cliffie Stone
"That's My Boy"	Stan Freberg
"The Gods Were Angry with Me"	Tex Ritter & Eddie Kirk
"The Lord's Lariat"	Tennessee Ernie Ford
"The Popcorn Song"	Bob Roubian & Cliffie Stone's Band
"Together Again"	Buck Owens (20 other artists)
"Try"	Stan Freberg
"Try a Little Kindness"	Glen Campbell
"Under Your Spell Again"	Buck Owens & Dusty Rhodes
"Watch It Neighbor, Watch It Friend"	Eddie Kirk & Cliffie Stone Band
"Wrong Time to Leave Me, Lucille"	Kenny Rogers
"You Gotta Have a License"	Tommy Collins

Songs Written Or Co-Written (includes)

Title	Writer(s)
"A Little Sooner"	Cliffie Stone & Joan Carol Stone
"Anticipation Blues"	Cliffie Stone & T. Ernie Ford
"B. One Baby"	Cliffie Stone & Stan Freberg
"Black-Eyed Peas & Cornbread"	Cliffie Stone & Herman "the Hermit"
"Bops-A-Lot Boogie"	Cliffie Stone & Mark Burnes
"Chopstick Boogie"	Cliffie Stone & Steve Stone
"Country Junction"	Cliffie Stone & T. Ernie Ford
"Country Rap"	Cliffie Stone & Jonathan Stone
"Dancing in the Arms of a Memory"	Cliffie Stone & Ginny Peters
"Divorce Me C.O.D."	Cliffie Stone & Merle Travis
"Gas Station Blues Boogie"	Cliffie Stone
"He's Left the Building"	Cliffie Stone, Ginny Peters, J.C. Parham, Dayne Rauton
"I Forgot What the Blues Was Like"	Cliffie & Joan Stone, John Hobbs
"I Only See You"	Cliffie Stone & Ginny Peters
"I'll Stop Lovin' You, Tomorrow"	Cliffie Stone & Joan Carol Stone
"John and Marsha"	C. Stone, Stan Freberg & Billy Liebert
"Jump Rope Boogie"	Cliffie Stone & Linda Stone-Hyde
"Lawdy What a Gal"	Cliffie Stone & Merle Travis
"Looking at You Looking at Me"	Cliffie Stone & Vivian Rae
"Lord, Thank You"	Cliffie Stone & Joan Carol Stone
"My Life Began"	Cliffie Stone & Joan Carol Stone
"New Steel Guitar Rag"	C. Stone, L. McCalliuffe, M. Travis
"No Vacancy"	Cliffie Stone & Merle Travis
"Riding Through the Purple Sage"	Cliffie Stone & Darrell Rice
"So Round, So Firm, So Fully Packed"	C. Stone, Merle Travis & Eddie Kirk
"Spanish Bells"	C. Stone, P. Freeman & Jimmy Dolan
"Storeroom of Memories"	Cliffie & Joan Stone, Larry Keyes
"Stuffed, Stacked, Fully-Packed"	Cliffie & Joan Stone, Mark Burnes
"Sunday Morning Tears For a Saturday Girl"	Cliffie Stone & Ned Miller
"Sweet Baby"	Cliffie Stone & Mark Burnes
"T N Teasin' Me"	C. Stone, Frances Kane, Claude James
"The Electric Cowboy Band"	Cliffie Stone & Curtis Stone
"They Said It Wouldn't Last"	Cliffie & Joan Stone, Larry Keyes
"(Touched by the) Magic of You"	Cliffie & Joan Stone, Mark Burnes
"Yellow Roses, Summer Sunshine"	Cliffie Stone & Joan Carol Stone

Bibliography

Stone, Cliffie & Joan Carol. *Everything You Always Wanted to Know About Songwriting But Didn't Know Who to Ask*. California: Showdown, Inc., 1992

Anderson, Bill. *Whisperin' Bill*. Georgia: Longstreet Press, 1989

Montana, Montie and Marilee. *Not Without My Horse*
California: Double M Company, 1993

Recommended Reading

Buscaglia, Leo, Ph.D. *Living, Loving and Learning*
New York: Ballantine Books, 1982

Frankl, Dr. Viktor E. *Man's Search For Meaning*
New York: Washington Square Press, Inc., 1964

Gibran, Kahlil. *The Prophet*. New York: Alfred A. Knope, Inc., 1979

Lee, Peggy. *Miss Peggy Lee*. New York: Donald I. Fine, Inc., 1989

McCormack, Mark H. *What They Don't Teach You At Harvard Business School*
New York: Bantam Books, Inc., 1984

Schuller, Dr. Robert H. *Move Ahead With Possibility Thinking*
New York: Jove Publications/Berkeley Pub. Group, 1986

Shemel, Sidney and Krasilovsky, M. Williams. *This Business of Music*
New York: Billboard Publications, Inc., 1971

Wallace, Irving. *The Fabulous Showman*. New York: Alfred A. Knopf, Inc., 1959

Disclaimer

This book contains the thoughts, ideas and opinions of its authors. What has lead to their success and/or the successes of others discussed in this book may not necessarily guarantee you the same results. The authors have never been shy to consult an attorney, a certified public accountant or a financial or investment advisor. You should consult the same for legal or financial advice and/or recommendations.

The publisher and authors disclaim any responsibility for any liability, damages, risk or loss, personal or otherwise, which may or may not be incurred as a result of its use and application of any of this book's contents. But be assured they truly wish you every success in your endeavors.

Tapestry of Friends

Speaking for Cliffie, as well as myself, I would like to thank all the people who have made up the tapestry of each of our lives. Since Cliffie knew thousands of people during his extensive career, it's impossible to list everyone. So if I left anyone out inadvertently, you know who you are. In alphabetical order, they are:

Adams, Berle
Adams, Michael
Adams, Andrea
Allison, Joe & Rita
Anderson, John
Antonovich, Michael
Armstrong, Billy
Arnold, Eddy
Arnold, Jack
Atkins, Chet
Autry, Gene
Autry, Jackie (Mrs. Gene)
Ball, Earl
Ball, Marlyn
Ballard, Evelyn
Bango, Laurel
Bare, Bobby & Jeanne
Barron, LeAnn
Bartley, Lary
Bates, Lori
Baxter, Dick
Beal, Kim
Bee, Allen
Bee, Molly
Benson, Ray
Bentley, Amy & Milton
Blaine, Hal
Blankenship, Johnny
Block, Billy
Boemecke, Bev & JB
Bond, Lincoln
Bond, Sherry
Boos, Dennis
Boris, Lenny
Boris, Marge
Boston, John
Bouille, Maryann
Bowsher, Carol

Boyd, Fran & Bill
Bradley, Don
Bradley, Harold
Bradley, Owen
Brosnahan, Kathy
Brown, Nick
Bruno, Al
Bryant, Jimmy
Burnes, Mark & Tami
Buttram, Pat
Campbell, Bonnie
Campbell, Glen
Carlson, Paulette
Carpenter, David Reeves
Cary, Bruce
Casalman, Charles
Castillo, Sean & Chris
Catino, Bill
Chesney, Kenny
Chapman, Elizabeth
Chapman, Marilyn
Chase, Charlie
Cihak, Carol
Clark, Dick
Coburn, Barry & Jewel
Condie, Gary & Mryna
Cooley, Al
Corbin, Paul & Marless
Corlew, David
Cox, Jimmy
Cox, Paula & Clem
Crakes, Chief Wright
Crook, Lorianne
Crowell, Rodney
Crutchfield, Jerry
Curb, Mike
Dahl, Steven
Daniels, Charlie

Daniels, Jack & Alicia
Darcy, Jo Anne
Davidson, Cheryl
Davidson, Lindsey
Dean, Eddie & Dearest
Dennis, Joe
Dickerson, Diane
Dietz, Jane
Doty, Gene
Dran, David & Sandy
Dran, Helen & Steve
DuBois, Tim
Duncan, Jim
Duncan, Steve & Yadira
Dunson, Van
Dykes, Tim & Wendy
Edwards, Skip
Elrod, Terry
Evans, Dale
Evans, Margie
Fagerlan, Jane & Ken
Fahnestock, Frances
Fahnestock, Ken
Farren, Chris
Farrington, Joan
Ferguson, John & Julia
Fleming, Wendy & Morry
Ford, Beverly
Ford, Brion
Ford, Buck
Ford, Tennessee Ernie
Foster-Wells, Holly
Frances, Archie
Frazier, Dallas
Freberg, Stan & Donna
Friedman, Brian & Jan
Friedman, Rick
Fries, Kurt

Frizzell, Lefty
Fuller, Jerry & Annette
Fulton, Steve & Salai
Gallico, Al
Gamblin, Marty
Gamblin, Cherry
Gibson-Palmer, Debbie
Gillette, Lee
Gould, Katy
Grant, Johnny
Grasso, Tom
Gray, Oren & Karen
Graydon, Joe
Gregory, Buck
Gurley, Cathy
Gustafson, Eric
Haggard, Merle
Hale, Monte
Hall, Susan
Hamblen, Suzy & Stuart
Hansen, Maxine
Harding, Fletcher
Hart, Freddie
Heatherly, Bob
Hendricks, Scott
Herman, Max
Hicks, Lyle
Higdon, Pat
Higinbotham, Galla
Higinbotham, Dan
Hinton, Bruce
Hobbs, John
Hoffman, Milt
Hornsby, Nikki
Howell, Linda
Huffine, Charlotte
Hughes, Brian
Hyde, Harvey
Jackson, Agnes
Jacobs, Teresa & Irwin
James, Billy
Kahrl, Joyce
Katalenic, Agnes & Carl
Kenny, Mary
Keyes, Larry & Melva
Kiczenski, Conrad
Kiczenski, Ed & Barbara

Kiczenski, Rob
Kiczenski, Ron & Cory
Kiczenski, Stan & Shirley
Kiczenski, Tim
Kienzel, Rich
King, Bob
King, John
King, Laurie
King, Loyal
Kingsley, Bob
Kraeger, Cathy & Steve
Krakowicki, Walt
Kriski, Mark & Sherie
Langford, Don
Lear, Norman
Lee, Peggy
Lerman, Candy
Lesink, Charlie
Levine, Marc
Levy, Leeds & Jaymes
Levy, Lou
Lewis, Luke
Ley, Mike & Michele
Liebert, Billy
Links, Sharon
Linn, Roberta
Litchfield, Liz
Loakes, Jim
Loe, Pam
Louvello, Sam
Lynn, Wendy
Mac Intosh, Kathy
Mack, Ronnie
Maness, Jay Dee
Maness, Luaina
Martinez, Zach
Masters, Mikal
Matchette, Carole
Maxwell, Kathy
Mayberry, Corky
Mayberry, Jamie
McConnaughy, Debbie
McConnaughy, Will
McKeon, Buck
Melton, Brenda
Meoli, Marge
Michaels, Danny

Milligan, Jody
Monroe, Smiley
Montana, Montie
Montana, Marilee
Moore, Arnie
Moore, Gail & Rick
Morgan, Denise
Morris, Earline
Mortimer, Chris
Moser, Cactus & Ellen
Musgrave, Jim
Nelson, Ken
Nelson, Willie
Nichols, Alice
Nona, Sharie & Bill
Norin, Gwen & Mike
Norman, Jim Ed
O'Dorn, Michael
Oehmler, Rosemary
Oermann, Robert K.
Orlove, Harry
Orr, Jay
Osterman, Louise
Osterman, Russ
Ott, Marsha
Overton, Gary
Owens, Buck
Page, Buck & Alwyn
Palmer, Alexas
Parks, Jane
Pasutti, Molly
Patterson, Rick
Pedersen, Herb
Pedretti, Mary
Peters, Ginny & Errol
Peterson, Bill
Phillips, Connie
Phillips, Garth
Phillips, Kay & Gregg
Phillips, Norm
Pierce, Alvin
Pond, Neil
Powell, Hope
Powers, Ann & Jim
Powers, Natasha
Preston, Frances
Quijada, Patti

242

Rae, Vivian
Raines, Bill
Rathbone, Glen
Ream, Julie & Bob
Reeves, Joanne
Reiser, Fred
Reynolds, Allen
Riccobono, Ric & Margo
Richardson, Linda & Lou
Riefler, Carl
Riefler, Charlene
Riefler, Joe & Hattie
Riggins, Pug & Rig
Rinkenberger, June
Rinkenberger, Larry
Roark, Marie
Roberson, Gene
Roberson, Adoree
Rogers, Dody & Tom
Rogers, Roy
Rogerson, Ken
Rollins, Loretta & Glen
Romeo, Bob
Roseman, Sandy & Gary
Rothman, Maria
Rowe, Red
Royce, Ramsey
Salamone, Joe & Angie
Salamone, Mary
Sands, Tommy
Saporiti, Bob
Schnathorst, Hank
Schnathorst, Mildred
Schneider, Stan
Schreiber, Carson
Scott, Larry
Sargent-Pettee, Gen
Sharp, Jim
Sheets, Dale & Joan
Shefrin, Paul
Sherman, Al
Shipley-Biddy, Shelia
Sill, Greg
Sill, Joel
Sill, Lester
Sill, Lonnie & Nikki
Siman, Scott F.

Sims, Tom
Singer, Linda & Al
Sitarek, Carol
Smochek, Bill
Smochek, Chet
Smochek, Helen
Smochek, Judy
Smochek, Mary Rose
Smochek, Ray & Ann
Smochek, Rose
Snipes, Pastor Bill
Sober, Paige
Sovine, Roger
Spielberg, Neal
Spiro, Mark
Squeo, Linda & John
Stegall, Keith
Stewart, Don
Striebel, Amy
Stone, Cathy
Stone, Ina
Stone, Tommi
Stone-Tucker, Lynn
Strait, George
Strange, Billy
Stroud, James
Sykes, Ted
Tarkanian, Anna
Tator, Joel
Tharp, Steve
Thompson, Fran
Thompson, Hank & Dee
Tibbs, Bucky
Tillis, Mel
Tippett, Jo Ann
Toast, Melba
Tolin, Steve
Travis, Merle
Travis, Merlene
Trust, Sam & Joan
Tucker, Jan & Gary
Tuttle, Mike
Tuttle, Wesley & Marilyn
Tyler, Stan & JJ
Van Horn, Randy
Vaughn, Cy & Barbara
Veluzat, Andre & Candy

Vescovo, Al
Virant, Sunny
Visnesky, Sally
Wagner, Kurt
Walker, Billy Joe, Jr.
Walker, Cindy & Bruce
Walker, Harvey & Linda
Walker-Meador, Jo
Wapensky, Russ
Ward, Bill
Ware, Holly
Weed, Gene
Weiss, Bob & Pat
Wendell, Bud & Janice
West, Jim & Cheryl
West, Speedy
Wilbor, Jo Ann & Denny
Willett, Tom
Williams, Charlie
Williams, Lund
Williams, Selma
Williamson, Cliff
Wipperman, Tim
Wise, Sunny
Wolf, Peggy & Don
Janet Woods
Woodworth, Ralph
Erv Woolsey
Worley, Paul
Yorkin, Bud
Young, Maryl
Zandstra, Linda
Zettel, Phil
Zettel, Virginia & Dick

243

Honoring Our Heroes

The following two poems won first place in their grade levels at the "Youth Poetry Contest" in conjunction with the "Sixth Annual Cowboy Poetry and Music Festival" held at Melody Ranch in Santa Clarita, CA, in 1999. The theme of these poems touched my heart, and I am honored to have received permission to reprint them.

"My Hero - Grandpa Ike"
By Shawnie Wise-Hawkins (Age 8)
1st Place - Grades 1 - 3, Sulphur Springs Elementary

We lost four great Cowboys this past year: Roy Rogers, Gene Autry,
Montie Montana and Cliffie Stone.
But if you ask me, none of them quite compare to my own cowboy,
Grandpa Ike. Issac William Wharton was his name,
and even though you did not know him, he, too, had his fame.
Grandpa Ike was only a baby when a wagon train he rode,
from Wharton County, Texas to the cotton and oil fields of Kern County,
where his parents searched for black gold.
Grandpa tried his hand at wildcatting - his derricks you still may see,
right off of Placerita Canyon, where he worked as a hired gun.
But for purposes of history he is known as the first man to cap steam,
and to bring water during World War II to the Philippines.
Legend is he could find water in the Mojave Desert...
where even snakes and cactus came up with just plain dirt.
Not only could he lasso and throw his rope around me,
but he could also ride a bucking bronco at a rodeo and live in a teepee.
Whisky Pete knew my Grandpa, and both of them are now shaking hands;
for I know Grandpa's joined the heavenly chorus and is singing in the band.
I am thankful that I knew him, and I will not forget...
the many hours we spent together - time, I can assure you, I will not regret!

"Our Nation's Greatest Cowboys - Our Hometown Heroes"
By Marie Wise-Hawkins (age 10)
1st Place - Grades 4 - 6, Sulphur Springs Elementary

In 1998, our nation's greatest cowboys rode beyond the Great Divide.
This time, however, they were not simply on another horseback ride.
Joining the flanks of many Ghost Riders up yonder in the sky,
are four of our matinee heroes - each one is riding high.
Roy Rogers, Montie Montana, Gene Autry and Cliffie Stone,
together they have traveled beyond the twilight zone.
Trigger gallops proudly with Roy Rogers on his back
trying hard to out run Montie Montana's rope
that to this date still makes a loud crack.
Gene Autry is crooning that lonesome cattle call,
while Cliffie Stone is strumming his bass.
You can tell they're all in for that long haul.
The memories of Roy Rogers and Gene Autry will be preserved,
not simply by their museums, but television shows to this day we still observe.
As for Cliffie Stone and Montie Montana - their presence will be sorely missed...at
the Tournament of Roses...September Sunday's at Newhall Park
near the Cowboy Walk of Fame.
Cliffie and Montie - these cowboys were our Hometown Heroes,
and with their help, most of us forgot our woes!
For Santa Clarita's Hometown Jamboree owes much to these great cowboys.
They were the real McCoys.
So Roy, Gene, Cliffie and Montie - I hope you've found that Happy Trail.
Don't forget we love you, and please sing one for us!
For truly in your searching, you will find the Holy Grail.

Index

249

Order Form

You Gotta Be Bad Before You Can Be Good

ISBN 1-880152-01-0 $17.95 + $3.50 s/h

Everything You Always Wanted to Know About Songwriting But Didn't Know Who to Ask

ISBN 1-880152-00-2 $16.95 + $3.50 s/h

Perfect gifts for any occasion!

Email: joancarol@cliffiestone.com Website: www.cliffiestone.com

Allow 4 - 6 weeks for delivery. Prices subject to change without notice.

Checks, cashier checks or money orders (no credit cards, cash or CODs), payable in U.S. funds to:

Cliffie Stone's SHOWDOWN, INC.
P.O. Box 9657
N. Hollywood, CA 91609-1657

You Gotta Be Bad Before You Can Be Good
Please send me ____ copies at $17.95 per book $ ____.__

Everything...About Songwriting...
Please send me ____ copies at $16.95 per book $ ____.__

CA residents, add $1.40 sales tax (8.25%) per book $ ____.__

Shipping/Handling charge, add $3.50 $ ____.__
(Add $1.25 S/H for each additional book) $ ____.__

Canada, $19.95 per book/add $5.00 S/H charge $ ____.__

TOTAL: $ ____.__

Enclosed is my ____ check or ____ money order in the amount of $ _____

Name _____

Address _____

City _____ State _____ Zip _____

A SHOWDOWN BOOK

Order Form

You Gotta Be Bad Before You Can Be Good
ISBN 1-880152-01-0 $17.95 + $3.50 s/h

Everything You Always Wanted to Know About Songwriting But Didn't Know Who to Ask
ISBN 1-880152-00-2 $16.95 + $3.50 s/h

Perfect gifts for any occasion!

Email: joancarol@cliffiestone.com Website: www.cliffiestone.com
Allow 4 - 6 weeks for delivery. Prices subject to change without notice.

Checks, cashier checks or money orders (no credit cards, cash or CODs), payable in U.S. funds to:

Cliffie Stone's SHOWDOWN, INC.
P.O. Box 9657
N. Hollywood, CA 91609-1657

You Gotta Be Bad Before You Can Be Good
Please send me ___ copies at $17.95 per book $ ___.___

Everything...About Songwriting...
Please send me ___ copies at $16.95 per book $ ___.___

CA residents, add $1.40 sales tax (8.25%) per book $ ___.___

Shipping/Handling charge, add $3.50 $ ___.___
(Add $1.25 S/H for each additional book) $ ___.___

Canada, $19.95 per book/add $5.00 S/H charge $ ___.___

TOTAL: $ ___.___

Enclosed is my ___ check or ___ money order in the amount of $ _____

Name _____

Address _____

City _____ State _____ Zip _____

A SHOWDOWN ⬥ BOOK